GAMING
AT THE EDGE

Sexuality and Gender at the Margins of Gamer Culture

Adrienne Shaw

University of Minnesota Press
Minneapolis • London

Published by the University of Minnesota Press
111 Third Avenue South, Suite 290
Minneapolis, MN 55401–2520
http://www.upress.umn.edu

Library of Congress Cataloging-in-Publication Data
Shaw, Adrienne.
    Gaming at the edge : sexuality and gender at the margins of gamer
culture / Adrienne Shaw.
    Includes bibliographical references and index.
    ISBN 978-0-8166-9315-3 (hc)
    ISBN 978-0-8166-9316-0 (pb)
1. Video games—Social aspects. 2. Electronic games—Social aspects.
3. Gender identity. 4. Sex role. 5. Sex. I. Title.
    GV1469.17.S63S53   2015
    794.8—dc23

                                                    2014005527

Printed in the United States of America on acid-free paper

The University of Minnesota is an equal-opportunity educator and employer.

20 19 18 17 16 15 14   10 9 8 7 6 5 4 3 2 1

Contents

Preface

In the late the 1980s, my mother, sister, and I lived in Japan for four years. Stationed on a military base, we received a steady stream of U.S. programming via the military broadcasting network and stateside relatives sending us VHS recordings of shows. Still, my earliest memories are of living in a place where the majority of people and media were not "like" me. Indeed, I spent a great deal of my childhood moving, always being out of place. Adding to that, growing up as a queer woman meant I rarely had mediated narratives to which I could fully relate.

One Christmas in Japan, my mother bought us a Nintendo Entertainment System console and a handful of games. All three of us played it regularly for many years. At the time and, indeed, for most of my childhood, video games were something everyone did. My mother played everything from the board game simulation *Othello* to the vampire hunting game *Castlevania.*[1] My sister and I fought over *California Games,* stayed up late playing *Tiny Toon Adventures,* and blew off the steam of adolescence on *Doom.*[2] My sister still plays with her husband and daughter, though as more of a spectator now (or so she claims).

Growing up, most of our friends played regardless of gender, race, or class, even though not everyone had a console in their own home. Because of all this, it never really occurred to me that gaming was something only a certain type of person did. In fact, it was only in my adult life that I heard people talking about the heterosexual, white, cisgendered male gamer as the norm. That is not to say such stereotypes did not exist also during my childhood and adolescence. Ads and popular representation did often construct a "boy" player as the main game audience. There was, however, a disjuncture between the audience hailed by these constructions and the lived experience of game play with which I grew up. I am fascinated with the way the male (white and middle class) image of the digital game player has become enshrined as common sense to the extent that it has eclipsed a much more diverse picture of the medium's history. One need only compare a 1982 feature in *Electronic Games Magazine* proclaiming that "women have officially arrived in the world of electronic gaming"[3] to numerous twenty-first-century articles that announce with surprise that "nearly half of all video-gamers are women"[4] to see that there is a disjuncture between how players are imagined and who actually plays games.

The stereotype persists despite the constant reaffirmation that players exist outside the common gamer construction. There has been a shift, however, in how this "unexpected female audience" is courted via representation. In 1982 Midway spokesman Stan Jarocki described how representation was shaped in honor of an already existing market: "*Pac-Man* was the first commercial game to involve large numbers of women as players. . . . Now we're producing this new game, *Ms. Pac-Man,* as our way of thanking all those lady arcaders."[5] In the 1990s and early twenty-first century, though, most discussions of representation in games were focused on pulling those who do not play into games by way of representation. Before, it was a problem of texts not responding to the existing audience, and now, it is a problem of people needing to be convinced to try this medium. Representation in games has always been tied to expectations about audiences, but throughout this book I question some of the easy assumptions made about which groups are particularly concerned with representation and why representation matters to audiences.

There are many ways in which this book grew out of those early formative experiences. I grew up taking what I could from media and my surroundings, even when they didn't exactly represent me. Sure, it was hard to find people exactly like me, but I could still find aspects of myself reflected somewhere in the mediated world around me. Sure, I wanted representation. At the same time, I remember cringing while watching movies and television shows that were supposedly about people "like me." In addition, game play has always been something much more omnipresent in my life than most definitions of gamer culture reflect. I am sympathetic to the project of making game spaces more open, but I also have spent my entire life playing a medium that never marketed to me directly. I have found my place in the many spaces that were supposed to be closed off to me. For these reasons, it comes as no surprise that my research has always focused on questioning the commonsense logics of representation.

I care about representation (a lot). At the start of my graduate research, I was committed to cracking open the underexamined area of representation in games. My first project was a virtual ethnography of a group of gay, lesbian, bisexual, and transgender gamers.[6] And it turned out . . . many of them did not really care about representation. This was a shock to me at first, but the more I dug into that project, the more it made sense. Homophobia in gaming communities was much more important to these players than was textual representation because many of my interviewees played games online. When it came to textual representation, they found and shared queer representations or queer readings as they found them, in games as well as other media. They figured that in time the industry would find a way to tap into the gay gamer niche the way other industries had. My studies of gaming in the Middle East, Finland, and India generated similar themes.[7] Over and over again, people kept telling me that they just did not care that much about having their group, whatever that group may be, represented in games even if they cared about representation in other media. Teaching classes on minority representation in games, I heard this refrain repeated yet again by my students. Video games are a niche medium; they are fantasy environments; and they are designed for a narrow market. Of course games are not diverse—so what?

I could have easily dismissed these responses as a desirability effect, cognitive dissonance, or false consciousness. But such a dismissal seemed both uninteresting and unethical. Instead, I adopted a position I had learned from feminist ethnographic media scholarship: I took my interviewees at their word. I set out to reconcile scholars' compelling research demonstrating the importance of representation with marginalized audiences' ambivalence about representation. What does a call for representation look like when we take both seriously?

In exploring this question, I realized that I recognized myself in my participants' responses. After all, I too grew up playing a medium for which I was not the primary market and media in which only certain aspects of my identity were ever shown. I recognized my interviewees' ambivalence as a coping mechanism of sorts, which pushed back against discourses that sought to make them responsible for their own exclusion. If the logic goes that I need to make myself knowable as a market in order to be represented in a medium I wish to consume, it is easier to not care than it is to articulate what I want, particularly when I have never had the experience of getting what I want from representation. Beginning there, this book explores how media scholars, within and outside game studies, might talk about the politics of representation in new ways. How do we talk about representation in a way that can embrace intersectionality and hybrid identities? How do we demand representation without raising the specter of niche marketing? How do we talk about representation from an audience-centric position? What new things can we learn about media consumption when we start at the edges?

Clichés versus Women

Moving beyond Sexy Sidekicks and Damsels in Distress

In May 2012 Anita Sarkeesian took advantage of the increasingly popular Kickstarter crowd-funding site to solicit donations for a series of five videos on female representation in digital games. Her project, titled *Tropes vs. Women in Video Games,* meant to "explore, analyze and deconstruct some of the most common tropes and stereotypes of female characters in games."[1] Her goal as a gamer and a feminist media critic was to identify the limited roles of women in digital games, including them being featured as "damsels in distress," "sexy sidekicks," and "rewards."[2] Given that feminist critiques of media are not new and that the criticisms Sarkeesian leveled at the games industry would not be particularly surprising to anyone who has taken even a passing glance at game texts over the past thirty years, what happened next is both troubling yet, perhaps, expected.[3]

Following the initial request for backers, Sarkeesian received an onslaught of misogynistic, sexist, anti-Semitic, homophobic, and generally vitriolic comments. Many of the attackers voiced a refrain with which many female players of online, particularly console, games are familiar—that women should either display their bodies or leave the virtual space.[4] Among the more violent responses were cartoon depictions of Sarkeesian being raped by video game characters.[5] Her Wikipedia page was repeatedly vandalized, as attackers replaced her images with sexually explicit ones and embedded links to porn sites.[6] Among the final malicious responses was a Flash game inviting players to "beat up Anita Sarkeesian."[7] In this game players could "beat" her to a bloody pulp by clicking repeatedly on her picture.[8] To this day Sarkeesian still receives regular rape and murder threats via Twitter, and the company refuses to close the offenders' accounts.[9]

1

Held up as exemplars of the sexism that plagues the game industry, and gaming culture more broadly, Sarkeesian's experiences are
common for women players, as games scholar Mia Consalvo and
journalist Leigh Alexander point out.[10] More important, however,
we must contextualize the sexism, racism, homophobia, and other
biases of game culture within broader systems of oppression. Violences in games, game culture, and the gaming industry are not
unique to gaming.

As Andrea Braithwaite describes in relation to her analysis of
fights over character dialog on *World of Warcraft* forums: "The range
of casual-to-vitriolic anti-feminism and misogyny in these discussions is not attributable to video game culture as a different kind of
culture, or to digital space as a different kind of space."[11] Treating
gaming as an isolated realm makes this misogyny a spectacle at the
same time it normalizes the oppressive behavior within mainstream
gamer cultures.[12] Similarly, to treat representation in games as being just about games, to do the same for any medium for that matter, fails to account for the ways in which violence against queers
(homo- or bisexual or not), women (cisgendered or queer or not),
and people of color (queer or not, cisgendered women or not) exists
everywhere, in all media, and in all institutions of power.

The silver lining of Sarkeesian's story is that in the face of such
violent responses, her fund-raising campaign succeeded (and then
some). While her initial goal was to raise $6,000, a mere month
after opening the Kickstarter project Sarkeesian received a total of
$158,922 from 6,968 backers. The added funding allowed her to
expand the project to twelve videos, hire a team to help develop
it, and deliver much higher production quality than she originally
planned. In the end the very sexism her project sought to reveal
was the catalyst leading to her fund-raising success. The controversy
surrounding Sarkeesian's project served as a call to arms for many
people with differing arguments about how, when, and why representation matters in this medium. In fact, her serial online video
project may have been the inspiration for a full-length documentary
called *Gaming in Color: Queers & Gaymers of the Pixelated World*,
which began its Kickstarter project with a $50,000 goal.[13]

Games are not the only contemporary texts that demonstrate
how and when representation comes to matter. In 2012, after the
books garnered a slew of awards and wide critical acclaim, the first

installment of Suzanne Collins's young-adult science fiction trilogy *The Hunger Games* was released as a major motion picture.[14] In the novels and film, the protagonist Katniss Everdeen and other children competitors from the twelve districts of the futuristic land Panem are pitted against one another in a battle to the death that is broadcast as a reality television event throughout the country, serving the political and personal interests of affluent Capitol audiences. Competing in the arena, Katniss befriends a young girl from another district named Rue, described in the books as having "dark brown skin and eyes."[15] Following the casting of Amandla Stenberg, an actress of African American and Danish ancestry, the Twitterverse erupted with fan complaints over the choice of a black actress to play the part.[16] One tweet in particular referenced that "awkward moment when Rue is some black girl and not the innocent blonde girl you picture."[17] Further complaints were raised over the casting of singer-songwriter Lenny Kravitz (of mixed African American and Russian Jewish ancestry) as Cinna, Katniss's stylist for the Hunger Games, despite the fact that Cinna's race and skin tone are never mentioned in the books. [18]

Despite Collins's clear description of Rue's appearance, some fans felt outraged by the fact that the character they perhaps identified with or felt attached to was not going to appear on the screen as she had in their heads.[19] In many ways, books are the original interactive medium, in that readers create many of the literary sensory elements in their heads. In regard to *The Hunger Games,* some fans felt their experience and memory of the text were devalued when Hollywood casting did not match the mental pictures they had created. I do not wish to defend their racial, if not blatantly racist, outbursts. These outbursts do indicate, however, that there are specific moments in which representation *can* matter to audiences, though it does not always matter, as I discuss throughout this book. In it I parse how people connect with media texts via the intertwined processes of identity and identification. Both inform how they talk about and react to media representation. The manner in which identity, identification, and thoughts about representation connect, however, does not necessarily follow a linear or static path. We get pleasure from texts that represent us, certainly, but we also enjoy those that do not. Media texts provide us with source material for what might be possible, how identities might be constructed, and what worlds we might live in. These are the reasons media representation matters, at least according to my interviewees. Representation provides evidence for what forms of existence are possible. It is this argument for representation that aligns with how we interact with media, more than those that emphasize realism. Moreover, it promotes diversity without relying on media effects or marketing discourses that are typical of many arguments for representation.

Of course, we must also consider the ways medium specificity shapes how representation comes to matter. Are the stakes of representation different for video games than for other media forms?[20] Sarkeesian had made a similar video the year before her Kickstarter campaign about filmic and televisual representations of women that at least according to her own account, was well received.[21] There was something particular about her critique of video games that struck a virtual cord. Online harassment of women in digital games culture is hardly new, as much of the coverage of and responses to the *Tropes vs. Women* controversies details.[22] Yet there seems to be something more at work in these attacks on a feminist gamer seeking to shed light on the long-documented sexism of digital games spaces and texts. Many of the attacks did not merely deny a woman's right to be present in a male-dominated virtual space but flat out rejected *anyone's* right to critique games as cultural texts.[23] It may be that the *Gaming in Color* documentary about LGBTQ[24] gamers and game industry members has received less vocal criticism than *Tropes vs. Women* because it addresses people involved in the production and consumption of games rather than critiquing game content.[25] As I detail, people often treat games as if there is something unique about them apart from other media forms, and I argue that discourse about representation is central to this treatment. In doing so, I demonstrate that understanding how representation comes to matter in games actually sheds light on how it comes to matter in other media, as well.

Throughout this book I also question some of the easy assumptions often made about which groups are particularly concerned with representation. Many of the attempts to rectify the under- or misrepresentation of women in games, for example, has focused exclusively on courting female players and designers via female-friendly game content. Sony Online Entertainment, for example, offers an annual scholarship for aspiring female game designers called GIRL: Gamers in Real Life. This program, however, privileges marketable audiences in its demands for representation and conflates audience and producer group membership with identities:

> G.I.R.L. helps raise awareness of the serious female gaming audience to the media in an effort to encourage the gaming industry to positively promote women throughout all facets of games, game production and into game management; which will hopefully impact the way females are depicted in video games and create and influence content to be appealing to women.[26]

This framing represents two key problems in discussions of representation in game texts. First, representation in game texts is consistently linked with the lack of diversity in the video game industry.[27] This linking, in turn, presumes that the mere presence of women (or members of any marginalized groups) in the industry will automatically result in more diversity in texts. To quote Charlotte Bunch, this "add women and stir" approach assumes that there are no structural limitations within the industry that preclude this representation, that men in the industry are simply incapable of creating texts that are not representations of themselves or their fantasies, and that all women are feminists.[28] Having a particular body and relationship to norms is neither necessary nor sufficient for having sensitivity to the nuances and importance of representation. Second, Sony's GIRL program and similar projects put the burden of creating more diverse representation on marginalized groups, insisting that if they invest in the industry as producers and consumers, representation will change. What I call for, in contrast, is a rejection of that burden. I demonstrate throughout that players/audiences, owing to the complexity of their identities, are able to have strong connections to people unlike them on a regular basis.[29] By using that fact as a starting point, the question becomes, Why does everyone in games, and other media texts, look so much alike? The industry, as well as scholars, must treat diversity as a goal in its own right, rather than an exception to the rule or the sole domain of those who are marginalized.

The *Tropes vs. Women* controversy highlights the importance of approaching representation through hybridity,[30] intersectionality,[31] and coalitional politics,[32] rather than through the more limiting discourse of identity politics.[33] For example, one productive respondent criticized Sarkeesian's lack of attention to race in her critiques of gender representation.[34] And beyond the venomous attacks, there were some fair critiques made about the very cursory, heteronormative, binary, cisgendered analysis of representation proposed for the video series. In addition, despite the sickening response from some sectors of the Internet, there was a sense of hopefulness created by the sheer magnitude of Sarkeesian's success. As journalist Helen Lewis describes, despite many examples of the "boys' club-ness" of 2012 gaming culture, an equal amount of social-cultural-political force had been pushing toward an at least gender-inclusive gaming sphere. She writes, "Thousands of people stood up and said to the perpetually incandescent sexists: You are nothing to do with us, or with gaming. And that has been the same throughout the year."[35] There is evidence to suggest that it is not just women, or marginalized groups generally, who care about representation in games and are invested in diversity.

Despite the broadening of video game audiences, the Sarkeesian controversy also demonstrates that some members of the gaming community continue to define "game culture" as something specific and particularly masculine, heterosexual, and white. In many ways, digital games seem to be the least progressive form of media representation, despite being one of the newest mediated forms. This is particularly surprising given decades of research on the importance of diversity in media and some other media industries' efforts to make texts more diverse (whether for politics, profits, or, more often, both).[36] Similarly, we have decades of critical theories of identity that demonstrate the shortcomings—and violence—of conceptualizing individuals though purely demographic-based, stable notions of identity grounded in identifiers like gender, race, and sexuality.[37] Finally, though the totality of media offer audiences more venues through which they might find representations that resonate with them, this pluralistic approach to representation does not seem to answer the social justice–oriented calls for media diversity in a broader sense. Despite a refrain in media studies and contemporary politics that "it gets better," I find myself as a media researcher and a player asking that if that is true, why hasn't it yet gotten better in games?[38]

After several years of researching the representation of marginalized groups in digital games, a few things continue to vex me. First is the point I just raised: despite the fact that digital games have developed alongside media representation critiques, numerous civil rights movements, and increased visibility of marginalized groups across popular media, it seems as though digital games are lagging. In my own work I have found that contrary to the progressive representation narrative that assumes diversity happens "in time," there are specific processes through which marginalized groups come to be represented in video games, as in other media.[39] Second, the players I interviewed from marginal groups often told me that representation in game texts was of little importance to them.[40] Third, and related to both of the previous concerns, is that demands for the representation of specific groups are always rather limiting in how those identities are articulated and rarely encompass the complexity and intersectionality of identities.

In this book I use dozens of in-depth interviews with people who play digital games and are members of marginalized groups to parse the connected but distinct issues of identity, identification, and media representation. Identification here is used not as the lynchpin between identity and representation but rather as an entry point into describing participants' complicated relationships with both. Identification also focuses primarily on the relationship between players/audiences and texts, while also noting the unique aspects of that relationship when games are played with others in a variety of contexts (online and off). Although this book does not explicitly address the representation of hegemonic notions of white, heterosexual masculinity, the approach outlined here could also be used to address this "mainstream" game representation in the future.[41] I build on feminist, queer, critical race, and postcolonial studies of identity and draw upon qualitative audience research methods to make sense of how representation comes to matter in an era of increasingly diversified, interactive, and niche digital media. I offer a textual critique model for game representation grounded in an audience reception study, arguing that the study of audience reception is imperative in analyzing texts designed to be interactive.

By breaking away from social categorization, in favor of social contextualization, I argue that we can better make sense of why representation is important in a broad social sense by first unpacking how it becomes important in an individual sense. Though I mostly focus on a single medium—digital games—the concerns about representation connect across media. To that end, in addition to talking to interviewees about digital games, I engage them in conversations about representation and identification in other media, as well. This allows me to see the edges of where and when representation is made to matter across media texts. In this book I demonstrate not only that arguments for game representation need to be made differently from how they have been made for other media but also that games demonstrate how representation might be discussed differently in other media.

Media researchers must rethink how we argue for the importance of diversity. Before arguing for the importance of media representation, we can do more work unpacking *why, when,* and *how* it is important. When does difference make a difference in how members of marginalized groups interact with video games and other media? The identity politics–based approach to studying and demanding representation simply does not work. More than that, arguing for the representation of cleanly defined, marketable identity groups excludes those at the margins of representation, those who do not sit comfortably in demographic categories, and those who exist outside the market. Arguably, these are the individuals who have the most at stake in demands for representation in a political, social justice sense. In particular, digital games in this study provide insight into how we might create critiques of representation that are politically engaged enough to resist market logics and nimble enough to encompass interactive, personalized, customized media texts.

In this book I focus on the relationship between identity, identification, and media representation in an effort to question (1) if and how people identify with media characters, (2) how a particular medium affects the process of identification, and (3) when and how representation is important to audiences. I demonstrate that identities are multifaceted and articulated in relation to particular social dynamics, that identification can occur in a variety of ways but is also not always important to audiences, and that representation does not always, or predictably, drive media consumption and reception. Building on this, researchers, activists, and interested producers need to engage more directly with the imaginative potential and pleasure of representation when arguing for its importance.

In chapter 1, I discuss the theoretical and methodological challenges of studying representation and marginalized gaming audiences and the advantages of the ethnographically informed approach used in this project. I also offer a brief review of the representation of marginalized groups in media generally and in video games specifically. I discuss the tendency of past research to isolate identifiers and approach identities in an overly simplistic manner.[42] I also describe the way qualitative audience research can help make sense of representation in a way purely textual studies cannot. Moreover, I discuss the importance of integrating a complex notion of identity into arguments for and analyses of representation in games and other media. The chapter also engages some of the political debates of good versus bad representation and the impact these debates have on studying representation from an audience perspective, setting the stage for the critique offered by this book as a whole.

In chapter 2 I outline the first of two sets of issues that must be unpacked in order to make sense of how people talk about representation in games. In a lot of work describing why representation matters, easy assumptions are made about identities and how people identify with media characters.[43] Although identification is most assuredly not the *only* way people relate to texts, a lot of the major scholarship on representation presumes that identification is a factor in media effects. Moreover, throughout my research interviewees consistently linked identification and their feelings about representation. As I discuss in this chapter, although people may identify *with* characters because they identify *as* members of a specific group, this is not the only way they form connections with media texts. The assumption that players/audiences with specific identifiers connect with characters who have those same identifiers trivializes the ways and reasons people identify with media characters. Identification *with* characters is not always a reason for playing video games or consuming other media, but examining how this works can generate a compelling argument for more diversity in game texts and media more generally.

In chapter 3 I disentangle interactivity and identification to make sense of how representation comes to matter in games versus other media. I use identification as a starting point for talking to interviewees about how they connect with game texts but discuss the many other ways representation is understood by players. In particular, I look at the ways game texts' ludic and narrative elements, contexts of play, and embodied interaction affect the experiences of identification. Studies of identification with game avatars or characters, particularly attempts to quantify it, often conflate interactivity with identification.[44] Just because *L.A. Noire* forces me, for example, to take on the role of Cole Phelps and interact in his 1940s-era Los Angeles through him does not mean I identify with Phelps as a character.[45] Moreover, researchers must also consider that different types of relationships between players and characters/avatars are made available in different types of game texts. Rather than simply critique the availability of certain identities in video games, researchers must also interrogate how and if players identify with those portrayals, how contexts of play shape those processes, and how options are made available in games.

In chapter 4, having demonstrated the multifaceted relationships interviewees have with their identities and how they relate to game characters, I turn to the question of representation more directly. I discuss how and if representation of their specific groups is important to interviewees and when media representation is important to them. As it turns out, representation is not necessarily important to members of a marginalized group by virtue of their membership in that group. How interviewees discussed the importance of representation was connected to their reasons for using a text, how they understood their identities, if and how the representation was made relevant in a given text, the context in which the text was consumed, and the social sphere in which the texts were created. Interviewees were also attuned to tokenization and bad attempts at representation. Some interviewees, furthermore, were fed up with media or simply did not think it was as important as is often claimed. Finally, when interviewees viewed texts as fantasy, the representation of reality was not seen as important. Rather than imply representation does not matter, this actually signifies that fantasy spaces are key sites of exploring diversity in new ways.

In the final chapter I address some very recent representation debates to help explain the stakes of this book at this precise cultural moment. I also interrogate the common theme across my interviews that representation and identification are "nice when they happen." Unpacking what "nice" means here, I contend that arguments for increased diversity in media representation can and must be made outside niche marketing, outside the refrain that a given group plays games, too, and thus must be accommodated. In order to accomplish this, researchers, activists, and interested producers need to demarginalize video games as a medium. In addition, I claim that while media scholars often talk about representation's importance in terms of its effect on out-group or in-group members, on the educative or the marketing potential of diversity, a better argument for representation can be made by focusing on the way diverse media gives us space to imagine the world differently.[46]

In the old national broadcast model of communication, analyzing what group a text is by, of, and for could illuminate social hierarchies in modes of production and cultural values. A new model is required to analyze representation, however, as emerging media technologies shift how audiences are constructed by media industries and user-generated content blurs producer/consumer roles.[47] At the very moment when media industries are pushing the burden of representation onto marginalized producers and audiences through new distribution platforms, niche media portals, and customizable content, we need to be more nuanced in our demands for representation. I demonstrate that contemporary representation studies, particularly in relation to emergent media, must begin with audience studies and that microlevel reception practices can inform macrolevel politics. By unpacking how representation comes to matter to audiences in the twenty-first-century U.S. media environment, this book articulates a new understanding of the stakes in representation debates. I offer a model for talking about representation, difference, and diversity beyond the logic of effects or marketing that focuses on how representation allows everyone to be part of our collective imaginings of possible realities.

From *Custer's Revenge* and *Mario* to *Fable* and *Fallout*

Race, Gender, and Sexuality in Digital Games

It was World AIDS Day 2009, and thanks to a reminder from a friend's Facebook update, I had worn my red argyle sweater vest over a button-down shirt to commemorate the day. As it had become finally chilly after an extended, mild fall, I donned my leather jacket and took the trolley into West Philadelphia. This was my second interview with Pouncy, rescheduled twice due to illness and other commitments.[1] I walked up the steps to the house they shared with eleven other people and several cats and knocked on the door.[2] As I entered, I said my hellos to the other housemates. One sat on the couch playing *The Sims*[3] on a laptop while watching a World AIDS Day movie marathon on Logo.[4] *The Gloaming* was playing.[5] Pouncy suggested that I should be interviewing this housemate because she had created a lesbian separatist community in *The Sims*. The housemate replied that, in fact, she was not currently playing with the lesbian separatist community. We discussed how recently they had all watched the Sims having sex. We laughed at the absurdity of sexuality in video games and how the digital characters' clothes seemed to disappear when they jumped into bed. I was then invited up to meet the two new kittens the house was fostering.

I watched the kittens wrestle and discussed my work with another housemate while Pouncy left to get a laptop to play on for the interview. Pouncy returned with a borrowed laptop, explaining that their own laptop had recently died. We settled on a couch by the window as the housemate began making curtains on a sewing machine nearby. As Pouncy took off their sweatshirt, the housemate commented on the fact that we were wearing similar outfits. Pouncy laughed and said that the woman who opened the door, upon seeing me through the window, said that I must be Pouncy's guest.

After struggling with the wireless connection for a bit, we moved downstairs to use the house's desktop computer. Grabbing a jacket, as the first floor was chillier than the upstairs, Pouncy opted not to take a leather jacket so that we didn't look too much like we were wearing "lesbian uniforms." Settling down at the communal desktop computer, we could hear the other housemates starting to watch *Brokeback Mountain,* the next offering in Logo's marathon.[6] My attention shifted back and forth between Pouncy's playing of *Settlers of Catan* and the housemates' discussion of the movie that ranged from the playful to the political.[7]

This fieldwork vignette encapsulates several themes central to this book: the uncertainty of research plans and the seeming omnipresence of cats in my fieldwork;[8] links between consumption and identities; the different types of sociality involved in media consumption; the way resources impact who plays video games and when; the fact that identities do sometimes guide consumption, but not always in the ways we assume; and finally, the different types of representation and audience activity made available by different media. All of these themes, in turn, offer insight into how media researchers might argue for the importance of diverse media representation in a way that can account for media as practice, using Nick Couldry's articulation of the term—not merely addressing the issue through textual artifacts, inequities in industry hiring practices, or audience constructions.[9] *Brokeback Mountain,* for example, is a mainstream film that taps into a history of queer readings of cowboy movies. As such, it demonstrates that although play and audience activity might be discussed primarily in relation to digital games, we can actually learn more about what is unique about the practice of game play when we look at it in relation to individuals' broad media consumption. What makes games unique in turn helps us make sense of individuals' articulations of the politics of representation in this medium and if and how they identify with game characters, as I discuss when I return to this example in the conclusion of this chapter.

Digital game studies is hardly a new field. Yet despite numerous books unpacking the intricacies of the games industry, game play and culture, and rhetorical/textual studies of games, research on the representation of marginalized groups in games has remained fairly limited and cursory.[10] Games research on the representation of marginalized groups tends to approach the issue by addressing gender, race, and sexuality as discrete and stable categories of analysis. The bulk of the literature on gender, for example, focuses almost exclusively on normative, binary gender identities and rarely looks at intersections with race, sexuality, class, etc.[11] Such researchers also assume that representation of these identifiers in game texts is the end goal for audiences and producers who are members of these specific marginalized groups. In other words, this approach assumes that all lesbian of color audiences (and lesbian of color producers) want lesbian of color characters in games to identify with.

One of my key arguments in this book is that the discourse about representation (from industry and academic points of view) is what needs to be transformed, not just the representation of particular groups in game texts. Although I use illustrative examples for the ways various groups are represented in games, my primary critique is that how representation is studied in games and media generally needs some rethinking. Toward this end, in this chapter I review the ways the representation of marginalized groups in games and other media has been previously studied by troubling how identities are deployed in critiques of representation, discussing the unique concerns of studying representation in games, and identifying the problems in how the importance of representation is articulated. I then describe the methodological choices I made in this project to redress those concerns. In particular, I focused on play that was not primarily social and players that did not necessarily identify as gamers and did not narrow the field by using one single text or site of play. All of this was done to emphasize social contextualization rather than categorization and to take individual players as the starting point for analysis on when and how representation comes to matter.

The Trouble of Representation

In this book I use a critical approach informed largely by feminist and queer theory to study representation in a way that takes into account the fluidity, performativity, and contextuality of identity categories. There is, as Bonnie Zimmerman describes it, "a price to pay for a politics rooted so strongly in consciousness and identity. The power of diversity has as its mirror image and companion the powerlessness of fragmentation."[12] Typically, stakeholders in media representation discussions focus on specific identifiers, often race, gender, or sexuality, in their analyses and arguments. The logic for this is similar to that of identity politics, arguing that representation functions as a type of "imagined community" formed for political ends.[13] It is, in a sense, like nation building in the way Stuart Hall describes it: "To put it crudely, however different its members may be in terms of class, gender, or race, a national culture seeks to unify them into one cultural identity, to represent them all as belonging to the same great national family."[14] We might also describe this as a form of "strategic essentialism" in the sense described by Gayatri Spivak.[15] Mary Bernstein, for example, analyzes how different deployments of gay and lesbian identity were useful in political struggles situated in different local contexts.[16] In this sense, identity politics, like identities, are momentary articulations of social relationships rather than essentialized entities. Bernstein argues that it is not useful to describe "identity" movements, monolithic entities inscribing inner and outer positions, but rather movements that use particular identities to specific ends. As Stuart Hall argues when thinking of political groups formed around a certain identity, "We should think of them as constituting a *discursive device* which represents difference as unity or identity."[17]

A major critique of identity politics is, however, that individuals do not fall within one identity category. Lisa Walker describes this in terms of her own identity: "A femme woman of color . . . will probably not be recognized as lesbian, first because she is not white and then because she is not butch."[18] Not only do all three of her "identities" not necessarily signify one another, but their very construction often presumes a mutual exclusivity. To argue that she has no essential identity is misleading, however, because she still wants to be recognizable in all of her identities. "Having destabilized the unitary subject . . . it is not yet possible to set aside our interests in identity and representation. . . . Postmodern politics do and must continue attending to issues of identity and representation."[19] Critical theorist bell hooks argues that, like feminism, postmodernism tends to act as an exclusionary discourse perpetuated by white, male intellectuals.[20] In its dismissal of identity politics, it tends to overlook the very real and lived experiences of being "other." She argues, however, that the critique of essentialism employed by postmodernism is still useful for members of marginalized groups:

Employing a critique of essentialism allows African-Americans to acknowledge the way in which class mobility has altered collective black experience so that racism does not necessarily have the same impact on our lives. Such a critique allows us to affirm multiple black identities, varied black experience. It also challenges colonial imperialist paradigms of black identity, which represent blackness one-dimensionally in ways that reinforce and sustain white supremacy.[21]

John L. Jackson Jr. similarly asserts that "our critical goal is not simply to expose race's enabling fictions; we must also find ways to rewrite them."[22] Drawing on these theorists' work, what I seek to do in this book is to deconstruct the relationship between the video game audience and game texts, a relationship that has enabled discourses about representation in games to focus on restricted and pluralized versions of diversity.

Media scholarship demonstrates that industries produce texts for a particular imagined audience and divide the market into segments based on the presumed value of those segments.[23] Media industry representatives often insist that they create only what audiences will buy, and in turn individual audience members assume that purchasing power is their only tool for demanding representation from media makers. Todd Gitlin demonstrates, however, the remarginalization implicit in this neoliberal logic:

So the magazine rack re-creates the long-lasting division of American culture into fragmented interest groups. . . . The result is a restricted pluralism of consumption. The market is formally open but can cater only to those interests that can be expressed as desires for commodities. By the *laissez-faire* logic that prevails in broadcasting today, the courts uphold the argument that, where there are so many channels, the free market will automatically end up serving minority tastes. If there are enough viewers who want unconventional movies, an entrepreneur will arise to serve them and succeed at it. By the same logic, however, if no such entrepreneur arises or if one tries and fails, the demand must not have existed. Demand knocks only after the fact.[24]

According to market logic, demand for representation must come from the audience. As Gitlin points out, however, representation is provided only as part of the "restricted pluralism of consumption." Groups are representable only insofar as they are marketable. Marginalized groups are excluded until they are profitable audiences or if their representation can draw other audiences.

Marginalized groups become reified by industrial logics that wish to shape texts to target niche markets. In *Fundamentals of Game Design,* for example, game designer Ernest Adams wrote an entire appendix devoted to instructing aspiring designers on how to appeal to women and children and how to address the issues specific types of disabilities pose to game design (race and sexuality are never mentioned).[25] Much of the industry-level discussion of representation presumes that a concrete group desire, such as that for representation, can be leveraged in production. Take, for instance, the following quote from video game designer and professor Brenda Braithwaite: "It took them a while, but developers eventually got hip to the fact that there are women out there who want to control female characters [in video games], and now they're getting hip to the fact that there are LGBT gamers out there who want to control LGBT characters."[26] Here, Braithwaite articulates a common assumption that there is a clear line to be drawn from identities defined by particular identifiers to a corresponding demand for representation to, if this identifier marks a profitable niche, some resultant form of representation. Notice, however, that by this logic women and people who are L, G, B, or T are described as separate, mutually exclusive categories of identity. If a player identifies both as a woman and as lesbian, gay, bisexual, or transgender, their video game wants are presumed to be different from those of the (assumed) heterosexual women appealed to previously by games made for "female players."

More than that, representations of people of color in games are often discussed separately from gender, meaning that much of the discourse about female representation in games implies white, female characters (similarly, discussions of race in games focus almost exclusively on men of color). Arguments such as these generally imply that if only the industry used a different or more expansive definition of their audience or, at least, more categories of audiences, diversity in game texts would inevitably follow. Such an argument obscures, however, the ways in which all audience constructions offer a limited view of the identities used to divide audiences, as I discuss in chapter 2.

Analyses of media representation often focus on texts, as the previous example shows. This is logical, as the texts do the representing. In the realm of game studies, the existence of nonheterosexual, noncisgendered-male, nonwhite characters has been discussed usually in terms of "good" and "bad" representation.[27] Much of this research is on representations of gender in video games.[28] There is less work on race/ethnicity/ancestry and sexuality in digital games.[29] In many, but not all, of these studies, the problem of representation is discussed in terms of media invisibility and stereotyping. Not being represented is essentially "symbolic annihilation" and exclusion from the sociocultural milieu.[30]

Being represented can pose problems, as well. As Stuart Hall asserts, invisibility is usually replaced by "a kind of carefully regulated, segregated visibility."[31] Who gets to "count" as a member of a particular group is limited, even as popular representation is made more diverse. As Katherine Sender demonstrates in *Business, Not Politics,* for example, attempts to court the gay market in the 1990s focused almost exclusively on white, affluent, gay men.[32] Marginalized groups are traditionally either cast in clearly demarcating "other" roles, exemplifying their threat to the mainstream, or made to be "model minorities," just like the mainstream, nonthreatening, and never challenging the status quo. Their difference may be displayed in a positive (assimilated) or negative (deviant) light. As Hall goes on to point out, although there was a time in which "nothing could have been done to intervene in the dominant field of mainstream popular culture . . . without the strategies through which those dimensions were condensed into the signifier 'black,'" even media texts produced by members of marginalized groups must be reflexive on their role in claiming to represent the experience of all who claim membership in those groups.[33]

The problem with media representation, regardless of who produces it, is that it is selective even when it is not necessarily distortive, as film scholar Richard Dyer discusses in "Stereotyping."[34] Whereas the previous argument insists that audiences must be represented in media, though not merely through stereotypes, Dyer points out that stereotypes are not necessarily negative nor false. He argues that their veracity is less important than their power. Stereotypes are used as disciplinary forces that clearly demarcate the norm from its "other." Dyer unpacks the complexities of stereotypes and distinguishes between "types . . . which indicate those who live by the rules of society (social types) and those whom the rules are designed to exclude (stereotypes)."[35] Rather than talk about whether stereotypes are true or offensive, it is better, he argues, to ask what purpose they serve in a text. Stereotypes are powerful symbols, but they are also highly precarious, as Angela McRobbie reminds us.[36] They must be constantly repeated and reaffirmed through media texts and social discourse to maintain their hold on the social imaginary. Part of the tension of stereotypes, in fact, is the inherent instability of signifiers like gender, race, and sexuality. What womanhood means, what blackness means, what queer means are contextual and malleable.

Just as stereotypes are neither inherently good nor bad, judgments about what counts as a "positive" or a "negative" representation are political questions and must be interrogated as such. As media scholar Julie D'Acci argues, many descriptions of the negative effects of television representations rely on a notion of a "real" world that mediated images distort.[37] Addressing media representation in terms of "correctness" ignores questions of cultural production. The relative positive or negative qualities of portrayals exist not within texts themselves but rather within the social hierarchies, disparities, and power relation to which they refer and that they support.

To say that a given portrayal offers a negative representation of a group implies both that the group is definable and that the group exists in the world in a singular way that is misrecognized. It is also highly problematic to separate out gender, sexuality, ancestry, ethnicity, race, religion, nationality, and so on in any analysis of representation. As a case in point, one can critique the infamous Atari game *Custer's Revenge* for its overlapping offenses of sexual violence, misogyny, racism, sexism, and colonialism (not to mention critiques of its game play).[38] Mystique, a developer of several adult-themed video games, released the game in 1982. It has been hailed as one of the worst and most offensive games in history.[39] In the game, players control Custer, who one online review states is "inspired by George Armstrong Custer, a United States Army cavalry commander who fought in the Indian Wars, directly taking part in the slaughter of thousands of Native Americans."[40] The goal of the game is to guide the mostly naked general and his erect penis through an onslaught of arrows toward a Native American woman named Revenge who is tied to a post on the far side of the screen. According to a 1982 article, the game's promotional literature states, "When he gets there he 'evens up an old score,'" by repeatedly raping the woman.[41] Atari ultimately sued Mystique for the damaging effects the game had to the console's image.[42]

Although it is an outlier in video game texts in some ways, pornographic video games like *Custer's Revenge* have a long if contentious history with the industry.[43] This game is also part of the game industry's long-standing tradition of commercializing women's bodies for a heterosexual, male gaze. It is a celebration of colonial violence and sexual violence, genocide and misogyny. Merely critiquing this game as offensive to Native American women on the basis of "truthfulness" would miss much of what is actually wrong with this representation. One might argue it is indeed a "truthful" representation of the era, carelessly reflecting just one era in which Native American people were subjected to all manner of violences, including sexual violence.[44] The game is quite realistic in that sense, even if the 8-bit graphics are not. The game also signals that although we might talk about how people of color and homosexual, bisexual, queer, cisgendered, and transgender individuals are represented in video games, any analysis that looks at any one of those identifiers in isolation will inevitably fall short. *Custer's Revenge* not only is offensive to those who identify as Native American and/or female but offends those who reject its world view, regardless of their personal gender, racial, or ancestral identities.

Academics and popular-media critics often tie the lack of portrayals of marginalized groups in video games to the fact that there is little diversity in the game industry's labor pool. This work draws on the cultural production literature, which argues that researchers must look at "the power relations (whether driven by economics, politics or other forms of social discrimination) which affect who is represented and how, who speaks and who is silent, what counts as 'culture' and what does not."[45] The homogeneity of the game industry is often given as a primary example of why games are dominated by what Stephen Kline, Nick Dyer-Witheford, and Greig de Peuter call "militarized masculinity."[46] This militarized masculine culture is typically a white and heterosexual one deployed, the authors argue, to appeal to the game makers and the audience they presume is like them. It is but one type of masculinity, moreover, representing a particular hybrid or intersectional identity in its own right.

In *The Business and Culture of Digital Games,* sociologist and media scholar Aphra Kerr outlines that one of the ways digital game companies have attempted to expand beyond the male market is by addressing the gender disparity in their companies, with varied success.[47] In doing so, game design companies assume that members of a marginalized group will represent that group best and that the representation of a marginal group requires the presence of members of that group in the media industry. Of Arab representation in film, for example, Jack Shaheen argues that "the industry has a dearth of those men and women who would be the most naturally inclined to strive for accurate and balanced portrayals of Arabs."[48] This is a prevalent argument in work on video game portrayals of women.[49] Such demands shift the argument from the positive or the negative quality of a given representation to a focus on authenticity and the producers' right to represent a given identity. That "we" can represent "our" group better is questioned in some of this literature, but the prevalence of this argument in popular and academic articles bespeaks the centrality of identity politics in media representation research.[50] This book extensively critiques the assumption that members of marginalized groups are "naturally" concerned with representation of a group in which they might be classified and argues that identity, identification, and representation are much more complicated than this model allows.

Studying Representation in Games

In addition to thinking about representation outside of "positive" and "negative" frames and without an overreliance on assumptions about how groups should be represented, in talking about media representation researchers must account for the unique qualities of each medium. Research on media representation often ignores medium specificity, though video game researchers tend to be more sensitive to the options made available in the texts they analyze. The limits, opportunities, and meanings of a given representation are shaped by its production and consumption, as well as how it is encoded and decoded.[51]

As others have argued, researchers must take into account the particularities of video games when they discuss the representation of marginal groups in these texts.[52] For one, the representational capacity of games is ever evolving and shapes how group representations manifest in this medium. For example, in Nintendo's famous *Super Mario Bros.* franchise, the title character, Mario, was not originally conceived of as an Italian American plumber.[53] Rather, the particularities of his design arose out of an assemblage of factors. His pudgy features, colorful costume, large nose, and bushy mustache—characteristics subsequently read as signifying his Italianness—were all designed to make the most of the limited graphics of early arcade machines and Nintendo consoles (Figure 1).[54] The hat saved programmers from having to make animated hair. The bushy mustache and large nose gave him character despite the low resolution, limited animations, and small size of the sprite.[55] His bright-red costume helped distinguish him from the dark background of the *Donkey Kong* game in which he made his original appearance.

Mario's Italian heritage, according to industry lore, was derived from a coincidental interaction more than from intended design.[56] Even his name wasn't intended to be Italian—originally, he was merely called Jumpman. Nintendo executives wanted to use him as a brand mascot in much the way the Japanese manga industry had deployed its iconic characters. During the localization of the game for an American audience, Mario Segale, landlord of the Washington warehouse in which Nintendo's American headquarters were located in 1981, visited his property to demand the past-due rent from then–Nintendo president Minrou Arakawa. Following a heated argument, the Nintendo representatives agreed to pay. Once Segale left, having noted a vague similarity between the landlord and their pixelated hero, Nintendo developers decided to name the new mascot Mario in his "honor."[57]

Mario was originally cast as a carpenter, a working-class occupation to which game designers assumed North Americans would easily relate. He became a plumber only later, as most of the original *Mario Bros.* game was set in underground pipes.[58] The final aspects of ethnic characterization merely fell into place, according to Nintendo game designer and Mario creator Shigeru Miyamoto: "Let's put him in New York and he can be Italian. There was really no other deep thought other than that."[59] The logics by which the world got

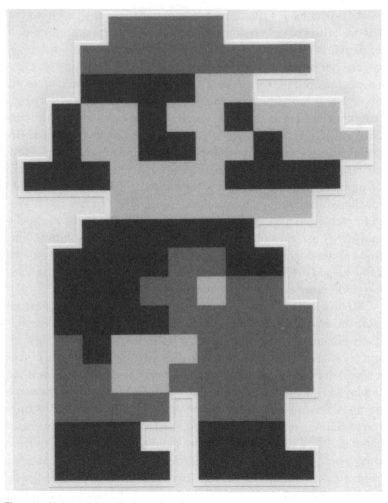

Figure 1. Picture of 8-bit Mario rendered as a sticker, showing the attempts to create a recognizable character with limited graphical capacity. Sticker produced by DecalNinja.com.

to know the now decades-old, goomba-stomping hero are unique to the particularities of 1980s game design processes. These particularities must be addressed in relation to the reception practices unique to the medium, as well, as I discuss later. Cultural critiques of Mario's ethnicization, as well as cultural critiques of video game representation more broadly, are strengthened by attention to medium specificity. To address merely the end version of a game or another media text is to divorce it from its context of creation and reception.

So if medium specificity is crucial to making strong critiques of video game representation, what then makes video games unique? What makes a game different from, say, a television show, a film, a novel, or a live theater performance? Unlike some scholars, I do not agree that video games are inherently more interactive than other media.[60] There is a lot to be said for active audiences in all popular culture.[61] This is true not just for the new media and fan activity Henry Jenkins describes in *Convergence Culture* but also for historical audiences, as Richard Butsch uncovers in *The Citizen Audience*.[62] What's different about games, though, is not just that audiences are *able* to be active but that they have to be. The game text is not as stable as other media texts, as a great deal depends on how one plays the game. This in turn has some important implications for how we critique and study representation in games.

Unlike most other media, some games give players the opportunity to create their own avatars/characters, make moral choices for their on-screen avatar/character, engage in a variety of romantic pairings, and choose dialog options that change the flow of the game texts.[63] This is particularly the case in the genre of role-playing games (RPGs).[64] As I demonstrate, however, the manner in which these options are made available can be critiqued just as readily as they can be celebrated. Optional same-sex relationships are one form of nonnormative representation unique to this medium. In games like *Bully, The Sims, The Temple of Elemental Evil, Mass Effect,* and *Dragon Age 2,* players have some options for engaging in homosexual or bisexual relationships.[65] Even in these games, however, we can see underlying assumptions on how sexual identities are articulated and formed. This is seen most clearly in the changes made between the three games in the *Fable* series.[66]

In *Fable I* my character can marry many men and women characters and remain married to multiple partners of any gender.[67] According to news articles on the game, this ability to marry multiple partners is the result of a coding error.[68] All of the villagers in the game are programmed to be able to fall in love with the player character. This makes same-sex romantic pairings possible, but it does not reduce such pairings to identity labels.[69] Whereas the nonplayer characters (NPCs) are not given sexuality labels, the player character is marked in an oddly rigid way. Before my male character (the only option in the first game) marries anyone in the game, his stat sheet lists his sexuality as "unknown" (Figure 2). When I cause him to marry a female villager, the stat sheet screen lists him as "heterosexual" (Figure 3). If I instead marry him to a male NPC, the stats screen labels my character as "gay"(Figure 4).[70] If I then marry him to a female villager, my character's label switches to "bisexual" (Figure 5). Significantly, in the game sexual practice and marriage are two separate actions, making it possible to marry one or more spouses and in turn be granted a sexuality label *without ever even having sex*! Indeed, in *Fable I,* I cannot have noncommercial sex until I am married, but I can employ the services of sex workers.

In *Fable II* the rigid emphasis on labeling and the clear distinction between identity categories shift. Unlike the first game, I can select a male or a female character at the start of the game. Gender choice in games is almost always a binary and collapses gender and sex into a single entity. Here, when I discuss gender without distinguishing it from sex, it is because performance (clothing, voice, gait, etc.) is the only way the game communicates either, and indeed, it often treats gender as sex (male and female). Interestingly, in the options

Figure 2. Screenshot from *Fable: The Lost Chapters,* where prior to marrying anyone, the player character's sexuality is listed as "unknown."

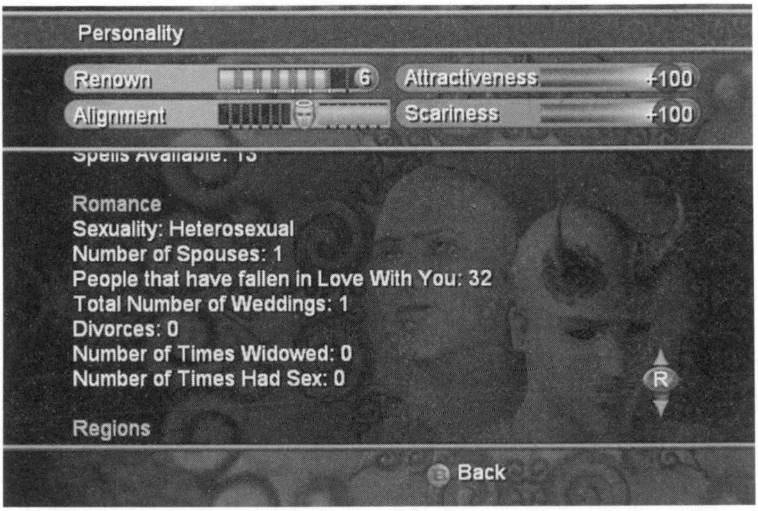

Figure 3. Screenshot from *Fable: The Lost Chapters*, where after marrying a female non–player character, the player character's sexuality is listed as "heterosexual."

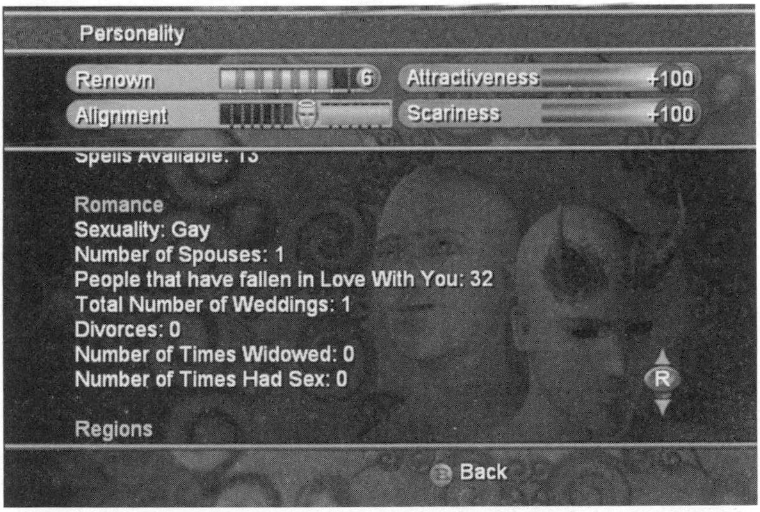

Figure 4. Screenshot from *Fable: The Lost Chapters*, where after marrying a male non–player character, the player character's sexuality is listed as "gay."

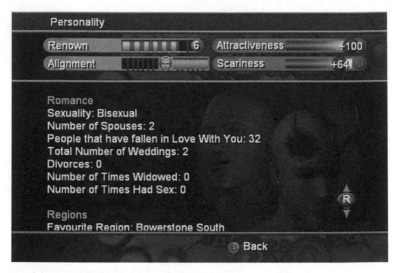

Figure 5. Screenshot from *Fable: The Lost Chapters,* where after marrying female and male non–player characters, the player character's sexuality is listed as "bisexual."

of young characters you have at the start of *Fable II,* there is not a great degree of gendered difference (Figure 6).

Either option is relatively androgynous, and largely, the difference is made clear only by the blue or the pink border around the images. Moreover, whom my character has sex with or marries no longer results in a sexuality label in the stats screen. My character can also have sex with or without being married, via seduction of the right person or by paying sex workers (Figure 7). NPCs, however, have encoded sexualities in *Fable II* (in contrast to *Fable I*). The player can highlight and scan the NPCs to pull up a screen that provides information on not only their personality and sexuality (either straight, gay, lesbian, or bisexual) but also the expressions you can perform and the gifts you can give them to win them over (Figure 8). If only dating could be this easy in the rest of our lives!

On the one hand, the type of representation in *Fable II* is more realistic than that in *Fable I,* as not everyone is open to dating people of all genders. On the other hand, what is not realistic—and quite problematic—is that any NPC whose sexuality marks them as potentially attracted to the player character's gender can fall in love

Figure 6. Screenshot of character selection screen from *Fable II*. The two options appear largely androgynous aside from the blue (*left*) and pink (*right*) borders used to signify their gender.

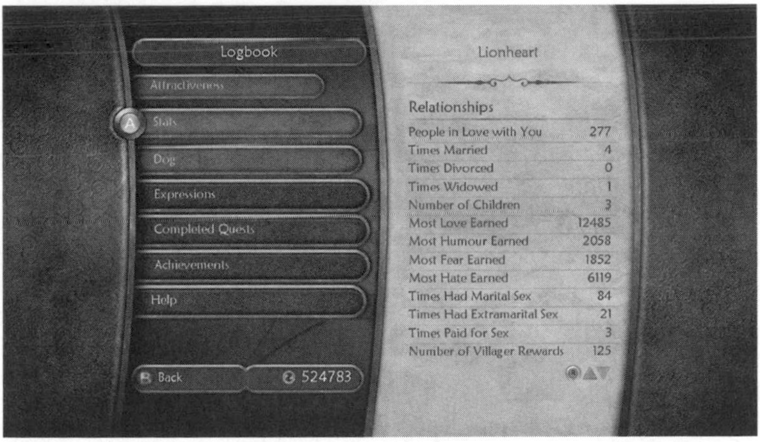

Figure 7. Screenshot of character stats screen from *Fable II* listing marriages and amount of marital and extramarital sex, but not a sexuality.

with the character. In other words, all lesbian- and bisexual-coded female NPCs and all heterosexual-coded male NPCs can fall in love with my female character, and all gay- and bisexual-coded male NPCs and all heterosexual-coded female NPCs can fall in love with my male character. Translating this into "real" life would imply that

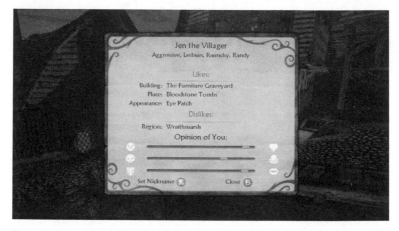

Figure 8. Screenshot of Jen the villager's info screen from *Fable II* listing her sexuality, personality, likes, and dislikes so that the player can better appeal to her.

all lesbians and heterosexual men could fall in love with me if I were a female-identified person and that all bisexuals could fall in love with anyone. Arguments about realism miss, however, what is most problematic about the way sexuality, sex, and gender are linked in the game. Specifically, a critical potential is lost when sexuality is treated as immutable and when fantasy is allowed to go only so far.

In neither game is sexuality treated as flexible. Identity labels like *straight* and *gay* are reduced to the sex you have (or whom you marry) and overdetermine with whom one might have sex in the future. As we know, outside the game many lesbians have had and continue to have sex with men, many straight men enjoy sex with other men, and many people of a variety of gender and sexuality identities end up attracted to and/or married to people they never would have dreamed of desiring at another point in their life. Further, we can be critical of the fact that children, guards, enemies, and other NPCs you cannot seduce notably have no sexuality listed. According to the game, it would seem that children have no sexuality and that NPCs' sexuality exists only as it impacts *me*. Moreover, all sex workers in the game (male or female) are coded as bisexual, which reproduces a tired and oppressive stereotype about sex workers and bisexuals as those who will screw anything that moves. Further, it assumes that sex work is *sex*, not work, and that it in turn defines one's sexual identity.[71]

Similarly, in *Fable II* although players can wear clothing designed for either of the two character options, the clothing is still clearly gendered. I can, for example, buy Noble Lady's Boots from various clothing vendors or choose to outfit my character in female or male versions of the Lower Class Outfit. Clothing meant for the other gender can earn my character "cross-dressing" stats and runs the risk of offending villagers: when I changed my male character's outfit from the Male Lower Class Outfit to a corset, a skirt, and Noble Lady's Boots (a mixture of class statuses but only one gender status), the tailor who owned the shop exclaimed, "That is just disgusting!" A female villager I was wooing, however, proclaimed me "radiant!" when I made a similar costume change in front of her and then reacted negatively when I switched back to the Male Lower Class Outfit. As in life, apparently, transphobia is not the automatic response of the NPCs. Regardless, male characters in dresses and female characters in male-coded pants are *always* coded as "cross-dressing," never merely as men in dresses or women in pants. Essentially, gender identity in the game (which is strictly controlled) overrides gender presentation in the game (which includes costumes).

Relatedly, after finishing the game's main story, the player has the option to collect one million gold, which takes a very long time, and buy Castle Fairfax. After completing these tasks, a quest becomes available by which the player can obtain the Potion of Transmogrification (Figure 9). This elixir changes the character from male to female or from female to male. At first glance, the fact that the game treats gender transformation as a reward might seem like a positive step in transgender representation. The resulting permanent transformation leads, however, passersby on the street to accuse, "Didn't you used to be a man?" Although transphobia is an everyday reality for many in real life, I doubt that the game designers were trying to highlight and critique its pervasiveness. Given that this is a fantasy game, one of the few places where gender transition might not be bound to "real-life" violence, why is it not celebrated? In other words, whose fantasy are we working with, here? Moreover, the game represents the reality of physical sex transformations as a reward for those who are able to reproduce the gender, racial, class, and sexuality norms of the system—whether that is the game or mainstream medical and legal institutions.[72] After my character's gender transformation, my spouses, unless they are labeled "bisexual," will no longer have sex with or be attracted to my character. The character's children refer to my character with a gendered parental term, *mom* for MtF characters and *dad* for FtM characters, and in the process they then use the reverse term for my character's spouse. It would seem that all of these revelations are meant as a joke, belittling the lived experiences of those for whom these sorts of reactions are everyday realities, as well as eliminating the realities of those who have supportive communities and partners (an option that seems outside the scope of possibility in the game). It also, as throughout the game, makes the relationships between sex, gender, and sexuality highly proscribed. While certainly there are real scenarios in which people leave their partners following a gender transition, many do not, and the game eliminates the latter as an option.

By the third installment of the series, we actually see a closing down of options in gender and sexuality when it comes to the player character. In *Fable III,* at the outset the player character is coded as gender normative and ostensibly heterosexual (unlike the androgynous, queer potential of the two child options in *Fable II*). At the start of the game, I can choose to play as either the prince or the princess (Figure 10). Once my butler wakes me up, if I chose to play as the prince, I must go meet my female friend after I get dressed. To show her the skills I have to "protect her," I have the option to hug or kiss her. If I chose the princess at the start of the game, then I go to the same spot to meet my male friend. I show him I am prepared to "fight by his side" by either hugging or kissing him. Thus, not only is my character positioned as heterosexual, but there is a heteronormative articulation of gender roles in the very first interaction with this NPC.[73]

All of these choices and changes are clearly tied to programmatic decisions. How NPCs react to and form relationships with my character are coded into the characters' artificial intelligence. Arguably, the goal in some of the NPCs' reactions is to enrich the experience of the game by making choices matter to the game play experience. That certain clothing options are read as cross-dressing, that sexuality is inscribed into characters' very code, and that gender and sexuality are statically defined demonstrate, however, that an oppressive world view defines the very structure of the game. In a fictional world where I can use magic on a regular basis, where faces carved in rock talk to me, and where I battle fantasy creatures,

Figure 9. Screenshot of the Potion of Transmogrification from *Fable II*, an irreversible potion that changes the player character's sex.

Figure 10. Screenshot of character selection screen from *Fable III*, with normatively gendered prince and princess options.

that particular types of reality and marginality are reinforced is both curious and indicative of larger systemic problems in how marginalized characters are incorporated into games. First, both sexuality and gender options are made available to players to use at their own discretion. Players are made responsible for making their game characters go against male, heterosexual norms in game representation. This is a very neoliberal approach to representation that puts responsibility for diversity onto audiences. If the player needs to push a "gay button," as game designer Anna Anthropy has termed it, to see same-sex relationships in games, then anyone who doesn't know or is unaware that the button exists can continue to consume the heteronormative-dominated texts.[74] Even in games with gay NPCs, the acknowledgment of their sexuality can be skipped over. In the game *Indigo Prophecy (Fahrenheit),* for example, the neighbor of one character is gay. In the one and only conversation with him, however, there is a path through the dialog trees in which he never reveals his sexuality (though other signifiers hint at his orientation).[75] If we conceptualize representation as important because it provides us with a chance to imagine the world differently, why can't that difference ever include a more open acceptance of gender and sexual diversity?

Race and gender choices are often available in games that allow players to design avatars/characters, but in many cases clear limits are placed on those options, as well. In *Fable,* I can choose only a male or a female character, for example, and the world I play in is a largely white one. In the hockey simulation game *NHL 2K5,* I can select how many inches around my various muscles are but cannot choose a female player or a dark-skinned player, despite the fact that both women and racial minorities have historically played in the National Hockey League.[76]

Role-playing games have endeavored to create a bit more diversity for players, given the integral nature of choice to the game mechanics. Unlike *Fable, Mass Effect* famously allows players to customize their avatar in terms of both physical and personality characteristics, as well as choose a backstory for their character.[77] Many of these choices are purely aesthetic, however, and sometimes obscure other problematic logics in the game code. In *Fallout 3,* for example, despite the fact that I can use a slider to change my character's skin tone, I am still forced to choose a race category first.[78] There are only four race options available: African American, Asian, Caucasian, and Hispanic. Caucasian is the default character option, though it appears third in the list.[79] In *Fallout 3* we can understand the need to pick a race as a programming decision. The character's father appears shortly after the start of the game and is rendered to look similar to the customized character, and perhaps the race choice is meant to be an algorithmic shorthand for the program to make that family resemblance possible. Yet game scholar Tanner Higgin argues this choice makes difference matter while being largely insignificant to playing *Fallout 3*. The game makes race into a rigid four-category system, reflecting the racialized violence of the "retro-futurist pre–Civil Rights world," but the game itself does not actually deal with racial conflict, outside of mutants who populate the postapocalyptic environment of the game.[80] This is particularly interesting given the fact that throughout the wasteland there is evidence that the United States' enemy in the war that led to this world was China. As is always the case in war, one would expect violence or epithets to be directed at the player character if they opted to play as an Asian character given the setting and backstory, and yet they are not. If one plays as a woman, however, there is plenty of misogynistic language to battle through.

Again, what I find most interesting about the optional representation made possible in digital games is that it places the burden of representation on players themselves. That is to say, rather than include diversity in games with set characters, most representation of marginalized groups and identifiers is placed in the hands of players. In some ways, optional and player-produced content could indicate the inclusion of queer reading practices into the game code.[81] In these games designers expand while still structuring players' ability to create their own textual experiences. At the same time, however, this optional representation must be understood as part of the neoliberal logic that dominates much of late twentieth- and twenty-first-century social and political life. Good neoliberal subjects are responsible for themselves and, thus, are responsible for their own media representation. It is also part of a long history of game industry reliance on immaterial labor from its consumers, according to Nick Dyer-Witheford and Greig de Peuter.[82] As Nick Couldry argues of digital media more generally, "We perform identity and develop public or quasi-public profiles within the constraints of platforms. . . . As a result, we risk a deep penetration by market logics into the very lineaments of self-reflection and self-expression."[83] Similarly, the way games structure how players get to alter representations, particularly when such optional content is the site of much of the potential diversity in games, indicates a particular type of marginalization made available by this medium. The industry shifts the burden of representation onto players, and diversity in turn is reduced to aesthetic pluralism.

In addition, translation and local adaptation complicate positivistic claims about representation, demonstrating how racial, gender, and sexual identities are understood quite differently in different national contexts. If this is so, how are we to read what happens when a player in Thailand chooses the racial and gender avatar options in a South African–made game? If race and gender are always local systems of value and *white* and *male* mean something very different in South Africa than they do in Thailand, given their different histories of colonialism, law, medicine, and media, what does it mean for the Thai players to choose a white, male avatar/character? Such variances make it difficult to analyze globally exported game texts as a single entity. As described earlier, the move of Jumpman to the United States is part of why we now have Mario the Italian American plumber. *Grand Theft Auto: San Andreas* is a Scottish development team's re-representation of 1990s Los Angeles gangsta culture captured through the lens of American popular media.[84]

Sometimes, the translation of games changes the implications of representation. Rumors of transgender characters in games, for example, are hard to research because of the localization process. Japanese audiences read the characters of Poison and Roxy from *Final Fight* as women. Representatives of Capcom's American division were worried that American critics would be upset that the game included hitting a woman, so the Japanese designers offered to call them transvestites.[85] This implies, of course, that Americans would have no problem with violence toward transvestite characters. When they ultimately released the game in the United States, Poison and Roxy were switched out for male characters, yet in video game culture lore, they are still claimed as early transgendered characters in video games (demonstrating a common problematic slippage between cross-dressing, transvestitism, and transgender identity in most discussions of nonbinary gender in games). Related to this, incidents of homosexual content being expunged from games and other media exported from Asia to the United States abound on the Internet but have proved difficult to verify.[86] If they were true, they would be further evidence of how choice about representation is done in concert with an imagined game audience. As this book demonstrates, however, what media makers expect audiences to want is not the same as audiences' self-described desires.

In addition, I argue that in order to study representation in video games, researchers must understand how players actually interact with games and how game play contexts shape the implications of a given representation. Espen Aarseth calls video games ergodic texts, which require nontrivial work in order for players/audiences to get through them.[87] It is important to remember, however, that as James Newman asserts, "Videogames are not *uniformly* ergodic."[88] Activity in games can be as complex as role-playing as a fictional character in a virtual world or as simple as shifting cards with a mouse in a game of solitaire. One may sit through filmic portions of a game (e.g., cinematics or cut scenes) or play a game without much thought while watching a television show on another screen. One may even watch another person play a game, acting as spectator rather than player. Indeed, games scholar and sociologist T. L. Taylor explores at length the multiple forms of "passive" spectatorship made available by these "interactive" texts in her study of the rise of professional e-sports.[89]

Although there is a long history of debate on narratological approaches[90] to games as cultural texts versus ludological approaches[91] to games as rule-bound play spaces, most games scholars now seem to accept that the best way to study video games lies somewhere between the ludology/narratology divide. Frans Mäyrä asserts, for example, that we can distinguish between core game play and representation when looking at games but that we must recognize the dialectical relationship between them.[92] Ian Bogost; Geoff King and Tanya Krzywinska; Gerald Voorhees; Torill Mortensen; and Garry Crawford make similar arguments, each articulating the way game structure informs how we might decode representational elements and the important insights to be garnered from looking at games as structures and games as representational objects.[93]

Games do not exist in a "ludological vacuum," but neither can we ignore the extent to which play affects audience readings.[94] We cannot look at representation by looking just at game texts, because the intertwined aspects of representation and play necessarily involve audiences' use of texts. Audiences matter, and as I argue, they are how representation comes to matter. In the realm of online gaming, for example, T. L. Taylor argues that avatar design is important because it "serves as the key artifact through which users not only know others and the world around them, but themselves."[95] In offline gaming, however, players may not always be as invested in their on-screen proxies. Still, as Derek Burrill argues, "The structure of the game engenders the mode of play and that the games interpolate the player, so that the player is forced into a specific identification with the avatar/character, narrative, and game."[96] Although they might be interactive, ergodic texts, games are structured in a way that promotes specific preferred readings, to use Stuart Hall's terminology.[97] Not all encoded play is equal, as some games very clearly define the gaming experience for players, including preassigned characters or clearly defined storylines and tasks. Others allow players to explore and have more avatar/character and narrative choices, thus including various player decisions in the game mechanics. Still other games can be played online, where the avatar is a representation of the player in an online social space. As I discuss in chapter 3, each of these contexts changes how players connect with game characters in important ways.

We also cannot discuss representation in games without taking into account the subcultural norms within and against which they are consumed. Speaking of the evolution of game culture over time, game designer and author Anna Anthropy points to the ways in which the games industry and its core audience have made games an exclusionary, if not inherently exclusive, activity: "The culture that this audience creates and exists within is one of in-jokes and brand worship, rituals to establish whether the participants are in or out of the tribe. It's an exclusive culture, an alienating environment that speaks only to itself. Its interactions with the outside world are decidedly hostile."[98] Textual content alone does not explain who consumes certain texts, nor can we unpack the meaning of representation in games without taking into account the context in which they are played, as I discuss in chapter 4.

It is beyond the scope of this book to offer a complete history of the representation of marginal groups in game texts.[99] I also do not delve deeply into the ways normative, white, heterosexual masculinity is depicted in games, as this project is interested in how those placed at the margins of the constructed center of gaming approach this medium. This leads to a different sort of argument for representation that could in turn be used to understand mainstream representation in a new way. Specifically, I argue that scholars can use the practice of game play to make more nuanced critiques of how representation works in video games, building on previous theoretical work that addresses games as interactive texts.

Does Media Representation Matter?

Building on the complexity of identities and the intricacies of analyzing representation in a medium-specific way, we can see that there are several problems with the way representation is made to matter in academic discourse. Media representation, some researchers argue, shapes social reality. Richard Dyer argues, for example, that "how we are seen determines in part how we are treated; how we treat others is based on how we see them; such seeing comes from representation."[100] Speaking of gender, D'Acci states, "Television representations of gender . . . have very profound effects on very real human bodies, societies, and economics."[101] Media scholars often argue that representations have beneficial or negative social implications for a given group.[102] What is beneficial or negative depends, however, on one's point of view and one's politics.[103]

Communication scholars, particularly in the social psychology tradition, stress the implications of representation through a dichotomous relationship between the marginal, disadvantaged group represented and the implied majority, empowered group who is (presumably) viewing.[104] The perspective a researcher takes, that of the in-group (those being represented) or out-group (those who are other to the group being represented), shapes their arguments about the importance of representation. Elihu Katz's seminal model for analyzing minority media representation, for example, stresses looking at whether a text is by, of, and for the minority or the majority.[105]

Looking at representation in relation to in-groups, some authors argue that it is important for individuals, minorities in particular, to see themselves reflected in the media. This is why Larry Gross argues in his book *Up from Invisibility* that representation has been especially important for sexual minorities. Unlike other marginalized groups, who are raised in communities of their own in-group, when members of gay, lesbian, bisexual, and transgender communities come out, they are often the only LGBT person they know, making media one of the only realms in which they might see others like them.[106] Several authors have described a lack of representation as a problem for queer people of color, in particular.[107]

It is important to push back against this assertion that we can posit differential importance for representation on the basis of specific social categories. The ways in which sexuality is hidden unless it is marked by socially intelligible signifiers have corollaries in many other types of identity (e.g., mixed-racial or religious identities). Indeed, the assumption that sexuality is not written on the body belies the experiences of those who fall outside the normative bounds of white, middle-class, gender-normative, male, nondisabled sexuality. Moreover, the assumption that sexuality is the only identity that can cause people to be markedly different from their families is shortsighted (e.g., cases of adoption or foster families, disabilities, neurodiversity, etc.).[108] The more general assertion that people want to see themselves reflected in cultural texts permeates discussions on media representation and is fairly consistent across the literature. The specifics of it are questioned, however, in chapter 4.

Alternatively, researchers argue that "good" representation of marginal groups is important because it can combat negative stereotypes and bigotry in dominant groups.[109] Conversely, in this argument "bad" representations can encourage negative stereotypes.[110] As Larry Gross asserts, "The media are likely to be most powerful in cultivating images of events and groups about which we have little firsthand opportunity for learning."[111] There is no clear evidence, however, that portrayals that address the needs of members of marginal groups to see themselves represented can properly address the issues of prejudice and stereotyping from out-group members. An overly positive portrayal of a traditionally disadvantaged group can serve to counter stereotypes the dominant audience might have but will not necessarily ring true to the experiences of members of the group portrayed. Furthermore, as seen in the work of Jacqueline Bobo on *The Color Purple* and Sut Jhally and Justin Lewis on *The Cosby Show*, a single text can achieve different ends in different audiences.[112] In Ben DeVane and Kurt Squire's study on portrayals of race in video games, for instance, the out-group non–African American members were more critical of portrayals of African Americans in *Grand Theft Auto: San Andreas* than were the in-group African American members.

> Peripheral social groups within the dominant class . . . enjoyed the
> satire of *GTA: San Andreas* but displayed concerns about stereo-
> typical representations of race. Conversely, participants from
> socially and economically marginalized groups . . . used the game
> as a framework to discuss institutional racism in society.[113]

In the case of the latter group, the young interviewees were largely
apathetic about racial representations in video games and used the
game as a way of discussing social inequality more generally. They
were less concerned with the game content in isolation and in fact
found the representation of urban life in the game to be very realistic. Moreover, the very idea that we can describe representations of
specific identifiers as "good" or "bad" implies a stability of meaning
of those identifiers that simply does not hold up to scrutiny, as I
discuss in chapters 2 and 4.

Regardless of the approach to analysis, throughout this literature
there are often two main arguments given for the importance of
representation for audiences. First, people want to see people "like
them" in the media they consume. This is part of the market-logic
argument: if you want people to watch/play/read something, you
put people "like them" in it. Second, it is important that people see
people unlike them in order to garner a broader view of the world.
This is the educational argument, and it tends to assume it is possible to define what is "good" or "bad" about a given representation:
good representation leads to equality; bad representation leads to
bigotry. In both cases there is a sense that researchers and marketers
can predetermine how people see themselves (i.e., identities) and
how they will position themselves vis-à-vis a given text (i.e., identification) and that this is why media representation is important.

A third way of understanding representation's importance is that
it provides evidence of what could be and who can be possible. According to Couldry, "Representations are the material site for the
exercise of, and struggle over, power."[114] Similarly, Jessica Davis and
Oscar Gandy Jr. assert that "media representations play an important
role in informing the ways in which we understand social, cultural,
ethnic, and racial differences."[115] This understanding of representation as broadly important, without assuming it defines consumption practices, is much more in line with the complex relationship
interviewees had with identities, texts, and how they understood

representation to matter. Looking at representation through the lens of audiences' relationship to these texts, as this book does, helps address these issues in a way that can take into account the contextual reasons that representation becomes meaningful.

Studying the Margins of Gaming

In the preface I discuss ways in which my own trajectory has shaped my scholarly work. For the same reason, I discuss, here, the details of this project, as they shape what conclusions I can make. As Elizabeth Bird asserts, "Methods matter because the choices made, along with the very characteristics of the researcher, play into and ultimately shape the conclusions of any research."[116] Though in many books methods are often relegated to footnotes and appendixes, I think its important that we as scholars recognize that in all research particular choices get made that determine the contributions we make to ongoing debates. Thus, methods are central, not peripheral, to our arguments.

The choices made in this project were done, for example, in conversation with the complexities of studying games as texts. Calls to have a diverse representation in video games hinge largely on proving that people who do not fit the norm (i.e., the popular and marketing construction) of the U.S. heterosexual, white, cisgendered-male, adolescent gamer stereotype do in fact play these games. In this book I take, and leave, this as a starting point in order to find out what people who are seen as on the edges of this constructed market think about representation and identification with game characters. Using an online survey and fliers posted online and throughout various Philadelphia neighborhoods, I sought out interviewees who were not male identified, not solely white identified, and/or not heterosexual identified. I wanted to avoid, however, assuming that the choice of these groups would necessarily mean either that the interviewees were concerned with representation of those identities or that those identities were particularly salient for them. To that end, I did not signal to those selected for interviews why I chose to talk to them.[117] In many cases this led interviewees to question why I wanted to talk to them, given that they weren't "your typical gamer." As game play has become an increasing part of many people's every-day lives, however, this was just the perspective I wanted. About half of my interviewees identified themselves as gamers, demonstrating that *gamer* as a term meant something more to them than "someone who plays games." Indeed, as I discuss elsewhere, gamer identity was described in relation to the amount of time, money, and socializing they spent on games, the genres of games they played, and their knowledge of gaming subcultural references.[118] Taken as a whole, they all played games fairly regularly, played a wide range of genres, and played on many platforms. In addition to the twenty-seven interviews from these participants, I also interviewed Chuck and Rusty, two white, heterosexual, male-identified video game players who were the partners of interviewees Carol and Tanner, respectively. Also, Elise, Julia's partner, was present at and took part in Julia's first interview, though she herself did not play video games and did not fill out the survey.[119]

Although I started with people who were members of particular groups, it was not to make claims about these groups in particular. Rather, the aim was to look at how members of marginalized groups discussed the importance of representation and their own connections to game texts. That is to say, I did not start with the a priori assertion that the categories of gender, race, and sexuality "mattered" to my participants or that being marginalized in some way shaped their media consumption. An overarching theme in this book is breaking away from social categorization in favor of social contextualization. In it I take seriously the insights of critical identity theories in rethinking how media researchers study and talk about identity, identification, and media representation.

Many authors have argued for the critical rethinking of the "essentialness" of identity.[120] There is empirical evidence that identities are experienced at the nexus of the individual and the social.[121] Many contemporary theorists have argued that identity exists between rather than within individuals: "Identity is a construction that is the result of interactions, relationships, and influences between individuals and institutions."[122] External forces do not, as structuralist theory would argue, wholly shape us; as Bruno Latour argues, although everything we do is inherently social, this does not mean that social structures determine our actions.[123]

Even though I used sexuality, gender, and race as starting points for selecting interviewees, I do not want to imply that these categories mattered to the interviewees' senses of self. Rather, I argue that these are identity categories whose representation has been made to matter in both popular and academic discourses (a mattering my own earlier work has been guilty of propagating). The challenge I pose is in leaving them as a starting point, not as a predetermining lens through which to interpret my results. If the identities do not matter or matter differently or challenge the ways in which these identities are assumed to matter, then I will have made my point.

The Venn diagram of interviewees maps their intersectional identities (Figure 11). I categorize my interviewees in relation to how they are positioned outside the white, heterosexual, male subject. It is important to note, however, that my positioning of interviewees (identified by their aliases) within these categories is not meant to imply an easy partition of the spheres. Devon identified, for example, as half Cuban and half European American. Growing up in Miami, people viewed him as white. When he moved to Philadelphia, people who found out he was half Cuban would say he was Spanish. He elaborated on this in the second interview:

> I look white-ish and I don't speak Spanish, so I was always the gringo in Miami. And then I come up here and I've had people say that I'm not white. And I'm always confused. . . . But I've had people, when they find out I'm half Cuban, they're like, "Oh, so you're not white." I'm like, "I . . . guess?" I don't know, that's weird. I've never not considered myself white. I mean, it's not like I'm sitting around— "I'm white, doot dee doo . . ." [laughs].

Some might call this an intersectional identity.[124] As Devon articulated, however, he did not see himself as at an intersection per se. He was both and neither, which resonates more readily with Homi Bhabha's notion of a "third space" than it does with intersectionality.[125] Also, his identity did not shift in different contexts, but how others interacted with him did.

In addition to not focusing on identifiers in isolation, in this project I look at game play as part of everyday media practices. Most game scholars and game designers treat video game play as isolated from other media. Players, like other audiences, as Janice Radway describes, "are cordoned off for study and therefore defined as particular kinds of subjects by virtue of their use not only of a single medium but of a single genre as well."[126] Much of the limited view of

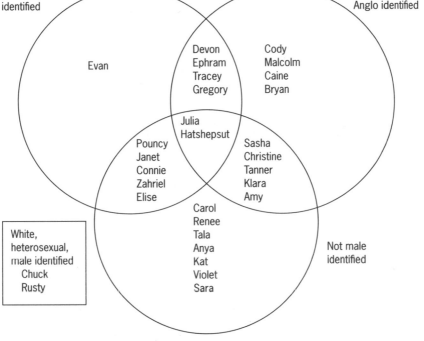

Figure 11. Venn diagram of interviewees.

gaming culture has stemmed from the industry's construction of the hard-core gamer as the ideal market, resulting in a lack of adequate attention paid, for example, to casual-gaming fans.[127] Using a similar narrowing of focus, game scholars often end up offering a representation of consumption that does not adequately address the totality of players' mediated experiences. By talking about game play in relation to the consumption of television, films, music, books, etc. and across different game texts, this book offers insight into connections between individuals' uses of media, the process of identification, and their thoughts about representation.

Although framed as an audience study, this is not a study of audiences per se; rather, it is a study of individuals' media use. In a review of audience studies, Martin Allor concludes that all previous models of the "audience" are problematic, as they continue to rely on distinct notions of the "audience," whether as a physical entity or an abstract position, and of texts.[128] As Ien Ang argues, through an overreliance on industry models media scholars have traditionally treated the audience as something that exists naturally in the world.[129] Allor asserts, "To take the social subject seriously, the heterogeneous practices that frame individuated engagements with texts, discourses, and ideologies need to be taken into account."[130] We must see media consumption as situated within the everyday lives of interviewees, as well as situate those experiences and individuals within wider contexts. This is, in fact, the only way to study meaning. As Radway asserts:

> We are forced . . . by the nature of meaning itself as the construct of a reader always already situated within an interpretive context, to conduct empirical research into the identities of real readers, into the nature of the assumptions they bring to the texts, and into the character of the interpretations they produce.[131]

For this reason we have to view the importance of representation as situated within larger contexts rather than focus only on a single text, a kind of audience, or a particular identity category. In the end we must look, as Allor asserts, "through both a microscope and a telescope at the same moment."[132]

How do we get at the reception of video games in a way that helps us make sense of when and how representation comes to matter in them? Seth Giddings argues that rather than study game texts, researchers should study the "event" of game play, the moment in which players engage with a text.[133] I think, however, that this is still too narrow. Rather, I examine video game play as part of media as practice. In this book I look at the whole environment of media flows rather than just audience consumption of discrete texts. As Couldry suggests, "By moving media research's centre of gravity away from texts (and their production or direct reception) and towards the broader set of *practices* related to media, we get a better grip on the distinctive types of *social process* enacted *through* media-related practices."[134] For this reason, this project does not focus on specific game texts or game play sites. Rather, I use video game play as a starting point in interviews for a conversation about the interconnections (and disconnections) between identity, identification, and representation.

Looking at game play as a form of media practice also entails looking at games in terms of everyday life. Methodologically, it makes a great deal of sense to look at media texts in the context of their production and reception.[135] Similarly, it makes sense to look at audiences in context of their whole experience of being audiences, across media, and in relation to social systems. In her essay "Travels in Nowhere Land," Bird argues that "we must try to see how media use fits into the entire complex web of culture, understanding how it articulates with such factors as class, gender, race, leisure and work habits, and countless other variables."[136] In sum, the key might be to see both media and identity as processes, not as end products. In retrospect this seems like an obvious suggestion, as communication is a process and media and identity are both types of communicative practices. Both media representation and identity are built upon shared meanings and are part of the circuit of culture Hall describes.[137] Rather than look at the representation in a text or a specific identity category, I look at the webs of meaning to which both are tied.

Instead of approaching the issue of representation in game texts, I use an ethnographic approach to study marginalized players of video games. I draw on the long history of ethnographic feminist media studies on audiences who are traditionally under- or misrepresented in media, on fans of disparaged media, and on generally disempowered audiences.[138] Ethnographies of media audiences have as their task the "thick description" of the complex process of media consumption.[139] As put by Faye Ginsburg:

> If there is some original contribution to be made by an ethnographic approach, it is to break up the 'massness' of the media, and to intervene in its supposed reality effect by recognizing the complex ways in which people are engaged in processes of making and interpreting media works in relation to the cultural, social, and historical circumstance.[140]

By engaging with individuals' use of media broadly, I address the ways identity, identification, and representation are contextually important rather than universally so. This project is informed by this ethnographic sensibility, though it is not an ethnographic study in the strictest sense.[141]

During the course of this project, I conducted at least two inter-views with each person,[142] the first being a traditional face-to-face interview and the second being a "gaming interview," as described by Gareth Schott and Kirsty Horrell and as used in one of my pre-vious studies.[143] Interviews were crucial to getting the type of data I needed in this analysis. I was interested in how participants ac-counted for their choices and experiences in game play and media consumption. I wanted to understand how, in their own words, they understood representation and identification. Over the course of the interviews, all of my interviewees talked about how they under-stood their identity, as well. Certainly, interviewees were always performing in some regard, and indeed, one interviewee described approaching the first interview like a job interview.[144] Multiple inter-actions offered the chance to get different information from partici-pants. It was particularly useful that some second interviews took place in a different venue from the first. I could balance a more for-mal first interview in an office with a more relaxed gaming interview in someone's living room. In addition, as one interviewee stated, having the second interview gave her an opportunity to think more about the questions I had asked previously and elaborate on her an-swers. Despite the odd nature of speaking to a stranger (me) about personal topics like identity and identification, more than a few people said, "I never tell anyone this, but . . . ." Several interviewees also contacted me after the interviews to provide more thoughts on issues we had discussed.

I would argue that by staying broadly scoped I was able to map relationships between identity, identification, and representation across an array of gaming and media experiences. More narrowly focused studies would have missed this. I was also able to hear more about the wide variety of games each person played and how their relationships to gaming shifted over time. I did this in the tradition of media studies scholars who take individuals and look at their me-dia use broadly to understand how identities are formed and re-formed constructions.[145] In doing so, however, I branched out from these studies in an attempt to speak to a diverse group of people. Again, my findings demonstrate important ways in which social po-sitionality does and does not shape participants' thoughts about the issues central to this book. Much remains unexplored in the realm of solitary offline game play (as well as social offline and solitary online game play), and that is what makes game studies such an exciting field. Further, by analyzing responses within participants' interviews and survey responses and identifying similarities in themes across interviewees, I was able to identify variances at the individual level, similarities among people who played different games, and differences among people who played similar games.

In several ways this was not a traditional ethnography, as there was no definable field for me to enter into—not even a contentious and quotation-marked-off one like the "Harlem" Jackson analyzes.[146] Researchers using more traditional ethnographic methods define their field in many different ways. One might study a specific region, as Mary Gray does in her study of rural queer youth or as Lila Abu-Lughod does in her study of television in Egypt.[147] One might also focus on specific communities of users defined by texts, genres, or online spaces.[148] Researchers look at how a specific geographic space and a sense of belonging to that space are played out through various media uses.[149] They locate consumption, historically or currently, in locations such as the home, public places, and online worlds.[150] Similarly, game studies fields are often defined in relation to sites, whether physical spaces of play,[151] virtual worlds,[152] or game practices.[153] Some studies have also focused on individual, solo game play.[154]

This book expands on this literature, focusing predominately but not exclusively on individuals playing on their own, largely in offline or single-player games.[155] Although I discuss online or group play at times, the primary focus of this project is individual video game play. Gary Fine in his 1970s ethnography of tabletop gaming argues that context of play is a key component in analyzing the frames of game play.[156] This is something that many games researchers acknowledge, yet so much research has focused very specifically on online gaming. If we are to take seriously that context matters to playing games, then more work must be done on the game play that often takes place behind closed doors. To that end this book focuses on solitary gaming, although I do discuss themes from interviews that offer insights into online and social game play, as well.

There are certainly limitations to using interviews as a method rather than the extended and ongoing participant observation common in most ethnographic research. Similarly, by focusing on game play broadly rather than the play of a specific game, this project provides only brief glimpses into each participant's relation to specific games. Some of the factors in the methodological decisions were purely logistical.[157] Given that I was targeting individuals who with some exceptions did not know me or each other, longer embedded work seemed like asking too much. Many brought me into their homes, while others traveled to meet me. They answered questions and played video games with me as a spectator. For my questions about how they described their game play, how they conceptualized identification, and how they discussed representation, two meetings with only a single observation session proved to be enough to achieve theoretical saturation.

Similarly, this is not a project about Philadelphia, but the location of this project within its geographic boundaries inevitably shaped with whom I spoke and what they said. Philadelphia is an urban center that contains several universities, and my interviewees came from diverse socioeconomic backgrounds, as well as places of origin.[158] Though my project is located in a specific space, it is influenced by the histories of interviewees' lives. A graduate student from Southeast Asia, an unemployed artist from Southern California, a city worker from rural Georgia, a child-care provider from North Philadelphia, and a neurologist from the Jersey Shore are just some of the individuals who make up the participant pool. These experiences influence the accounts analyzed herein.

My focus on solitary gaming is not meant to deny the sociality of gaming. As I later describe in detail, solitary game play is inherently informed by social process. I also do not focus on interviewees' experiences and solitary game play to reify the individual. As Couldry argues, "To reflect on the individual experience of culture does not mean turning our backs on the social; instead, thinking about the individual story plunges us immediately into the web of relationships out of which we are formed."[159] Approaching issues of identity, identification, and representation through individuals' interpretations can offer a more grounded understanding of all three and demonstrate the ways sociality is intertwined with them.

I am aware of my own relationship to my interviewees, in a manner similar to that described in Patrick Murphy and Marwan Kraidy's review of ethnographies in global media studies:

What emerges from a reading of these different forays into textual self reflexivity is a sense of the ethnographers as self conscious dancer. The ethnographer has entered the dance floor to dance with the others, but who the others are to the ethnographer shapes the ethnographer's way of moving and interacting, indeed, of the ethnographer's own sense of self and community.[160]

During several gaming interviews, interviewees asked me about the games I played, the research I did, and what game they should play for our interview. As I watched interviewees play, I knew that I was changing the experience of playing the game, because most people are not used to having a stranger watch them play, outside of the professional gamers Taylor describes.[161] To correct some of this imbalance, I played along with interviewees in some cases and even refrained from recording audio in others to make it seem less awkward and staged. Playing with participants allowed for new research moments to appear. It broke down many of the barriers between me, as the researcher, and participants, as the researched. One interviewee, for example, was taciturn throughout much of the first interview, but once he started playing a game in the second interview, he talked for three hours straight with little prompting. Another interviewee sat opposite me with his arms crossed until we began talking about shared childhood popular culture loves, at which point he leaned in on the table and became animated.

Following the interviews, I was in email or personal contact with several interviewees. For example, some emailed follow-up thoughts after interviews or would discuss my research with me if we saw each other in another setting (Philadelphia is a surprisingly interconnected city for its size). In this book I draw heavily on my own video game play and media consumption, and in addition, I made it a point to seek out games or other media texts with which I was unfamiliar if interviewees mentioned them or played them during interviews. Finally, I draw on media coverage (online and offline) of the representation of marginalized groups in video games and other media and online discussions, as well as on informal conversations I have had about video games, media representation, and identification.[162]

Conclusion

This is a study of representation that does not look primarily at texts. It looks at game play within the everyday lives of players while focusing on offline rather than online play. It studies marginalized groups without focusing on specific identifiers in isolation. I argue that these are necessary shifts from the typical approaches and help produce a different kind of knowledge about identity, identification, and media representation in video games. I "back into" media use, as Elizabeth Bird and David Gauntlett describe, by starting with the audience as people rather than as types of players or markets.[163] I thus start, as Radway suggests, with a group of people (though using one medium as an entry point) to see where, when, if, and how they interact with media in order to get a more complete view of media consumption broadly speaking.[164]

It is often proclaimed that interactivity and play make video games unique as media texts.[165] Audience activity is not, however, the sole province of games. Returning to the field note that begins this chapter, *Brokeback Mountain* is a particularly fortuitous counterpoint to a discussion of video games and audience activity. The film was heralded as a major mainstream portrayal of homosexuality, yet it recalled a history of queer readings of presumably "straight" cowboy films. The movie itself was the fodder for a slew of parodies, offering queer rereadings of everything from *Teenage Mutant Ninja Turtles* to *Entourage*.[166] Games like *The Sims* offer a similar type of activity, but one encoded into the very core of the game. It too was celebrated as a landmark in gay media representation for being one of the first games to allow same-sex relationships.[167] Though the game has limits to the number of options it offers, one can create a lesbian separatist community almost as readily as one may make a heteronormative, 2.5-offspring fantasy.

Audience activity need not just imply an active reworking of the text. While I watched Pouncy play *Settlers of Catan,* I heard the housemates discuss whether Jack and Ennis, the two protagonists in *Brokeback Mountain,* were both actually gay in the movie (no conclusion was reached). Reception and meaning making are always active, communal processes and are produced through engagement with a variety of media texts. Play is not the sole domain of games, either. There was a lot of playful banter among the housemates watching the film, between Pouncy and their online game competitors, and between Pouncy and myself. Games are not always part of an active consumption process; watching others play is not only the domain of scholars like myself, as Taylor also discusses.[168] Media consumption is social in ways that are not readily apparent in research that focuses on audiences as either masses or individual viewers or in game studies that focus on fandom and social gaming. There is a sense, however, throughout the interviews conducted in this project and my previous research, as well as in literature on video games generally, that there is something about video games that is unique.

Unlike most movies or TV shows, in video games identifiers like gender, race, and sexuality are not always integral to representation. *Settlers of Catan,* for example, is a board game that was subsequently released as a computer game, a version of which my interviewee Pouncy played online with other people. Players try to control portions of the digital game board, which give them access to the different resources necessary to build up their settlements. This all takes place on a visually abstract screen (Figure 12). As is discussed in the following chapters, however, in several ways the intersections of identity, identification, and media representation were relevant even in this abstract setting.

What is different about video games, then? According to my interviewees, mostly and quite simply, it is the fact that they are games. Two primary ways they described the effect of this fact were through the linked issues of identification and the politics of representation. Although not universally, interviewees described connections with

Figure 12. *Settlers of Catan* board game, which has been re-created in both official and unofficial form for online game play. Photograph by Angel Bourgoin, October 6, 2013.

most video game characters often as different (sometimes non-existent) from identification with other media characters and game characters with developed backstories. They also felt identification, when experienced in games, was the same process they experienced in other media. Thus, identification in games is like other media reception, but the texts do not always engender or, even, need to engender identification. Moreover, interviewees viewed the representation of marginalized groups in games as relatively unimportant. The reasons for both differences, as well as the fact that interviewee after interviewee noted the close relationship between identification and representation, help us make sense of what is unique about video games. They also direct us to reconsider, however, what is important about media representation and identification more broadly. That is to say, through a medium in which both seem unnecessary, we can question how and if identification and media representation are necessary in other media. Taken together, they provide an argument for diversity in video games and media representation that does not rely on niche marketing, identity politics, or neoliberal logics.

2

Does Anyone Really Identify with Lara Croft?

Unpacking Identification in Video Games

In the 1980s Clair Huxtable of *The Cosby Show* was my mother's TV-mom idol.[1] She was exactly the type of mother that my mother wanted to be: strong and independent yet caring and always there for her family. If I were to analyze this as a researcher investigating identification and representation, there would be many ways in which I might approach this viewer/character relationship. I might signal it as an instance of surprising cross-racial identification (my mother was white, and Clair was African American) or, conversely, an expected same-gender identification (both my mother and Clair were women). I might claim that it was a case of aspirational class identification: Clair was a lawyer married to Bill Cosby's character, Dr. Cliff Huxtable, whereas my mother was a working-class single mom. Knowing my mother, however, I doubt that any of those analyses were particularly true. Rather, there was something in Clair that my mother both recognized in herself and wished for herself that made her feel connected with Clair. She saw both their similarities and their differences.

The complexity of this relationship between my mother and a fictional television character is so familiar to so many of us that it may seem academically uninteresting. Yet when taken down to the level of actual viewers, the broad strokes of research that describe identification as a result of either sameness *or* difference are rendered obviously flat. What interests me in this example is that the phenomena we see vary greatly with what identifier we as researchers deem important. Research on representation and identification often assumes that identifying *as* a member of a particular group means identifying *with* a media character. Theoretical and empirical research into playing as "other" in video games, for example, often uses identifiers like gender to interpret players' relationship to their avatar/player character/game.[2] Researchers tend to extrapolate identities from identifiers (gender, ancestry, sexuality, etc.) while ignoring the ways in which identifiers are unstable signifiers. Identities are often used as the independent variable in audience-based studies (and the social sciences generally) through which results are interpreted. As Judith Butler puts it, "It seems that what we expect from the term *identity* will be cultural specificity, and that on occasion we even expect *identity* and *specificity* to work interchangeably."[3] Yet what it means to be a woman, Asian, or bisexual, not to mention how each is inflected in audience relationships to texts, is relative and contextual.

In this chapter I explore how interviewees understood the process of identification. I disentangle the ways individuals identify *with* video game and media characters in ways that do not always correspond to identifying *as* members of specific marginalized groups. This is not to say that identities are irrelevant to how we engage with media or articulate the importance of representation. Rather, I show that we can get a better sense of what representation means when we unpack the nuanced relationship we have with texts. Identification proves a useful entry point into these discussions. I describe how players identify with and as fictional characters, as well as the relationship between identification and disidentification. I also discuss identification's ties to perceived realism and its relative unimportance when it comes to texts used for fantasy and escapism. These relationships also influenced if and how interviewees identified with game characters, as I discuss in chapter 3, and how they viewed the importance of media representation, as I explore in chapter 4. The escapism that is central to much of game play, linked with the relatively low importance of identification-like relationships to interviewees' game play, supports an argument for representation that highlights diversity in what is possible rather than the marketability of niche audiences.

Identification and Representation in Games

Often, critiques of textual representations are based on how the audience is constructed. Whatever group the researcher thinks is the intended audience for the text shapes the researcher's analysis of that representation. David Leonard and Dean Chan, for example, discuss the relationship between player identities and the race of player and non-player characters in digital games.[4] Both argue that most representations of minorities in video games are structured in a way that implies one might play at being a minority but that the player is not presumed to be a member of the marginalized group. A game like *True Crime: Streets of L.A.,* for example, "pro-actively cultivates a sense of relative cultural 'otherness.' . . . It constantly reminds the gamer that this is the 'other' side of Los Angeles."[5] The implied audience is the dominant identity (white), opposed to the minority one depicted (African American, Latino, or Asian). Geoff King and Tanya Krzywinska propose that this could help explain the pleasure for Arab players in games like *Underash* and *Special Force,* which were created by Arab companies and organizations for Arab players:

> Does a powerful impression of agency created within a game reinforce broader cultural/ideological notions of agency—or does the pleasure involved lie in some level of acknowledgement of the fact that such agency is, precisely, *not* available in the outside world?[6]

Other literature on Arab representation in video games relies on similar assumptions, implying that games by Arab companies represent Arab protagonists better than those produced elsewhere.[7]

Some scholars look at how gender shapes audience interpretations or experiences of game texts.[8] Playing as Lara Croft in the game series *Tomb Raider* is assumed to mean different things whether a player is male or female, as one implies cross-gender role-play or objectification and the other assumes same-gender identification. The train of thought that presumes playing as a character necessarily entails identifying with that character is exemplified in the following passage from Anne-Marie Schleiner's essay "Does Lara Croft Wear Fake Polygons":

> The predominantly male players of games like Tomb Raider are drawn into identification with the female avatar, immersed in the combat and puzzles of the game. . . . Rigid gender roles are broken down, allowing the young boys and men who constitute the majority of Tomb Raider players to experiment with "wearing" a feminine identity, echoing the phenomenon of gender crossing in Internet chat rooms and MUDs.[9]

This quote clearly demonstrates a problematic conflation of online role-play and identification with closed-game avatars. Maya Mikula argues that based on the way the game has been marketed, *objectification* rather than *identification* more aptly describes the primarily male audience's relationship to Lara Croft.[10] Schleiner goes on to identify the many different readings of Lara Croft available to different types of players but links these readings to player identities in a highly problematic way. For instance, she makes the compelling case for Lara as a queer character but argues that such a reading is solely available to queer women. Though I would concede that queer audiences are better versed in finding queerness in otherwise mainstream texts, the persistence in linking the interpretation of characters to the identities of players is something I question in this chapter.

Tomb Raider is a particularly interesting example when trying to make sense of the complex connections between identities, identification, and representation in video games. The franchise's archaeologist heroine is "an upper-crust thrill seeker, an 11th generation Countess who rejected a life of comfort, learning rugged self-reliance at an early age."[11] The game's original developer, Core Design, released two games in the 1980s featuring a male Indiana Jones–esque character named Rick Dangerous with modest success. These earlier games have been identified by some as precursors to *Tomb Raider*.[12] The decision to create a female protagonist in a sea of games in which women existed almost entirely as victims or decoration was meant as a hook to help the game stand out in a crowded marketplace.[13] Understanding this decision as a hook rests on the assumption that it was the first time men were asked to play as a female character (1982's *Ms. Pac-Man* and 1986's Samus Aran from *Metroid Prime* notwithstanding).[14] The game was also meant to foreground new 3-D graphics technology, which may in part explain Lara's ever-increasing and much-critiqued breast size. Her visual design took greater advantage of 3-D graphics than did that of the flat-chested, straight-hipped male protagonist Duke Nukem, whose 3-D game was released the same year.[15]

How the intended audience was constructed helps us critique the decisions made in developing Lara. Looking at the early design process, for example, we can see the inherent intersectionality at play when a character is created, as well as critique the developers' limited imagination of who could be a strong heroine. During the game's development, designers proposed several different designs:

> Sociopathic blonds, muscle women, flat topped hip-hopsters and a Nazi-like militant in a baseball cap came and went. Eventually, they settled on a tough South American woman in a long braid and hot pants, willing to go to any lengths to win the greatest trophies lost to history. An Olympic-level athlete, an expert of antiquities, a born survivor. [Artist Toby Gard] named his creation Laura Cruz.[16]

Higher-ups at Eidos, the video compression and editing software company that had acquired Core Design, insisted that they "wanted a more 'UK-friendly' name," ultimately settling on Lady Lara Croft.[17] According to Katie Salen and Eric Zimmerman, "Originally conceived of as a cross between riot grrrl icon Tank Girl and British pop star Neneh Cherry, Lara developed into a buxom female version of Indiana Jones."[18] Her class, race, sexuality, and gender presentation were made normative, and thus, the only challenge she posed to mainstream game representation was in her performance of gendered labor.

At her inception Lara could have been a kick-ass, intelligent, woman of color, feminist superstar. Market logics, imagined audiences, and an assumption that men could not identify *as* Lara led, however, as Sheri Graner Ray describes, to "a hypersexualized female caricature that is, essentially, 'eye candy' for male players."[19] Lara, according to Stephen Kline, Nick Dyer-Witheford, and Greig de Peuter, "represents a revised approach to game design that more prominently incorporates women into the game world but in a way that intensifies appeal to the male market."[20] The marketing and programming of *Tomb Raider* largely implied a male player.[21]

Despite these histories, the act of playing Lara within the game series can mean many different things to different people. Marketing might attempt to anchor her as a plaything signifier, but as Helen Kennedy argues, within the context of the narrative and the play of the game Lara does not necessarily fall into the typical sex-kitten role.[22] In addition, Kennedy asserts that although Lara might be gender normative in terms of dress, her sexuality is never discussed in the game narrative. At the same time, she goes on to say, Croft bares many of the signifiers of female objectification, including breasts that are overly large for her physical size and revealing clothing that seems poorly suited to traipsing through danger-filled tombs. As Mikula details, after Toby Gard left Core Design subsequent games in the *Tomb Raider* series upped the sexual ante for the heroine.[23] Moreover, the *Tomb Raider* paratexts, including the film franchise starring Angelina Jolie, have overdetermined player interactions with the game, as Mia Consalvo and Bob Rehak describe.[24] She is presented, for example, as having relationships with men in the film adaptations of the game, though having sex with men certainly does not have to define her sexual identity.

In the recent reboot of the series, Crystal Dynamics has attempted to make Lara a more nuanced character. The marketing of the game demonstrates, in fact, a shift in how the company is positioning the audience in relation to Lara—largely, from an emphasis on accompanying and/or learning about Lara to an emphasis on becoming and/or identifying as Lara. Whereas the box for 2006's *Tomb Raider: Legend* invites players to "take Lara back to the tombs," in the 2013 release we are invited to "experience Lara Croft's intense origin story."[25] The Best Buy synopsis is even more explicit, stating that players of this release can "step into the role of Lara Croft," as opposed to ads for previous releases, which invite players to "accompany" or "play with" Lara.[26] Although the new edition of the game invites players to take on the role of the heroine, the box imagery and the game content itself portray Lara as more vulnerable. The *Legend* box shows Lara staring out confidently (Figure 13), whereas the box for the reboot shows Lara bending her head, gripping an injured arm, and gazing downward and away from the player (Figure 14). Similarly, there has been much debate about the 2013 game's inclusion of an implied threat of sexual assault and the ritual sacrifice of female characters at the hands of an all-male group of cultists.

We could take the developers' word that they wanted to go beyond the sexualized pinup of old and create a more vulnerable Lara.[27] The visual depiction of Lara as more athletic, reasonably proportioned, and wearing cargo pants (rather than the series' norm of short-shorts) is encouraging.[28] The choice to include the threat of sexual assault, however, demonstrates an assumption that players of the game have never feared or been the targets of sexualized violence, at least to the extent that it would deter them from purchasing the game. Furthermore, it is questionable that when the series is inviting

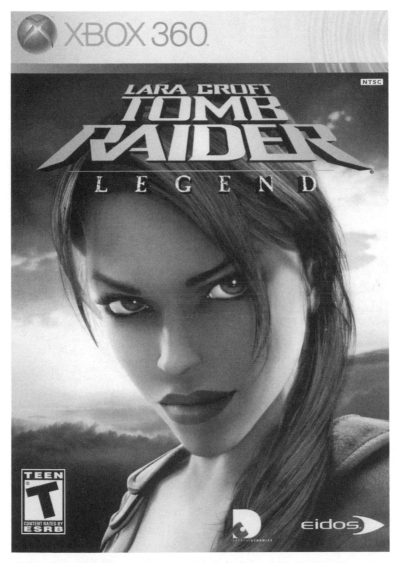

Figure 13. *Tomb Raider: Legend* box cover showing a strong and self-possessed Lara Croft staring directly at the prospective player.

players to identify with Lara, her strength is being framed in relation to a victimization narrative. Marketing logics presume that a strong woman is not a character with which male players could connect. Reviews of the game by some feminist critics claimed that reports

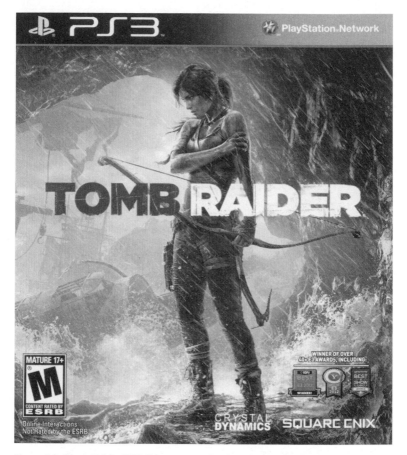

Figure 14. *Tomb Raider* (2013) box cover showing a battered Lara Croft looking down, head against the rain.

of Lara's victimization were overblown, fueled by the developer's discussion of the game prerelease.[29] And yes, the sexual assault threat scene most often critiqued is brief and over early in the game, but the game clearly uses sexualized advances as a threat, which is not something that typically happens to male game protagonists. Throughout the game Lara is scared, not as confidently self-possessed as she is in other games in the series, and loses many people close to her in an attempt to add complexity to the character's backstory. Furthermore, throughout the game her enemies pepper their threats of violence with sexist language. Threats of and actual sexual assault against female characters are not unique to games, of course. In novelist Stieg Larsson's widely popular *Millennium* trilogy (later adapted as both a Swedish and a U.S. trilogy of films), rape and domestic violence are used to explain the drive of hacker heroine Lisbeth Salander.[30] For male characters in popular media, whether the television show *24*'s Jack Bauer or film action hero Indiana Jones, threats of violence tend to be nonsexual in nature.

The cyber-bimbo feminist icon and vulnerable young girl readings of Lara tell us more about how Lara is positioned by producers than what she means for different audiences. Although we can interpret Lara as a character with all of the tools of film theory, semiotics, and cultural production, those approaches, while valuable, do not tell us about how fans interact with her evolving characterization. As Mikula writes, "She is indeed a sex object; she is indeed a positive image and a role model; and many things in between."[31] For this reason among many, this book focuses on audiences rather than texts as it addresses the many readings these texts make possible. Analyzing texts tells us how the audience was constructed and about the inner workings of industry logics, but an audience study helps us make sense of where these meanings go after they are constructed.

Identification and Identities

When we say we really *identify* with the main character in a book, the sidekick in a movie, or a particular character in a television show, what does that word mean? Do we mean the same thing when we say that we identify with our avatar in a video game? When we say representation is important to marginalized groups, is it because identifying with people who share our marginalized status feels validating? Similarly, are nuanced, positive, and good representations of marginalized groups important because we want to believe that if out-group members could only identify with them, inequality and bigotry would end? As discussed in chapter 1, part of the problem in the perceived relationship between identities, identification, and the importance of media representation is the assumption that identification *with* a character is the same as identification *as* a member of a specific group. As I explore in this chapter, although identity is an important part of the identification process, the act of identifying *with* a fictional character is slightly different. This is particularly true if we conceptualize identification as contextual, fluid, and imaginative. In turn, this helps us rethink how and when representation is important.

A major problem with identification is that researchers do not clearly or consistently define it as a theoretical concept. In part this is because as a concept identification spans sociology, psychology, communication, media studies, and numerous other fields, as outlined in wonderful detail by Kelly Boudreau.[32] In the article "Defining Identification," Jonathan Cohen argues that media studies scholars often talk around identification without clearly explicating or studying it.[33] Some authors describe identification as taking the perspective of a character.[34] Others define identification as the process by which a viewer/player/reader takes on the role and mind-set of a fictional character.[35] Many of these are cognitive-based approaches that seek to quantify audience relationships with media characters. Scholars in this vein define identification as forms of homophily,[36] parasocial interaction,[37] empathy,[38] transportation,[39] presence,[40] and combinations thereof.[41]

Instead of using these theories, I approach the issue of identification through theories of identity, in part because identifying as a member of a group is part of the process of identity formation. As Stuart Hall describes in his essay "Who Needs Identity?" identities and subjects are made in specific moments, through a sense of connection and via a process we can call *identification*:

> The notion that an effective suturing of the subject to a subject-position requires, not only that the subject is 'hailed,' but that the subject invests in the position, means that suturing has to be thought of as an articulation, rather than a one-sided process, and that in turn places *identification*, if not identities, firmly on the theoretical agenda.[42]

Hall argues that a focus on identification is potentially more useful than a focus on identity, as it allows for the contextual self-definition of the individual, rather than defining them from the outside.

Representation studies often start by looking at how one specific identity (gender, race, sexuality, etc.) shapes audiences' identification with and interpretation of a text.[43] Such studies tend to essentialize identities and their impact on audiences' approaches to texts. Although it is important to analyze what identities texts make available for identification, media cannot simply transmit identities from above. Caroline Evans and Lorraine Gamman argue, for example, that gaze theory is complicated when one looks at the fluidity of identity categories: "Because identity itself is not fixed, it is inappropriate to posit any single identification with images."[44] One way I have sought to enter into the conversation about representation and audiences' identities is through the process of identification.

If one is asking audiences about representation, when and how particular aspects of identity become relevant in the process of consuming media is important. This examination usually involves starting with a specifically defined audience and seeing how it relates to a representation of their identity, however operationalized. There are some methodological problems with studying representation without presupposing the relevance of certain identity markers.[45] However, arguing that marginalized groups should be represented in games so that members of those groups have characters to identify with collapses *being identified as* a member of a group into *consumer demand for* representation. Identifying *as* a member of that group is also assumed to shape how players want to identify *with* video game characters. How might one get at which identities are relevant in these texts and what it is about representation that is important without presupposing which identifiers matter? Rather than talking to players about how they connected with particular characters and then using their demographics to interpret those relationships, I began the discussion of representation by asking interviewees if, how, and why they identified with media characters generally as well as video game characters or avatars. This method allows me to see the expansiveness at work in how audiences connect with media texts—sometimes, in unexpected ways.

The relevance of particular identities in particular social interactions helps explain how people identify with media characters. According to French philosopher Louis Althusser, subjects are made through interpellation. In his seminal work "The Ideological State Apparatus," Althusser uses the metaphor of a person being hailed by a police officer shouting, "Hey you!" He asserts that it is "in the turning" that a person realizes she or he is the "you" being called and, thus, becomes a subject of the state apparatus.[46] Subjects are produced as such within specific moments, as Graeme Turner explains:

> For Althusser, the notion of an essential self disappears as a fiction, an impossibility, and in its place is the social being who possesses a socially produced sense of identity—a 'subjectivity'. This subjectivity is not like the old unified individual self; it can be contradictory, and it can change within different situations and in response to different kinds of address.[47]

Building on Althusser, Michel Foucault interrogates the way institutional discourses shape how people think about themselves as subjects. The individual is the product of this historical process and becomes a subject through the obfuscation of the connection between this process and individual identity. Identities for Foucault are thus produced through power relations, not simply limited by them.[48] This subjectivity requires agency, however: "Power is exercised only over free subjects, and only insofar as they are free. By this we mean individual or collective subjects who are faced with a field of possibilities in which several ways of behaving, several reactions and diverse comportments, may be realized."[49] In turn, critical race and postcolonial studies explore, as Paul Gilroy describes, "how 'subjects' bearing gender and racial characteristics are constituted in social processes that are amenable to historical explanation and political struggle."[50]

Continuing this line of interrogation, Judith Butler argues that identity is a performance. For Butler it is not just that practices and discourses are shaped by powerful institutions but that subjectivity is constantly performed and made natural by subjects.[51] The concept of performativity highlights the absence of internal identities but also explains that structures themselves are *empowered* via performance. Identities are performed, but only within the context of systems of meaning that allow those performances to be intelligible. Performativity is, for Butler, not akin to Erving Goffman's dramaturgical self.[52] People are not simply playing parts in different social contexts. Rather, performance of gender is more like a speech act.[53] That is to say, the performance of gender is what constitutes gender.

These performances must draw on a broader system of meaning that helps render those utterances, those performances, intelligible. Media representations and connections with them via identification are deeply connected with this process.

In her more recent work, Butler has proposed that precarity works hand in hand with performativity.[54] *Precarity* refers to the ways one must perform identities in an intelligible way, in a way that others can read, in order to be recognized. One might perform in a variety of transgressive ways in order to destabilize categories, but "to be a subject at all requires first complying with certain norms that govern recognition—that make a person recognizable. And so, non-compliance calls into question the viability of one's life, the ontological conditions of one's persistence."[55] Here, she is discussing recognition at the level of the nation-state and citizenship, in particular the way marginalized populations are harmed by the violences of neoliberalism and nationalism. I argue, however, that her articulation is useful in the realm of consumer culture because precarity allows us to argue for a politics of representation that values the edges, rather than reimagining the center. Butler writes, "Performativity has everything to do with 'who' can become produced as a recognizable subject. . . . Precarious life characterizes such lives who do not qualify as recognizable."[56] What Butler's latest articulation allows for, as has been debated and reformulated throughout the history of social and cultural theory, is that we can conceive of the self, the individual identity as the result of a momentary, fraught, and complex intersection between the social and the individual.

Many of the studies of representation reviewed in the previous chapter argue that part of the reason the representation of marginal groups is so important is that media representations serve as points of recognition that help validate those identities, both for those who identify with those representations as well as those who do not. Drawing on Butler's discussion of precarity, media representation makes certain identities possible, plausible, and livable. In using the charged term to refer to the sphere of consumer culture, I do not mean to diminish precarity's ties to life and death. Rather, I think drawing on it helps make an argument for representation that really stakes a claim for the political importance of visibility beyond a simple reconstruction of who counts as a marketable audience. It also lends itself to an argument about media representation being important because it articulates what might be possible without focusing so explicitly on what is "true" or "good."

Unpacking Identification

Certainly, identification is not the only entry point into understanding the relationship between identities, audiences, and representation. Many qualitative researchers address the multifaceted pleasures fans can have with media, particularly media that are often disparaged by critiques of "low culture."[57] Identification is, however, a much theorized and measured type of connection to texts, and it is rarely grounded in audiences' understanding of the term and process. It is also implicit in the many arguments about the potential impact of representation, in particular in arguments about the importance of representation to members of marginalized groups. Building on feminist media studies, I argue that analysis of media consumption is one part of unpacking how research participants construct and perform their identities in the face of precarity. Ethnographic methods, like those that inform this project, are one way of making sense of the wide variety of phenomena subsumed in this concept of identification. As Elizabeth Bird asserts, "Only ethnography can begin to answer questions about what people *really* do with media, rather than what we imagine they *might* do, or what close readings of texts *assume* they might do."[58] As I argue throughout this book, the focus on the microlevel practices of people who play video games and are members of marginalized groups can help us make sense of these macrolevel concerns about the intersections of identity, identification, and media representation.

Rather than start with a set definition of identification, I instead asked interviewees to tell me whether they identified with video game or other media characters and what identification meant to them. The order of my questions came out of a trial-and-error process. Asking interviewees to define identification first resulted in several of them describing, as Pouncy put it, "the little card you show the cops." Tanner made a similar reference; identification to her was "another symbol that could represent you." Both of these statements cite an identification process that entails *being identified as a member of a particular group* and *representable as* a subject.

Digging into the issue a little further, Renee described identification as being able to express one's connection with a specific category: "You don't necessarily consider yourself identified with it until you use a word to describe it, like until you are able to label what that relationship is. . . . It's the words that give that the meaning." This definition of identification as identity is much the same as Hall's.[59] Identification is one way of making sense of who one is in terms of being intelligible to oneself and to others.

Asking about identification *with* media directed interviewees first toward a more media-specific identification process. Most people I spoke with had not thought of or had trouble working through the definition of identification and coming up with examples of characters they identified with. This is hardly surprising given the diversity of definitions offered by scholars and the fact that the concept is rarely made concrete. I asked the question during both interviews, and while no interviewee could remember their previous answer, the core of their definitions was fairly stable. Similarly, although each person defined identification somewhat differently, there was one tying thread—finding a connection with a character. For example, according to Tanner, who was a neurologist, "We started watching *Bones* recently, and I guess I kind of identify with the main character there, just being sort of a strong-willed, independent woman in a field that is male predominant. . . . But I don't really feel a strong connection; it's more like entertainment." Although she identified *as* a similar sort of woman as the character, she did not identify *with* the character per se. Distinguishing identification *as* and identification *with* was also present in interviewees' comments on if and how they identified with media characters. Hatshepsut said, "I think there's a lot more to identification than what's obvious. I think it really has to do with the person, thoughts, beliefs, feelings." Beyond thinking of identification as something tied to demographic categories, we see here that it is much more about affective connections.

Perhaps one of the reasons studies of identification have used such wide-ranging definitions of the concept is that individual experiences of identification run the gamut from parasocial interaction to homophily to empathy.[60] Combining them in reference to identifying with media characters generally, Tala said, "I empathize with them. I see qualities of myself within them." The ways interviewees connected with media characters encompassed the expected identifiers, as well as life experiences, personalities, senses of humor, actions, and choices. In general it was described as an emotional or intellectual connection (or both) or what Cody called a "gut feeling." Emotionally, this connection could be sympathetic or empathetic. Some interviewees said, however, that these feelings occurred in lieu of identifying with characters. They sympathized and perhaps even empathized with a character in a show, but they did not feel that this meant they identified with them.

Given the diversity of responses, it might seem that identification is not useful as a theoretical concept here. I think, however, that the variety of connections interviewees have with media demonstrates that identification provides an excellent entry point into making sense of how audiences/players relate to media texts. Not everyone approaches media in the same way, and in my interviews this concept helped open up conversations about media use in ways I had not anticipated. Rather than making the concept more specific, researchers could embrace the diversity of those experiences. In turn, this could empower us to move beyond arguments that focus heavily on specific identifiers and types of identification in making sense of why representation is important.

Carol described several different kinds of identification. One entailed saying that a particular actress would play her in a movie; another involved seeing herself in a character and identifying *as* that kind of person:

> But there's other kinds of identification. I'm a big *Buffy* fan. I would get in these conversations with other fans of the show, and we're talking about them like they're actually people. . . . Or I would get worked up and emotional during certain plot points. I know they're not real. So there's that kind of relating.

Carol's comments referenced parasocial interaction, identifying *with* the experiences of fictional characters but also identifying *as* a particular type of person who might be represented by a particular actor. She also described the affective pull of texts that make us feel for characters, even when we know the characters are "not real." Identification, then, is not about a static, linear, measurable connection to a character. Rather, it is about seeing ourselves reflected in the world and relating to images of others, both of which are critically tied to arguments for representation that focus on media's ability to create possible worlds.

Most research on identification discusses it in terms of books, movies, television shows, and games. For several interviewees, however, music engendered a great deal more identification than did other media. Evan said, for example, that he identified very strongly with the music he listened to; it evoked particular emotions and fantasies. As he listened to music while running, he would imagine he was a heroic figure: "Somehow, I saved an entire city or town or village or something." Several interviewees described identifying with and identifying themselves in terms of the music they enjoyed. Music opened up an imagined potential reality.

Christine felt an emotional connection to her favorite music and said it reflected how she saw herself. She identified with a particular musician, KiD CuDi. She said, "He's not a person you can really classify as any one type of way, so people are kind of confused by him. And I feel the same way about myself, which is why I immediately took to his music." Sasha described occasionally having emotional connections with singer Mary J. Blige, but that her connection to the singer was only one type she experienced:

> I relate to people in different ways. So it depends. Like sometimes when I'm sad, I like to listen to old Mary J. Blige. Like back when she was depressed, her songs were the shiiiit. . . . And I'm like, "Wow, I really, I understand what you are saying." Some people, just like some celebrities, I'm like, yo, I would really wear that.

This latter form of identification, which she called "superficial," was a type of identification *as* the kind of person with a particular type of style, but her connection with Blige was a more specifically affective identification *with* the singer's music and experiences. Although she shared gender, sexual, and racial identifiers with Blige, those were not the reasons she identified with her. Rather, it was the affective connection that Sasha considered contextually and temporally important. Like Sasha, many interviewees described similar life experiences, histories, and life approaches as ways of identifying with fictional characters or media personalities that were more meaningful than identifiers like gender, race, and sexuality.

In fact, interviewees pointed out that identifiers like gender, race, and sexuality led to only surface-level connections. Kat said, "At first glance you're going to automatically assume that someone your age, race, gender is going to be someone you'll connect with more because you assume you'll have a common way you'll see the world." Kat and others saw this first-glance form of identification as fleeting, and other ways of connecting with characters led to more meaningful connections, as Christine explained:

> I feel like there are certain aspects and values about a person that they can sort of pinpoint in themselves, and identification is when you can recognize that in other people or other things. . . . Not on a shallow level though, not just being a woman or something like that . . . just a connection based on similar interests and goals and values in life.

Identification can also entail other forms of connection. Julia did not identify with media characters at all, for example, but said she might "connect" with them if she saw "where they were coming from." Identification, when viewed as a flexible concept, encompasses a wide variety of textual experiences.

When interviewees mentioned specific identifiers, some asserted that they identified with characters because of these characteristics only in the absence of other, deeper ways of connecting with characters. Caine said, "[I can identify with] a character who I can relate to on some level, whether it's in terms of actions . . . skin tone, racial, or religious identity. Large part of it is actions I can identify and empathize with, and that's the baseline, and the others are sort of additions to that." Hatshepsut said that in video games where characters were less developed, she might identify with characters based on physical characteristics. In other media with fleshed-out characters, she could find other ways of identifying with characters. That is not to say, however, that identifiers cannot lead to a deep level of connections. Rather, it matters how such identifiers are used in the text. Ephram discussed this at length in regard to one particular film that he could not name at the time, but based on his description, it seems he meant Wong Kar-wai's *Happy Together*:

> It's about this character, these two gay characters, where they have to live in a different country, but they are both originally Chinese. . . .

And I think it was a good example of how you could have a gay character but not have it completely be about the whole experience. . . .
I just happen to identify with you closer because you are gay. I can
understand your experience, but you are also going through this
real human issue and problems. That was a lot more relatable, and
I could identify as him.

As a gay man of Chinese descent, Ephram certainly shared two axes
of identity with the movie's lead characters. He connected with the
film, however, because of the nuanced representation of the characters' experiences, not their shared identifiers.

Sharing identifiers like race, gender, and sexuality can certainly
entail having similar life experiences. Often, though, studies that focus on these identifiers conflate these two different forms of relating.
In the context of nationality, Gilroy argues, "Consciousness of identity gains additional power from the idea that it is . . . an outcome of
shared and rooted experience tied, in particular, to place, location,
language and mutuality."[61] Although identifiers can be shared points
of connection in this way, shared experiences do not arise *only* from
these shared identifiers, as Kat, who identified as a white woman in
her early twenties, described in her interview:

I would be able to identify with a fifty-year-old black man who was
also from Georgia and also went to my high school much more than
I would be able to identify with a twenty-one-year-old white female
who lived in Canada and was like a scientist or an engineer and like
I couldn't relate on a personal or social level. I think that common
geography and common history bonds people.

Her age, race, and gender identity are described here as surface-
level identifiers rather than as intrinsic to how she connects with
others. She describes history and geography, different types of embodied experiences, as more meaningful in making connections
with others. This is not because race, gender, and age do not matter
but because they are not *all that matters.* In much the same way that
identity categories cannot encompass all of the people who possess
the identifiers associated with those identities, individuals encompass multifaceted ways of identifying with characters. In all types of
identification, we identify simultaneously with multiple identities,

a fact that troubles all overarching identity group categories. Eve Sedgwick emphasizes, for example, that categories such as gay, straight, and bisexual cannot encompass the diversity of individuals within those groups.[62] Assuming that any particular identity, like gay, white, or transgender, will be the primary salient identity of a given individual is overly simplistic. Sedgwick further argues that the importance of identifying *as* a member of a group does not preclude identifying *with* other groups.

Simply because a person chooses to watch one film or television show because it reflects their sexuality does not mean that they are unable to enjoy a film or a television show that does not or that they undergo psychological contortions in order to do so. For example, Malcolm, originally from Sri Lanka, enjoyed the show *Girlfriends,* a UPN situation comedy about a group of African American women that now airs on BET. He liked the show despite the fact that he did not identify with the characters or their experiences:

> There was this one show, *Girlfriends.* . . . It's about four black women and the issues that they deal with. Absolutely no identification, as you would say, for me. Now granted, they were attractive, but there isn't a shortage of TV shows with attractive people on them. It was just that it was so well written and so amusing that I would watch it on a regular basis, even though I had no identification with that.

His enjoyment of the show was not about seeing himself reflected in it, in direct contrast to many of the reductive arguments for how and why various groups should be represented in media. Similarly, Renee, who was white, said that Malcolm X's autobiography was one of her favorite books. She went on to say, however, "I identify very little with him . . . but I think it's awesome, and I really like it. And I don't seek materials out, going, 'Ooo look, it's about a thirty-year-old, somewhat overweight girl traipsing through life.' . . . It's cool when it happens, but I don't seek out media or anything that does it." Often, interviewees described identification or representation as "nice when it happened," a theme I return to in chapter 5, but they did not actively look for either.

Several interviewees pointed out that they found many different ways of connecting with characters in media texts. Zahriel identified very strongly with all types of characters across media forms. She discussed this as part of her experience of being an actor:

> Well, there's an element of living vicariously through the character. You know, putting myself in their shoes so to speak. . . . At my most romantic I think I tend to try to find a happy medium between what I would want being me in that situation and where the character wants to go. . . . So if we ever met in, you know, some alternate future universe or something, they'd be like, "Hey, you played my game. Good job. I like what you did there." You know?

Zahriel saw people as inherently multifaceted and believed that anyone could identify with anyone else if they made an effort. Not all of my interviewees shared this view, of course; not everyone could identify easily with just any character. Pouncy described this in relation to their multidimensional identity, noting that there were clear limits to which characters they could connect:

> I feel like my personality is very broad and I have a lot of diverse traits in my personality and I'm able to extrapolate that into a diverse character base. I feel like, like I can go the very nerdy, steampunk route in one thing but also find myself in a gladiator character in another thing. I mean, it's all fantasy, but its different aspects. But also, like I wouldn't be able to do the womanizing space man per se [laughs].

Being able to find oneself in many characters does not imply that identity is wholly meaningless in defining how audiences connect with texts. After all, life values, politics, what we find funny, and what we find abhorrent all shape the types of characters to which we relate. As Tanner described, "You're not going to be drawn to something that has no relevance or no commonality to you. . . . But I don't think that I actively seek or gravitate towards the things that are most like me." Identifier-based identification studies fail to account for this important nuance. The assumption that identifiers define or shape identification is then conflated with an identity politics approach to media representation arguments that lend themselves to pluralism in amount of representation (i.e., niche marketing of texts) but not diversity in texts broadly.

Identification and Disidentification

Much as identity can be both positive and negative, identification and disidentification are parts of the same process. I draw here on José Esteban Muñoz's discussion of disidentification as a media consumption practice utilized by queers of color.[63] As he puts it, "The version of identity politics that this book participates in imagines a reconstructed narrative of identity formation that locates the enacting of self at precisely the point where the discourses of essentialism and constructivism short-circuit."[64] In his book he describes the processes by which we might see ourselves in texts that are not inherently coded to connect with us while simultaneously recognizing that disjuncture.

Muñoz asserts that "disidentification is the third mode of dealing with dominant ideology, one that neither opts to assimilate within a structure nor strictly opposes it."[65] He connects this with Stuart Hall's discussion of oppositional readings, in contrast to preferred or negotiated readings.[66] Disidentification becomes a reading and a production practice, an act of reception that is also a performance: "Disidentification can be understood as a way of shuffling back and forth between reception and production."[67] As such, it has clear links to the way games as interactive media blur the lines between producer/text/audience. This is part of the reason games provide such an intriguing site for rethinking how we understand identification, as I discuss in the next chapter.

In her explanation of Muñoz's concept, Janet Staiger states, "Disidentification is an instance in which an individual sees another individual and both assumes some commonality that might result in normal identification and simultaneously realizes that the two are not the same."[68] There is an assumption implicit in this formulation about what would constitute "normal" identification, one that assumes identification *as* is related to identification *with*. Muñoz is arguing, however, for an understanding of identification that entails identifying *with* a character despite any ruptures that might exist in one's ability to identify *as* the same social position as said character. That is not to say, though, that identification as a member of a group requires a positive connection. Gilroy, for example, describes identity in terms of difference:

> Selves—and their identities—are formed through relationships of exteriority, conflict and exclusion. Differences can be found within identities as well as between them. The Other, against whose resistance the integrity of an identity is to be established, can be recognized as part of the self that is no longer plausibly understood as a unitary entity but appears instead as one fragile moment in the dialogic circuits.[69]

In the case of identification *with* a character, the relationship between positive and negative identification is somewhat different from identification *as*. A woman may articulate her identity as such because she does not identify as a man or genderqueer. In the case of identification *with*, however, one might identify *with* an Asian character even though one identifies *as* Latina.

For some interviewees, identification entailed finding a similarity with a character. Gregory said of identification generally, "Do I think it represents me or my group of people whether it be black or gay or middle-aged men living with their parents [*laughs*]?" There is a problem when researchers and marketers assume that this type of identification *as* becomes a determining factor in media choices. Certainly, some people cannot identify with certain types of characters. Evan said, for example, that he could not imagine identifying with a female character. Devon said that he needed to find some sort of similarity with characters in order to connect with them. These similarities could be in terms of physical or social characteristics like race, gender, sexuality, religion, ancestry, body type, nationality, class, and so on. Devon felt, though, that more ephemeral life experiences, personality, and humor were also major ways he identified with characters.

Based on interviewees' discussions, it is perhaps best to consider disidentification and identification as part of a simultaneous process. Disidentification arises when one connects with a character because of some characteristic but feels distanced from them based on another. Building on disidentification, we can look at the way texts meant to hail us as audience members can in fact distance us from them. Evan explained that he had struggled with his own identity over time and that he tended to identify with heroic characters.

He stated, "I don't think I identify with people like me. . . . I'm a transman. . . . They're not really depicted in movies, and if they are, they're not really heroic per se." He sought pleasure through media that allowed him to image himself as heroic, strong, and capable. He did not see any texts with transmen that created that possibility, so those were not characters with which he identified. In video games Evan really identified with the hero Link from *The Legend of Zelda* but not Mario from *Mario Bros.*, despite their assumed shared heritage.[70] "The neighborhood I grew up in was all Italian American, but I didn't even get that Mario and Luigi . . . It wasn't like, oh, Italian American middle-class plumbers, that's like my family. It wasn't like that! It was just fun and colorful."

There was, for many interviewees, a disjunction between what they sought in media in terms of identification and what they saw of representation of themselves. In many cases it seemed like they connected more with texts that were affectively familiar, even if the identities of the characters were radically different from theirs. Communication scholars Johan Hoorn and Elly Konijn similarly find that "although similarity may enhance involvement and dissimilarity may elicit distance, positively charged dissimilarity or negatively charged similarity may simultaneously increase both involvement and distance, and may lead to ambivalence."[71] Ephram asserted that sometimes it got frustrating identifying with the minority position: "It just got to the point that I just got tired of it. And I just want a break. . . . If I hear one more coming-of-age of a minority overcoming adversity, I'm just going to scream." In the same conversation Ephram's partner, Devon, said that he would go through periods of watching lots of movies made by and for gay men only to be repeatedly disappointed by their quality and failure to reflect his experiences. As this shows, we can enjoy texts that are in no way about us, just as we can feel excluded from texts that presume to be about us but fail to ring true to our experiences.

Identification *as* or *with* Video Game Characters?

Research on identification in digital games often assumes that because these games are interactive, players automatically take on the role of the main character/avatar. Sabine Trepte and Leonard Reinecke argue, "The more the user 'becomes' the media character, the more he or she identifies with the character."[72] Dorothee Hefner, Christoph Klimmt, and Peter Vorderer propose that identification in games is distinct from other media precisely because the point is to feel no distance between the player and the player character.[73] This, they argue, is "true" identification. In a later study they and additional coauthors, Christian Roth and Christopher Blake, find that players who identify more with their player character demonstrate more alliance with implicit associations with the role played in the game.[74] I will not dispute that being more "into" a game might lead to learning more associations made by the game. Indeed, when tied to the vast underrepresentation of marginalized groups in games, this possibility is quite frightening to anyone concerned with social justice.[75] I do question, however, what exactly is being demonstrated in studies like these. Identification seems to be standing in for other processes, often meaning interactivity or engagement in a broad sense.

According to my interviewees, identification requires a distance between audience member (viewer, reader, player, listener, etc.) and a media character. This harkens back to film theories much more than it does to the aforementioned game studies articulations of identification. Interviewees needed to see a game character as a distinct entity from themselves in order to feel as though they could identify with it. We can put interviewees' descriptions of identification in psychoanalytic terms: "Recognition is thus overlaid with misrecognition: the image recognized is conceived as the reflected body of the self, but its misrecognition as superior projects this body outside itself as an ideal ego."[76] Identification *with* a character requires that people see what they are identifying with as separate from themselves. In this sense, we can think of identification in much the same way as Butler:

> Identification always relies upon a difference that it seeks to overcome, and that its aim is accomplished only by reintroducing the difference it claims to have vanquished. The one with whom I identify is not me, and that "not being me" is the condition of the identification. Otherwise, as Jacqueline Rose reminds us, identification collapses into identity, which spells the death of identification itself.[77]

Given that much of game studies work on identification presumes the complete taking on of a character's role or investment in the avatar as an extension of the player's self, it would seem that distanced identification with game characters is nearly impossible. If players are active agents in playing the game, if they *become* the avatar/character, where does identification lie?

Much of the qualitative work on identification in self-contained digital games relies on textual analyses.[78] Player-focused analyses tend to rely on quantitative measures. Jonathan Cohen's 2001 analysis of the various ways the concept has been defined in communications research led him to develop a scale for measuring what he defined as the core of identification. Many quantitative studies of identification in games in turn use adapted versions of Cohen's identification measures.[79] Others researchers, like Trepte and Reinecke in their analysis of avatar similarity to player, identification, and enjoyment, ask players merely if they identified with an avatar.[80] As I have shown, however, people have very different definitions of the term, so we cannot be sure what prior studies' participants meant in their responses to such a question.

To make sense of these competing definitions and examine identification across different types of games rather than within a single text, I used some of Cohen's questions developed to measure identification in film and television as talking points for most of the gaming interviews. Using these questions as discussion points in qualitative research, I found that interviewees felt the questions addressed game involvement more than what they understood as identification.[81] Using interviewees' individual understandings of identification, their responses to these questions, and follow-up questions about whether what they experienced in the games was the same as what they would call identification, I was able to parse interactivity and identification into two distinct themes. The following is a brief overview of interviewees' answers to the six Likert-scale items adapted from Cohen's questionnaire.

1. *To what extent would you agree with the following statement: While playing the game, I forgot myself and was fully absorbed?*

Most interviewees answered affirmatively that this happened at least some of the time when they played video games. This was often a qualified yes, however. Usually, it was contextually dependent in that several interviewees expressed that this was more likely to happen if they were playing alone. For others context and reason for play mattered to involvement because wanting to win, as noted by many interviewees, was a reason for getting absorbed in video games. Sasha said, for example, that she got more absorbed when playing against men because she felt she had to prove herself. She was a very skilled player. She beat me five rounds in a row at *Marvel vs. Capcom* (a fighting game), and I am hardly a novice player.[82] She indirectly related her expertise and absorbed play to gendered dynamics. They motivated her because, she said, "When I'm playing a guy, I get fully absorbed because I really have to win. Because he just expects me to lose anyway, because I'm a girl." She played against her brother and his friends in order to get better because gaming was highly competitive for her. Her mother walked through during part of the gaming interview and actually insisted that I should really talk to her son, who was the "real gamer." Upon watching Sasha play, however, she said, "But she's doing alright," and left the room. Sasha seemed annoyed by the exchange.

Interviewees described spending a significant amount of time playing as both a cause and an effect of this kind of absorption into the game. Caine and Malcolm described the ways game interface disrupted this absorption, something James Newman has analyzed, as well.[83] As Caine described, "By nature of any games, its user interface pulls you out from the game a little bit." While playing the game *Diablo II,* Malcolm stated, "When things are complicated, you might be in the game, but then you know you go from point A to point B and pick this up and oh it doesn't fit; that sort of pulls you out of the game."[84] In games with complex inventory systems like *Diablo II,* a lot more than characters' mind-sets is going through players' minds, as players must engage in what Malcolm referred to as "inventory Tetris" (Figure 15).

2. *To what extent would you agree with the following statement: I think I have a good understanding of my character?*

When it came to understanding their characters in the game, interviewees' answers varied greatly with the kind of game they were playing. Interviewees were evenly distributed between answering affirmatively and negatively to this question. In part, this had to

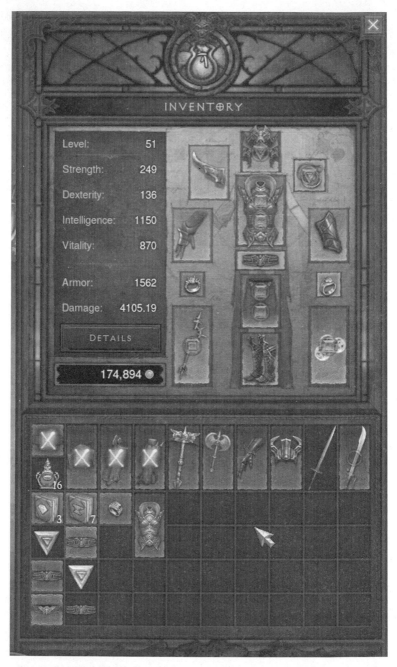

Figure 15. Screenshot of character inventory from *Diablo III*, illustrating the Tetris-like methods required for organizing items collected throughout the game. Image by Todd Harper, October 17, 2013

do with the fact that some characters were too abstract to connect with, especially for interviewees playing *Wii Sports*.[85] Several people discussed this in relation to Miis, the avatars used to represent different players on the Nintendo Wii console. These avatars represent different accounts saved on the console and can also be used to play various Wii games like *Wii Sports* or *Wii Fit*.[86] Renee found it hard to connect with Miis, because "they don't have feet!" Kat said, too, that she didn't identify with the Mii, "because it doesn't have legs."[87]

In games with strong narratives, understanding the story allowed players to get a sense of their characters. Interestingly, narrative can pull players into games even if they're populated with nonhumanoid characters. Zahriel discussed this in relation to the 1989 puzzle game *Adventures of Lolo*.[88] In this game based on the Japanese *Eggerland* series, players control a small, round, blue character named Lolo whose love, Lala, has been kidnapped by the evil King Egger. Players guide Lolo through a series of puzzles to unlock rooms in the castle until they find and free Lala. In describing her connection to the game, Zahriel said, "I identified with Lolo, every now and then. Poor little guy stuck in this place . . . I would curse the guy that put me in this stupid thing and stole my girlfriend" (Figure 16).

Julia did not identify with fictional characters in general, but when she played one of her favorite games (*God of War*) for her gaming interview, she had a sense of the character Kratos's goals because of the narrative.[89] Hatshepsut played the same game in her interview but unlike Julia had not played the game before and so had less of a grasp on the story and thus felt like she understood the character less. Similarly, when Violet played *Assassin's Creed*, a game in which players control the Crusades-era assassin Altair, she did not follow the storyline and therefore did not feel as though she really got inside the character's head.[90] As I discuss in the next chapter, narrative was identified as the key ingredient in helping players identify with their on-screen proxy.

3. *To what extent would you agree with the following statement: While playing, I felt I could really get inside the character's head?*

4. *To what extent would you agree with the following statement: At key moments in the game, I felt I knew exactly what my character was going through?*

Figure 16. Nintendo cartridge for *Adventures of Lolo* that pictures the fuzzy, round hero of the game escaping the evil King Egger.

When answering these two questions, interviewees generally said that these statements were not true for them in the context of the games they played for the interview or in video games in general. In terms of feeling they knew what their characters were going through, Ephram and Devon said that this was true in *Left 4 Dead* only on the most basic level—the "oh shit, zombies are coming to kill us" level.[91] Unless they had intertextual references, most interviewees felt that video game characters were not developed enough for them to make those kinds of inferences. Games with strong narrative components, however, made it possible for them to get into characters' heads.

In terms of both questions, the interactive aspects of video games made the process of identification qualitatively different from that of other media. Tala said, "I'm going through it with the character. So I'm going through dealing what they are going through but reacting a little bit differently. I'm not like, 'Oh shit a zombie!' [*laughs*]. But the spirit is there." There is less identification *with* or even *as* a character here. Rather, the self-referentiality of video game play does not allow the distance necessary for identification with characters. Some players actively experience the in-game situation, which calls upon a form of engagement different from an emotional or intellectual connection with a character. They think about what they are doing, not what the character is doing or what they as the character are doing.

5. *To what extent would you agree with the following statement: While viewing the program, I wanted the character to succeed in achieving his or her goals?*

6. *To what extent would you agree with the following statement: When the character succeeded, I felt joy, but when he or she failed, I was sad?*

The last two questions often resulted in smiles or laughs from interviewees and almost entirely resulted in affirmative responses from them. Largely, this was because the goals of the character were the goals of the player in most cases. As Tracey articulated, "No one wants to be a loser!" The goal of the player is often winning the game, and if winning fulfills the characters' goals, all the better. Even when Renee and Malcolm answered no, it was because they did not care what the character's goals were and only their goals mattered.

For question six, most interviewees stated that they did not necessarily feel sad so much as frustrated with the outcome. On a few occasions players described crying because of events in the game, but they did not necessarily articulate this as feeling aligned with the character. Tala said, "I would say more satisfied when they succeed and irritated when they fail [*laughs*]." Evan said he was not sure if he was feeling the character's emotions or feeling his own emotions in relation to what the character was going through. He told me that the first time he played through *Call of Duty 2: Big Red One* a few years ago, a soldier from his team (the only female in the group) was killed.[92] He called to his then girlfriend in the next room, "They killed her!" To this she replied, "So? Why do I care?" He said that her reaction pulled him back and made him remember that it was not real. It also effectively shamed him into disavowing an emotional reaction to the game text. Interviewees described reacting emotionally as one way of relating to characters, but it was not necessarily the same as identification with the characters. It was also, because of the fictional, frivolous framing of games, seen as an inappropriate reaction. Indeed, many interviewees described strong identification with media characters as somewhat embarrassing, an issue worthy of further investigation.

Is Identification Important?

The interactive aspects of games were part of the reason these questions proved difficult to answer. Interactivity made it hard to parse involvement in a video game and identification as defined in other media. As Tanner described, interactivity in games fulfilled some of the need she satisfied by identifying with characters on television:

> I think I can more identify with characters portrayed on the [television] screen more readily. Which seems weird because I have no control over those characters on the screen. Yet, I'm the one who is working the avatar on the video game screen. So that's kind of strange, I guess. Maybe I don't feel the need to identify with something that I am controlling. I would like to engage in a different way by identifying with a character in a story on a [television] screen.

Games as activities could be absorbing, but the added connection of identification did not always seem important to interviewees. None of their answers demonstrate the kind of involvement Cohen is interested in when it comes to identification.[93] Interactivity is enjoyable, yes. The enjoyment it promotes, however, does not necessitate identification.

Identification is not a necessary part of media enjoyment generally. Sasha's favorite television show was CBS's *NCIS*, a crime drama about a group of naval investigators. In fact, it was on in the background, muted, during our first interview, and as I had watched the show myself, we built rapport by discussing our favorite characters.

Despite her clear enjoyment of the show, she did not identify with any of the program's characters, either in the sense of identifying *as* a member of a particular group (there are no characters who "look" like Sasha on the show) or identifying *with* any of their experiences or actions. Like Sasha, other interviewees did not always see identification as an important goal. In part, not needing to identify with characters occurred because individuals fulfilled different needs through their media use. Several interviewees described playing video games as a way to zone out, for example. Not all interviewees wanted or needed to identify with characters, in video games or in other media. Most had trouble coming up with examples of characters or media personalities they identified with, even though all were eventually able to come up with definitions for the term *identification*.

For many interviewees, connecting to media characters was about experiences more than anything else. Anya did not feel identification drove her media consumption, but if she was going to identify with a character, she said, "I have to be able to see myself in their shoes. It doesn't necessarily have to be age, race, or anything like that. More of what they are doing in the situations they are in." To feel a connection, she did not need to see a character who had emigrated from Russia to the United States as a young girl, worked as a public health researcher, or was a white woman in her twenties. Between our two interviews, she saw *Up in the Air* with George Clooney and identified with the film because she saw the characters as going through things she or people she knew had experienced. When it came to games, she did not feel like she identified with characters, because they rarely engaged in activities she herself did. She used games to imagine other realities, like creating a utopian version of Philadelphia in *Sim City*. She played tennis games on the Wii because she cannot play tennis in real life but would like to learn. She played *Guitar Hero* with her friends but of real life said, "I hate the stage. I hate being the center of attention, so it's a complete opposite of what I am actually in life." That said, she would not play violent games, because she identified as antiviolent, and avoided the Wii boxing game, though her boyfriend was a boxing fan. Her play choices connected with how she identified with herself, including selves she aspired to or was happy to imagine being.

Amy was probably the most resistant to saying she identified with media characters. She was also adamant that representation in media was not important, a point I return to in chapter 4. Interestingly, though, when she created avatars, she always made them look as similar to her as possible. This was not because it made her identify with them more but simply because she wanted to see if she could make them look like her. When it came to media characters, Amy could not think of many characters she identified with, though in the first interview she said that if she did identify with media characters it was only in terms of personality. She built on this in the second interview and said, "I think it's more the actions. Like, if I would do what they would do. So like, it could be a balding elderly man or a night elf; it's just a matter of doing, if they are doing the same stuff that I would be." When it came to games, however, she did not feel as though she identified with characters/avatars. According to her, television shows and books had more-developed characters, with personalities and actions that unfolded as the text progressed. For games she might be drawn to characters because she liked the way they looked, but she did not feel that she ever related to them on an emotional level. Even though identifying with characters was not important to Amy, she said, "If I think they are doing something that makes no sense, that really agitates me." This resonates with Alice Hall's interviewees' assertion that "something was realistic if the audience could either feel the characters' emotions or have an affective response to the characters as they would a real person."[94]

A few interviewees mentioned that relating to or feeling as though they could be friends with media characters was a better description of their relationship than was identification, if identification was a matter of seeing themselves as the character. Connecting this to games specifically, Violet felt that caring about a character was more important than identifying with a character. When she identified with book or film characters, she saw herself in them, but when it came to games, that rarely happened. She really felt attached, however, to characters in the game *Kingdom Hearts* and, thus, felt an emotional connection to that game.[95]

The ways interviewees identified with characters made up their "narratives of self," to use Anthony Giddens's phrase.[96] Creating such narratives can help individuals connect even with nonhuman characters in games. Connie, for instance, chose a car in the racing game she played for the gaming interview because she once owned the same model. This was a momentary articulation of the self. As Hall describes:

> The fully unified, completed, secure, and coherent identity is a fantasy. Instead, as the systems of meaning and cultural representation multiply, we are confronted by a bewildering, fleeting multiplicity of possible identities, any one of which we could identify with—at least temporarily.[97]

For the same reason a researcher should not look at a single avatar created by a player for one MMORPG and assume they can read the player's identity from it. Narrative approaches offer the chance for a more complex picture of interviewees' identities. Néstor García Canclini asserts that "identity is a narrated construct. . . . The narrative proceeds by adding up the feats through which the inhabitants defend their territory, order their conflicts, and establish the legitimate ways of life there in order to distinguish themselves from others."[98] If and how people identify with media characters is a part of these narratives, and representation shapes which narratives are possible.

Given how central identification has been to the interpretation of media representations, as well as to arguments for why representation matters, it was surprising how little identification mattered to my interviewees, at least in a positive sense. Interviewees largely did not view identification as an important factor in their media consumption. Yet feelings of distance or disidentification could shape whether they liked a text. As Caine explained:

> Part of the reason I avoid playing the *Grand Theft Auto* games is because I have no particular desire to play a character who winds up going around and stealing cars and murdering people. . . . Or I read a book where the protagonist is utterly despicable, and I say, "Wow, I don't really want to read this."

Similarly, Janet said, "It's more of a negative than a positive identification that's important to me." She discussed this particularly in terms of physical, human-on-human violence, which she did not enjoy watching. She was more likely to avoid media that portrayed scenarios or characters with which she did not identify than to prefer texts with which she did identify. These disjunctures are important to recognize when building arguments for representation. If people simply do not like some games or cannot connect with them and those games are the only ones in which there is diversity of representation, then what has been accomplished? Similarly, are people who disidentify with particular actions or forms of humor pushed out of consuming certain genres or media? If you would not play, for example, a game with misogynistic, homophobic, racist, and/ or transphobic humor, then you would be excluded from playing many games. Furthermore, if characters are added to media texts for the sake of aesthetic diversity but are not characters audiences are asked to identify with, then scholars' critiques of those texts would necessarily have to be reframed.

Accordingly, researchers should look at the way identification makes certain identities relevant. Referencing the work of Manthia Diawara, Janet Staiger states, "The basic dynamics for identifications with characters exist for all spectators regardless of identities. However, if textual ruptures occur, a spectator might recognize a personal identity (such as black, Marxist, gay) that is separate from the characters with whom the spectator is identifying."[99] While playing through *God of War* in the gaming interview, Hatshepsut said that identification could be this kind of momentary process: "Sometimes, there's certain moments or certain things that happen that I can identify with." In other instances, however, Hatshepsut felt dissimilar to the character. With some characters, she said, "There can be certain aspects that I do identify with, but I really feel like I'm an individual person, and although we might have a lot of things in common, there's always going to be a lot of differences, too." This is similar to the way in which different identifiers become salient identities in specific contexts. Identification, linked with identity, is also both positive and negative. I know who I am not only because I identify with that kind of character but also because I do *not* identify with another kind of character.

When market logics dominate decisions about whether to include more diverse representation in games, caricatures often stand in for these kinds of connections. As Connie pointed out, "I don't think people should follow stereotypes, but I think people will be more immersed in the game if they find themselves in the game, or find part of themselves in the game, regardless of what the character looks like." As this demonstrates, even disidentification requires some feeling of recognition with the text, even as audiences feel their difference from the characters. When trying to enjoy games or other media, however, people cannot feel so disidentified with the text that they cannot get pleasure from it.

Identification and Fantasy

Over the course of the interviews, many participants described interacting with video games as different from interacting with other media. In part, this may be because they tied identification to realism. For example, Bryan said that he could identify with a character "that was believable," but that did not mean he was able to see himself as that character: "[I'm] not necessarily like, 'That could be me'—I don't think I identify that way. . . . The whole point of enjoying entertainment is to go somewhere else." Realism and identification here have a co-constitutive rather than a linear relationship with each other. Interviewees did not identify with characters who were "really like them" but rather with characters they could imagine were real.

When identification occurred, as discussed in terms of representation in chapter 4, interviewees stressed that realism was a necessary factor. Julia said that she did not identify with video game characters, because they were too fantastical: "Nothing that I have experienced in my daily life has ever, you know, been like that." Speaking of the game *God of War,* in which players battle as the white Spartan warrior Kratos to take Ares's throne in a fantastical ancient Greece, she said, "To identify with someone there has to be some point in time where you found yourself in that situation. For me, I've never fought harpies in a loin cloth [*laughs*]." She did not connect with the avatar's affect, experiences, or representation. Gregory said that formal factors might help explain this difference: "Maybe because we got a sense that even though it's dialog and it's written, there's still the idea of real people being there—seeing real people—instead of the game, which we know is animated and stuff like that or to a certain degree is fake." Games as digital texts created a distance for him that made identification more difficult, unlike television shows or films with live actors, which felt more indexical and, in turn, more relatable.

For some players identification was beside the point, as fantasy and escapism defined their media consumption. Rusty did not identify with characters, though he said, "I sometimes wish I could be that FBI agent saving the day." He made a distinction between escapism and identification:

> Probably one of the reasons I love to play video games is because it lets me either be the guy conquering the world or he's slaughtering people or saving the world—the kind of things that I don't do in real life. So, in that kind of thing, I'm pretty comfortable with my identity. I do play video games to escape.

The escapist aspects of games allowed him to enjoy "playing a strategic game where you are nuking cities," he said, "That's the kind of thing I would be horrified with in real life. But if it advances the game, sure." His description of escapism demonstrates the importance of representation as imaginative possibility. Games and other media gave him the space to imagine whom else he might be. It is important to point out that Rusty was one of two heterosexual, white, cisgendered-male interviewees. The racial, gender, and sexual identifiers of these subjects are represented in games more often than those associated with racial, gender, and/or sexual minorities. Although identifiers do not dictate identification, their presence or absence in media texts do present a world in which only certain types of bodies get to do certain types of things.

People who are not represented in these games can still use them to escape, of course. As Hatshepsut said, "Typically for me, the games I play, they're like things I would never do in real life. So that's another reason I don't identify." Similarly, Tracey, who was the most uncomfortable with answering whether he identified with media characters, made aspirational connections with characters: "I don't think it's somebody I identify with. I just think that it's somebody that you just like, just has a cool power." He described this particularly in relation to his comic book consumption. The trouble is that even in representing worlds that might be, games and much of mainstream media represent very homogenous worlds. Players/audiences are not always given or forced into a space that allows them to escape into, aspire to, or imagine worlds where marginalized groups are not defined by their marginalization.

When fantasy and identification did connect for my interviewees, they seemed to involve aspirational identification. Indeed, Chuck called identification "escapism to the next level." Understanding identification as a form of imagining oneself otherwise directly links representation and identification to the pleasure of media consumption. Referencing video games, Zahriel said:

> It is kind of an idealized self in most situations. Knowing that I'm the fat, lazy one sitting on the couch playing video games—it definitely inspires me to go out there and do more things, but at the same time it's nice to know that if I can't, I can always come home and live vicariously through somebody else's creative vision.

At times we want to see ourselves in the place of characters who are as we wish to be. At other times we use media texts as fodder for imagining what else might be possible in our everyday lives. In either case, while identification *as* a member of a group does not define how audiences identify *with* media characters, representation of different types of bodies remains crucially important to shaping what types of worlds we can imagine.

Conclusion

Chantal Mouffe argues that understanding identities as complex and contextual requires that we rethink political identity in two ways.[100] First, "the political community should be conceived as a discursive surface not as an empirical referent."[101] We can, as explored in this book, view identity in such a way. Identity is a starting point for discussions about the importance of identification and representation, not an independent variable through which they should be studied. Second, she promotes "citizenship as a form of political identity that is created through identification with the political principles of modern pluralist democracy."[102] Similarly, I argue that representation becomes important through identification but that its importance does not lie solely in the ability of marginalized audiences to identify with texts. This is because, following from the first point, identification can occur on a variety of axes. Important to note, Mouffe argues that identification with a group identity necessitates that "*equivalence* does not eliminate *difference*."[103] That is to say, the ultimate point of this research is not to assert that everyone can identify with anyone and that we therefore do not have to worry about diversity in media. Rather, because identifications are not predetermined, producers' reliance on representing only groups they market to is unnecessarily narrow. Indeed, diversity in and of itself (though not done solely for the sake of diversity) can be an attractive media feature. Moreover, audiences, drawing on a notion of coalitional politics as explained by Bernice Johnson Reagon and developed by Judith Butler, can argue for diversity as a social imperative rather than succumb to industry demands that they make themselves legible as markets.[104]

Based on my interviewees' responses, we might define identification as a process by which we come to feel an affective connection with a character on the basis of seeing that character as separate and yet a part of us in some way. Traditional media studies seem unable to fully account for this process, as its focus on specific identifiers has created an oversimplified understanding of how audiences relate to texts. Separating identification *with* from identification *as* demonstrates that people are able to connect with characters in a multitude of ways. Researchers and marketers cannot take for granted that players actively identify with video game characters. After all, audiences do not always want or need to actively connect with fictional texts. Researchers, activists, and video game makers alike can argue for the importance of representation in a way that takes advantage of this fact. People are able to connect with characters for a variety of reasons, which implies that texts can be created to appeal to a wide range of people without focusing on specific identifiers or niche markets.

Identifying with experiences was the main way interviewees connected with characters across their media consumption. Anthropologist Elizabeth Chin finds a similar phenomenon in her ethnographic study of poor African American children in Hartford, Connecticut. She finds that although "adults tend to assume that the physical aspects of toys—their gender, skin tone, hair, determine how children will use and relate to them," children connect with dolls in much more complex ways.[105] Rather than wanting dolls that were physically similar to them, the children expressed "the desire for dolls who lived like them and the kids they know."[106] They felt more underrepresented in terms of their class than their race. The issue the children had with Barbie was not that she was a skinny, white, blond woman but that her dream house and glamorous life-style were so contrary to everything they experienced. Artist Justine Shaw describes a related anecdote about her fan letters for her comic *Nowhere Girl*. Although her comic is about a twentysomething Asian American lesbian, many of the fan letters she received were from adolescent males "who didn't fit into the straight-male pecking order at school."[107] They identified with the experience of being an outcast, not the identifiers of lesbian or Asian. Additionally, Melanie Green's research demonstrates that transportation is influenced by whether individuals have previous experiences that lead them to connect with a fictional character more readily.[108] Similar to Alice Hall's interviewees, for my participants the "personal experience not only served as evidence, but also established a standard to which specific media portrayals were compared."[109] As discussed in chapter 4, this has implications for how people understand and critique media representation, as well.

Not only is the process of identification diverse and multifaceted, but so is the object of the identification. What people connect with in media and how they do so is a complex process made more complex by context-, medium-, and genre-specific elements. If identification is about more than seeing oneself directly reflected in characters, more than merely sharing gendered, racial, or sexual identities with characters, how might we make arguments for diversity in games beyond just looking at these categories? Moreover, how do we make such arguments in an era in which digital media texts are themselves so shaped by audience input? This is to say, we can argue for the importance of representation in a manner that gets away from assumptions about how people see themselves in relation to digital game characters and that takes advantage of games as play spaces. Games provide many different types of identification that must be parsed in order to better understand the failings and the possibilities of the representation of marginalized groups in this medium.

When it comes to representation, James Paul Gee argues, "Video games have an unmet potential to create complexity by letting people experience the world from different perspectives. Part of this potential is that in a video game, you yourself have to act as a given character."[110] Others conceptualize identification with game avatars through the identification-as-simulation lens, in which the player thinks and treats the avatar as though it were the player.[111] Bonnie

Nardi compellingly argues, however, that performance rather than simulation is the best way to understand the embodied activity of game play in *World of Warcraft*.[112] Even while James Newman concedes that the relative importance of this type of identification or immersion may vary, he argues, "It is unlikely that players fail to bring any investment and understanding of characters to the game."[113] As I explore throughout my interviews, however, it was precisely this disinvestment in the characters that was a very common theme, part of which might stem from my primary focus on solo, offline rather than collective, online gaming. Although a game experience *might* produce an indexical player–avatar relationship, particularly in online gaming, assuming this is something good games simply do ignores a wide variety of game-play experiences. More than that, by uncovering how players do or do not identify with game characters, we might better understand when critical reflection on cultural differences could be something encouraged via games. As I discuss in the next chapter, this requires more than simply placing a person in the position of controlling an avatar or character "other" to them.

3

He Could Be a Bunny Rabbit
for All I Care!

Like game researchers, game designers speak at length about the importance of identification in player character/avatar relationships, but without clear definitions of the term. In *Fundamentals of Game Design,* a widely referenced textbook for game designers, Ernest Adams states that the goal of character design "is to create characters that people *find appealing* . . . that people can *believe in,* and that the player can *identify with* (particularly in the case of avatar characters)."[1] He goes on to say that men do not identify with their avatars as much as women do, though no supporting research is cited in his text. Nowhere does Adams delve into what identification with the avatar means outside of caring about how the narrative unfolds. He outlines several different types of relationships that players have with avatars, along lines similar to what I detail in this chapter. Despite acknowledging these different kinds of player–avatar relationships, however, he again asserts that the avatar "must be a character the player can identify with."[2] Identification is central to game design, at least according to Adams, yet what that means remains elusive.

Although identification may be what some designers expect to provide, it is not necessarily something players desire, at least not all of the time. Crucially, the interactivity of game play may overshadow the importance of identification, at least in relation to how identification is understood in other media. The title of this chapter comes from Julia, who identified as an African American, gay woman in her late thirties. She was speaking of Kratos, the player character in the game *God of War.*[3] She went on to say, "He's just the thing on the screen. He's holding the knives; that's all." Importantly, her inability to identify with this character was not simply because their gender, race, sexuality, and temporal context were different.

Julia did not see the need for connecting closely with her on-screen proxy in general. She was not the only interviewee who felt this apathy, though most were more ambivalent than apathetic. My interviewees' responses deeply trouble the dominant assumption that players identify closely with player characters or avatars.

According to some scholars, active control over the outcome is the appeal of games.[4] Scholars argue that interactivity makes new media different from old media.[5] Yet I demonstrate that this is an overgeneralization. Interactivity is certainly important to how researchers understand identification in video games, but what is meant by interactivity is an unsettled question.[6] Interactivity in video games is not just about pushing buttons and making things happen on the screen. If that were the case, then there would be little difference between using a video game controller and channel surfing with a remote control. It is important to make sense of what interaction means in order to make use of it as a concept. Games are interactive in terms of their ludic and narrative properties, but they are also bodily and socially interactive. These factors shape players' relationships with game texts and if or how they identify with on-screen characters.

In this chapter I discuss how games' ludic as well as bodily and socially interactive aspects result in players identifying *as* themselves rather than *with* characters/avatars and how narrative aspects of games help players identify *with* characters. I address the way play as an embodied and a contextually specific experience shapes players' relationships to their avatars/characters. Finally, I outline how these issues intersect by demonstrating the ways games that contain set characters, character options, and customizable avatars promote empathic identification or self-referentiality (i.e., identification as sameness).[7]

In addition to challenging assumptions about new media's interactivity, I want to push back against the easy assumption that interactivity promotes identification. Many authors assert that identification is stronger in games than in other media because interactivity lessens the distance between players and their on-screen representatives.[8] Often, these assumptions are derived from autoethnographic accounts. Shelia Murphy asserts, for example, "When I game I am both player and character simultaneously."[9] Geoff King and Tanya Krzywinska explain this claim as follows:

> The activity of the players is essential to the realization of much of
> what unfolds in the playing of games, even where the parameters
> are clearly established in advance. As a consequence, the player
> can seem more directly implicated than traditional media consumers
> in the meanings that result.[10]

Some of my interviewees said that digital games' interactive properties made them feel more connected with their characters. As
Cody described it, "Generally, you have direct control over the guy
in a video game, whereas you are watching someone in a movie."
Hatshepsut reported, "The more control I have over the character,
the more I feel I'm in the character." This connection, however, was
not seen by interviewees as identification. When it came to identifying with digital game characters, Hatshepsut said, "It's a game.
Like if you go play tennis, you're not trying to identify with the ball
or something." Interviewees may have seen the character as their
proxy, but they did not necessarily identify with the character in the
emotional, distanced way described in the previous chapter. This
responsiveness to player input masks the way the choices available
in games are structured and limited.

Although the definition of identification offered in the last chapter (identification as a push/pull of distance and sameness) would
seem oppositional to literature that defines identification in digital
games as the lessening of distance between player and character,
both are at play in James Paul Gee's discussion of the "tripartite play
of identities" in digital games:

> The tripartite play of identities (a virtual identity, a real-world identity,
> and a projective identity) in the relationship "player as virtual charac-
> ter" is quite powerful. It transcends identification with characters in
> novels or movies, for instance, because it is both *active* (the player
> actively does things) and *reflexive,* in the sense that once the player
> has made some choices about the virtual character, the virtual char-
> acter is now developed in a way that sets certain parameters about
> what the player can do. The virtual character redounds back on the
> player and affects his or her future actions.[11]

As Gee points out, the player's proxy is that which is and is not the
character, which is akin to identification. What he focuses on here,

however, is again a problematic conflation of interactivity and identification. It also presumes a particular approach to game play and
that this occurs in all games.

Certainly, identification is not the only way players connect with
game texts.[12] Gordon Calleja identifies agency (the ability to change
the course of events) as one of the key differences between games
and other media.[13] Agency fundamentally shapes how identification can be experienced. He goes on to outline several types of involvement in games that shape what he calls incorporation into the
game. Incorporation is defined as "the absorption of a virtual environment into consciousness, yielding a sense of habitation, which is
supported by the systemically upheld embodiment of the player in
a single location, as represented by the avatar."[14] Incorporation via
involvement is not the same as identification, given the definition
of identification offered by my interviewees. As the player actively
experiences what is going on in the game, what is going on in the
thought process of the character may prove relatively meaningless.

Previous studies have demonstrated that players can have very
close connections with their avatars. Zach Waggoner investigates
player–avatar relationships in his three-part study of role-playing
games (RPGs).[15] The games he uses, however, promote a very specific type of connection between players and avatars. He also acknowledges that he chose games that would elicit strong feelings
of identification in players familiar with RPG systems. Further, his
definition of identification seems to refer to the way players' offline
identities impact choices they make for their avatar. As I discuss,
there are other facets of identification and game play for which Waggoner's approach cannot account.

Other scholars have demonstrated that identification in games
can be fleeting. In her analysis of three separate single-player games
(*Mirror's Edge, Alone in the Dark,* and *Fable 2*), Kelly Boudreau
posits that "hybrid-identity" exists between a player and their
player character.[16] She finds that "hybrid-identity in single-player
videogames is generally fleeting" and that it is "a lot more difficult
to identify exact moments of its occurrence during the gameplay
process."[17] Similarly, looking at "ordinary play" versus role-play in
World of Warcraft, Ragnhild Tronstad distinguishes between two
different forms of identification: sameness identity and empathic
identity.[18] Sameness identity describes feeling that one has become

or is the character (for example, feeling like I *am* Lara Croft when playing *Tomb Raider*). In contrast, empathic identity describes an emotional connection with the character's experiences that is predicated on feeling separate from the character (for example, feeling emotionally connected to Lara Croft as a separate entity). Empathic identity is much more akin to identification as understood by my participants. Sameness identity better describes the intersection of the game as interactive text and the context in which it is played. Sameness identity refers to the way games make players think about their actions in terms of themselves rather than in relation to characters in the text as separate beings.

In addition to emphasizing the fleeting quality of identification or the nuanced ways identification works in games, some scholars have suggested that immersion rather than identification is a more fruitful focus, though Katie Salen and Eric Zimmerman dismiss the goal of full immersion into game worlds as the "immersive fallacy."[19] This fallacy is behind the assertion that players ideally become their avatars and identify with them completely. The danger this fallacy poses to game design, Salen and Zimmerman argue, is that "if game designers fail to recognize the way games create meaning for players—as something separate from, but connected to the world—they will have difficulty creating truly meaningful play."[20] They go on to argue that players undergo a double-consciousness and move through cognitive frames fluidly, "shifting from a deep immersion with the game's representation to a deep engagement with the game's strategic mechanisms to an acknowledgement of space outside the magic circle."[21] Similarly, Frans Mäyrä describes three different types of immersion involved in game play: sensory, challenge based, and imaginative. This last type is most closely linked with the concept of identification.[22] The interplay of all three types of immersion helps us make sense of the variety of ways players describe their relationships with their in-game characters.

Tronstad argues that "as computer games are not primarily narrative media," imaginative or empathic forms of identification are "much harder to accomplish and almost impossible to sustain should [they] occur."[23] Games can have narratives, of course (setting aside debates as to whether they are primarily story- or game structure–driven texts).[24] Indeed, my interviewees said they identified with characters largely through story elements. Evan strongly identified, for example, with the character Link in *The Legend of Zelda*: "Like, I wasn't actually sitting Indian-style on the floor in the basement in front of the TV. I was this little dude with a sword and killing monsters." In fact, identification was one of the main appeals of digital games for Evan. This was not because he felt the interactivity made him the character but because in most of his media consumption he identified with heroic characters, and in turn he played games with such characters. His example also points to one other key distinction in understanding how and when players identify with game characters: the difference between characters and avatars.

Characters or Avatars?

Before delving into when and how identification occurs in games, it is important to distinguish between digital game characters and avatars, as Rune Klevjer, Ragnhild Tronstad, and Zach Waggoner also argue.[25] A digital game avatar is the visual, digital embodiment of the player in the game world. The term *avatar* cannot be applied to all game characters, however, since it implies self-representation very specifically. Its original meaning refers to the physical manifestation of a Hindu deity on Earth, the embodied form of an ephemeral being.[26] When I create a representation of myself in an online or offline game, that is an avatar. Additionally, an avatar might be a proxy that I create for a specific game, even when it is not meant as self-representation and thus doesn't look exactly like me. Even if I decide to choose a seemingly random selection of options from a character-customization screen, I must momentarily reflect on how much I care about how I am represented in the game space. It is the notion of player self-representation that determines whether a person in a game is an avatar.

Digital game *characters* are entities unto themselves that players then control. Lara Croft of *Tomb Raider,* Mario of *Super Mario Bros.,* and Master Chief from *Halo* are characters more than avatars.[27] Although a player can sometimes change the costumes or weapons of their character, the character is not a self-representation of that player. Klevjer makes a further distinction between avatars as characters/personas (those with narratives) and avatars as proxies through which players experience agency in the game, like tokens in a board game.[28] As I discuss, all of these distinct player–character and player–avatar relationships promote different types of engagement with games. Further, not all of these relationships manifest as identification.

Ludic Texts and Interactive Narratives

Broadly speaking, the games industry constructs games, and audiences view games as responsive to players' wishes. This responsiveness is often used by both groups to distinguish games from other media, which is not to say that this engagement is better or more thoughtful than that which accompanies other media. Responsiveness and engagement are coupled with narrative and representational elements.[29] Players are not just reading or viewing stories to see where the characters end up, as they do with films and novels. In games they engage with texts that often, though not always, have end goals and rewards. According to Violet, "Because I'm actively doing it . . . it's definitely not that I identify with him as a character, but just the act of doing it." This causes two disruptions to the way we usually think about identification and representation. First, the player's goals and the character's goals are typically conjoined. The player is not rooting for a character to succeed, in the way they might with a book, a film, or a television show, as much as they are rooting for themselves as they try to win the game. Second, the story and the act of playing are not always distinct. As Bryan described:

> I don't feel like, "Oh my, that's me!" You know? It's still like I have the objective. And in that sense I feel outside of the character, but it's still like there are certain parts of the narrative and the story where it's totally like, oh yeah, that's why I'm playing this. . . . And then in *Bard's Tale*, there's no separation there. . . . I'm going to tell this person off because that board was really hard and I had to go through it ten times and now you are giving me fifteen cents for my troubles, fuck you. That's much more identifiable, and I feel much more a part of that.

When Bryan says "identifiable" here, he means identification as sameness, in Tronstad's sense.[30] Getting frustrated with constant failure, which Jesper Juul has identified as central to game play, does not constitute identifying *with* the character.[31] The failure implicates the player more than the character/avatar. Though I may occasionally blame the on-screen character for screwing up a jump or shout, "Why did you die!" it is not because I think the character is an entity separate from myself—quite the opposite. I know that I am the one who screwed up the jump or killed the character, but I use such comments to further distance myself from the frustration. Despite assumptions in the literature described that since players are actively controlling avatars, they identify more strongly with these characters, this is not *necessarily* the case.

Erik Bucy asserts that "interactivity should be regarded primarily as a perceptual variable" and that the fact that players view games as interactive is an important difference from other media.[32] After all, video games don't just allow players to be active—they require it. As T. L. Taylor describes, "Players do not just consume, or act as passive audience members of, the game but instead are active co-creators in producing it as a meaningful experience and artifact."[33] Yet this is not to say that video game reception is always or inherently active. Evan described how his father passively consumed games: "I don't think he ever touched a paddle in his life. He only watches. He still does. . . . My father sits in his recliner, and my brother sits on the sofa, and my father just watches him play." Evan's father even got mad at Evan's brother for finishing a game while he was not home. Elise, Julia's partner, also enjoyed watching games unfold but did not wish to play herself. She is an example of the secondary player James Newman describes: "The secondary-player role is frequently taken by players who like the idea of games but find them too hard and is just one example of the ways players appropriate videogame experience in manners often not intended by producers (or observed by researchers)."[34] Similarly, in their work on competitive gaming, T. L. Taylor and Todd Harper both point out that spectatorship forms an important aura in the experience of gaming.[35] We should be wary of using interactivity as the sole defining characteristic differentiating games from other media. After all, filmic, television, and literary audiences are not passive dupes thoughtlessly absorbing mediated messages. These audiences interact with nongame media texts by questioning them, critiquing them, remaking them, and actively creating meaning out of them to serve diverse purposes. When it comes to interactivity, games are both like and unlike other media forms

Although medium specificity is important and games differ in important ways from other media forms, it is crucial to keep in mind that games often contain those other media forms in their design (and thus aren't so radically distinct from them). This has important implications for interactivity, as we can consider the way that people playing games might feel disengaged from the activity. Cut scenes, the filmic portions of games, are a key example of the multimedia nature of games and demonstrate how inactivity or a lack of engagement is sometimes an important part of game play.[36] Bryan recalled that after a long day of work, he would sometimes sit down and watch the beginning half-hour cinematic opening of *Disgaea*.[37] Another common form of disengagement is button mashing, in which players smash all the buttons their fingers can reach as often as they can rather than thinking strategically about moves. Players might button mash to get through a three-minute fight in a game like *Soul Calibur*, as Hatshepsut did in her gaming interview.[38] People may, as Christoph Klimmt points out,[39] shift between the two different forms of involvement during a single text, as Hatshepsut did while playing *God of War*: "While I'm playing, I don't think about it, but like say a cut scene comes on between levels, I'll pay attention to what they are saying if I think it's going to help me when I'm playing. But while I'm playing, it's gone. I'm just playing." Here, we see a clear distinction between the ludic and the narrative elements of the game, which in turn can be used to define the line between empathic identification and identification as sameness.

Even active moments in games can feel passive. This was particularly obvious in the gaming interview I had with Sara. Sara worked for a nonprofit that represented Philadelphia art and cultural institutions. She grew up in the Midwest and New England but went to college near the city and remained there afterward. Her apartment was covered in music posters and dominated by a large collection of vinyl records. A record player held a place of status in the living room (dwarfing the handful of games and the console on the shelf under her television). As I settled in for the interview, one of her cats inspected my bag on the couch next to me.

Sara was already in the midst of playing the *Wii Sports* bowling simulation game when I arrived. It was her regular after-work ritual. She played sitting down, unlike most of the Wii players I had watched in person or seen in Nintendo's advertisements, making barely noticeable motions with the Wii-mote controller. Bored with bowling, she shifted to baseball and then golf. She hit her knee with the controller when she messed up a putt and swung the controller in a downward motion to make the golf swings. The cat that had been sniffing me lost interest and walked to the kitchen. Sara switched back to baseball and, as she played, leaned over, elbows on knees, making very subtle motions with the Wii-mote, which were translated into exuberant swings by the Mii. Her Mii avatar looked a lot like her. She sat up straight when batting, as it was not going well, yet despite her intensity of focus, her approach to it overall was relaxed and dazed. Sara played for nearly two hours straight while I watched, and her affect was that of someone trying to zone out at the end of a long day. Indeed, in contrast to her approach to discussing music, an area in which she was animated and knowledgeable, her approach to games was very passive. She did not feel she identified as or with the avatar; she merely reflected on herself playing the game. Although Sara was clearly engaged with her games, exhibiting the interactivity the aforementioned scholars insist is central to what makes games different from other media, her mode of interactivity was more passive than active.

Similarly, Janet played games because they allowed her to engage in an activity that took up mental energy without being emotionally engaging. As she put it, "I do client-support training for a living, and pretty much all of my jobs have involved dealing with the public in some kind of intense manner, and I just like to relax by, like, I'm going to move the squares around in a box." Janet clearly was not actively identifying *with* her game in the ways some assume games are always experienced. As described previously, game studies has often conflated interactivity with identification. Interactivity can sometimes be passive, though, as Janet and Sara demonstrated. According to my interviewees, active reflection was seen as necessary for identification, but not all game necessitated reflection.

Sometimes, active and passive engagement are intertwined. For instance, Klara played to take up time as she faced postcollege unemployment. Her game play might be understood as a response to the lowered employment prospects following the 2008 economic collapse; she felt she was being productive even as she waited to hear back on job applications. Sara, Janet, and Klara's game play can also be read as useful escapism made possible by the games medium.[40] Escapism can be understood as something games offer even to disengaged or disinterested players. None of these interviewees felt that they identified with the characters on-screen. Rather, they were self-referential. They largely did not think about what the character on the screen wanted or planned. They thought about their actions only in terms of their own progression in the game. The activity of playing the game was the point for them, not emotional connection with a character.

Given these responses, some games are perhaps more usefully understood as reactive rather than interactive texts.[41] In many games players are reacting to a system that provides them with stimuli rather than interacting with spaces that passively wait for their input. Often, games move too quickly for players to have the requisite time to contemplate their characters/avatars, time that identification requires. As Renee explained the experience, "You've got thirty seconds to not screw it up too bad [*laughs*]. There's not a whole lot of backstory involved." Ludic elements shape how players can or cannot engage in the process of identification. For many interviewees this lack of time prevented the distancing process necessary for identification to take place. Playing was about their success as players in the game system rather than the experience of the character/avatar per se (with some exceptions).

Identification, according to interviewees, occurred largely through the narrative, non-medium-specific aspects of games rather than through their interactivity. The ludic aspects of games (rules, systems, goals) often caused interviewees to be too self-referential to identify with their character, whereas interviewees asserted that the narrative aspects of games allowed them that identification. When identifying with characters, they thought about their actions often in terms of the history of the character, which was communicated via narrative. While playing a wrestling game, Cody said, for example, he could identify with his avatar when playing through the *WWE* storyline. When playing other sports games, he said, however, "I like [avatars/characters] kind of to look like me or act like me." Again, the narrative game elements could lead him to empathic identification, but other types of play resulted in identification as sameness. Interestingly, many of the interviewees who played *Zelda* identified with the protagonist's story and position. Connie said that she really identified with Link because "he's kind of like little underdog elf guy that rose to the top because he was smart." This characterization, being a smart underdog, was part of the personal narrative she gave when I asked her to tell me about herself in the first interview. For both Cody and Connie, identification was tied to the *narrative* elements of the game rather than the *interactive* elements.

The identification that my interviewees experienced with games was akin to their identification with other media—games were not a radically distinct media form in this case. For many, though, identification was not the point of playing games. Renee, for instance, felt a strong attachment to Mario:

> I'm always Mario. Always. To the point where my six-year-old nephew, I come over and he's like, "Here aunt [Renee], you're Mario." It's good. But in that one, like, it's his game, it's his world, it's his space; it's my game, my world, my space. But I don't feel like I'm an Italian plumber, you know what I mean? But in books and in movies you have a different kind of characterization, so you, like, you identify more with the words that they are using or the clothes that they are wearing or whatever. But in video games it's a little different; you kind of identify with the adventure, I guess.

The interactivity of games as a medium altered what type of connection was possible for Renee. Unlike with other media, her attachment was to the experience of play more than to Mario. As Christine put it, "I'm only really thinking about what I'm doing and how my actions are affecting the character's actions." Revisiting the ludic/narrative divide, Malcolm said that in games there were two senses in which one could understand a character. The first was in terms of using the character's skills and abilities optimally. The second was when deeper games allowed players to get a sense of what kind of choices the character would make and to feel encouraged to make those kinds of choices as they played. In those instances where players identified with a character, it was because of the narrative.

As Anthony Giddens argues, motives are intimately tied up with a concept of the self as autonomous.[42] When it comes to playing a game, the motives of the player and the motives of the in-game character are neither wholly distinct nor wholly the same. While the player actively experiences what is physically happening to the character in the game, they are not necessarily concerned with the emotional or cognitive life of that character. Tala described this as being "one with the character but not of the character." An exception would be games with developed characters in which the player wished to play as that character. In that case, players may attempt to understand the character's thought processes rather than merely controlling their actions. Often, however, it does not matter what the character is thinking, as the player ultimately decides what to do next. Similarly, the character's goals are in many cases the same as the player's goals. Kat described, "As far as winning and losing, I could sympathize with the character in that regard. . . . But the avatar probably wasn't feeling that; it was probably me putting my emotions there." For Kat the motivations of the character were relevant only insofar as they were part of the goals of the game.

Part of what scholars (and game makers) must be more willing to embrace is that the text alone does not define how the player interacts or connects with the characters or avatars. Subjective reasons for play and personal preferences drive the very personal experience of identification much more than textual elements can. We can see the different ways people approach identification in games by comparing two interviewees' thoughts about identification during a cooperative gaming session. On a late November afternoon, I sat on partners Devon and Ephram's couch as they debated which game to play for the interview. We stared at the tall bookcases, chock-full of various console and PC games, hugging both sides of the large television on the opposite wall. They finally settled on *Left 4 Dead*, a first-person-shooter, cooperative, zombie-apocalypse survival game.[43] In the game, players could pick one of four protagonists to control: (1) Zoey, a young, white, female college student; (2) Lewis, an African American, male, information technology professional; (3) Francis, a burly, white, male biker; and (4) Bill, a gruff, white, male Vietnam War veteran (Figure 17). The computer controlled any character not chosen by the player(s) and fought alongside them as they tried to escape the flesh-eating hordes. The main goal was to complete individual short "chapters" by getting from one checkpoint to the next. Each "book" of the game comprised five chapters.

Left 4 Dead was not the kind of game either man typically played, though they had already played it multiple times and often played it when friends were over. It was cooperative and had discrete end points, making it ideal for the interview setting. It also gave them

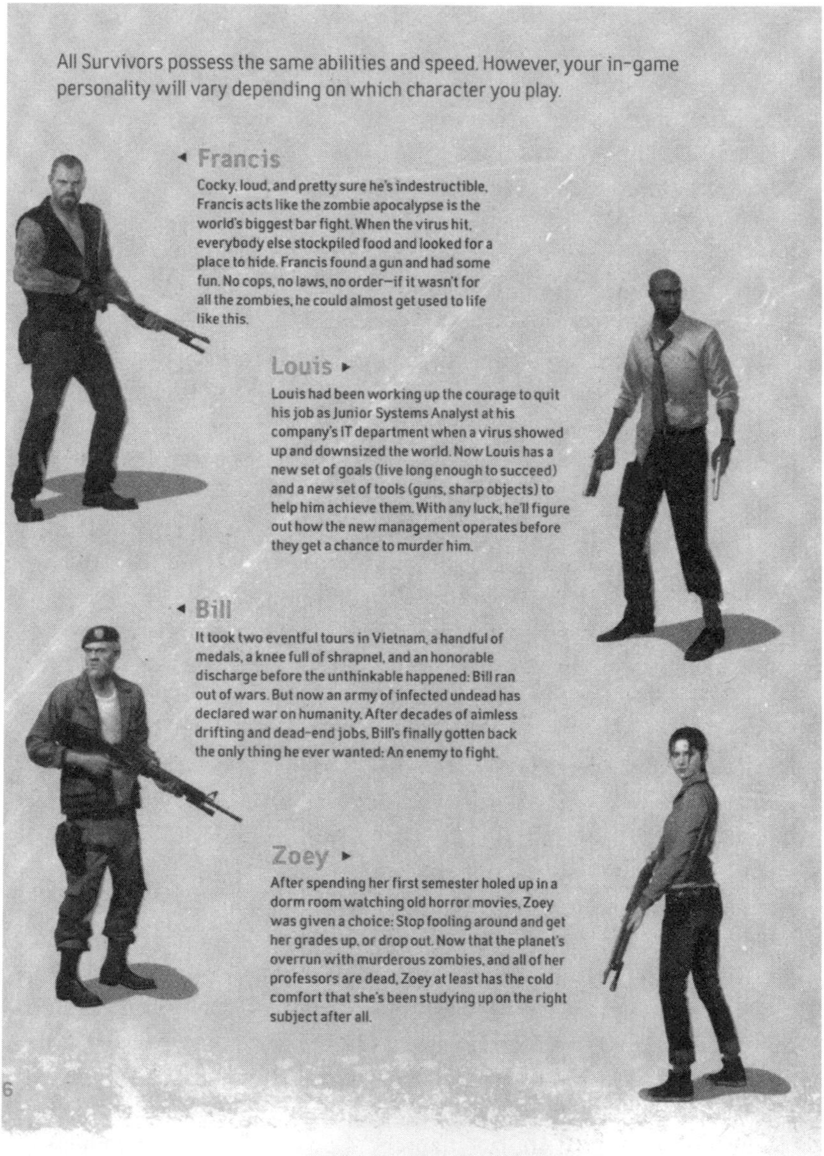

All Survivors possess the same abilities and speed. However, your in-game personality will vary depending on which character you play.

◄ Francis

Cocky, loud, and pretty sure he's indestructible, Francis acts like the zombie apocalypse is the world's biggest bar fight. When the virus hit, everybody else stockpiled food and looked for a place to hide. Francis found a gun and had some fun. No cops, no laws, no order—if it wasn't for all the zombies, he could almost get used to life like this.

Louis ►

Louis had been working up the courage to quit his job as Junior Systems Analyst at his company's IT department when a virus showed up and downsized the world. Now Louis has a new set of goals (live long enough to succeed) and a new set of tools (guns, sharp objects) to help him achieve them. With any luck, he'll figure out how the new management operates before they get a chance to murder him.

◄ Bill

It took two eventful tours in Vietnam, a handful of medals, a knee full of shrapnel, and an honorable discharge before the unthinkable happened: Bill ran out of wars. But now an army of infected undead has declared war on humanity. After decades of aimless drifting and dead-end jobs, Bill's finally gotten back the only thing he ever wanted: An enemy to fight.

Zoey ►

After spending her first semester holed up in a dorm room watching old horror movies, Zoey was given a choice: Stop fooling around and get her grades up, or drop out. Now that the planet's overrun with murderous zombies, and all of her professors are dead, Zoey at least has the cold comfort that she's been studying up on the right subject after all.

Figure 17. Page from *Left 4 Dead* manual showing the four character options with brief bios, emphasizing that "all survivors possess the same abilities and speed. However, your in-game personality will vary depending on which character you play."

a starting point for talking about other games during the interview. As Devon and Ephram started up the game, their dog sat next to me and pushed his nose under my hand anytime I stopped petting him to take notes. Fortunately, I was familiar with the game and could follow the rapid-fire pace of the game play fairly easily and reconstruct my notes afterward.

In the frenzy of action on the screen, Devon and Ephram occasionally shot one another's characters and their computer-controlled teammates. They came within feet of completing the book they had selected but died at the last moment and, after shouting in frustration, opted not to continue. Turning to the interview questions, the couple acknowledged that they had discussed their separate first interviews after I had left. My discussions with each of them about identification had gone on for some time and were still on their minds when I asked them about identification in relation to *Left 4 Dead*. Each saw the process of identification differently:

DEVON: I would say identification is when you feel that you and the character are going through similar situations. Not necessarily, you know, saying, I have fought zombies before. But saying that you could identify with the character if you're like, "Oh, if I was in that situation, I would do the same things." Or even though the situation is different, I can see similarities between—yes, I've never fought zombies, but I've been stuck with three people that I don't know very well, and we've had to work together, and people snipe at each other or whatever.

ME: And accidently shoot each other [*all laugh*].

DEVON: And accidently—shit happens. So . . . [*shrugs and chuckles*].

EPHRAM: I think there has to be something that ties the two together. Like, there has to be some kind of similarity. Whether it's coming from the same background or coming from the same experience, there has to be some kind of commonality between the two people. I don't know; it's kind of similar to the way you [to Devon] were talking about, you know, you can kind of identify with the experience they are going through. But for me it has to be a little more, I guess, more concrete? I don't know if that makes sense. Like, I think we had this discussion after . . . [referring to the first interview].

DEVON: Yeah, we had the discussion afterwards.

EPHRAM: And I was kind of like, I can identify with an Asian person, or I can identify with a gay person, or and to a lesser extent, I can kind of identify with other minorities. But it's more of a, I guess, an empathy or sympathy towards it versus identification. I don't know.

Even though Ephram focused on identifying *as* someone in a similar social position, he said that this was not the same as identifying *with* the character per se. Identification *as* might result in empathy or sympathy but not the taking on of that character's role. In the first interview Ephram said, "I have to be able to not just kind of empathize with the situation but really be like that person is me. That person is a gay person or is a minority and is really struggling because of that." Identifying *with* the character, however, as Devon pointed out, does not necessitate that type of concrete connection. He could identify with the character's situation, experiences, and personality regardless of whether he shared identifiers with the character.

When I asked them why they chose the game characters they did, their choices encompassed the various reasons players might do this. Devon chose Lewis, described in the game's manual as a "junior systems analyst in an IT department." Ephram chose to play as Zoey, described as "a college student home from school." All of the characters had the same basic mechanics and abilities, though Ephram noted, "[Zoey] is smaller, so you can shoot around her." Some of their reasons were aesthetic. According to Devon, the other two male characters were a bit "grizzled." In contrast, Lewis was a white-collared and relatively jovial character, considering the bloodthirsty, zombie-filled world in which they found themselves. Devon stressed that he also felt an affinity for what little of Lewis's personality he could glean from the game's short opening sequence and his occasional vocalizations and jokes through the game.

As I have described, narrative elements could engender identification as long as there was something the interviewee connected with in the character's persona, but ludic aspects of game play made interviewees self-referential, superseding their identification with the on-screen proxy. Moreover, the context of game play could shape how and why identification was relevant.

Sociality and Contextual Play

If we are to heed Paul Dourish's caution that researchers need to account for the complex interaction between context and embodied activity in human–computer interaction, researchers must be more explicit about the way the context in which games are played (online or offline, with others or alone) necessarily shifts players' relationship to their avatars or player characters.[44] Dourish suggests that context is more usefully understood as practice rather than as setting. Following this suggestion, we can assign a "central role to the meanings that people find in the world and the meanings of their actions there in terms of the consequences and interpretations of those actions for themselves and for others."[45] Furthermore, as Bart Simon argues, newer motion-sensitive consoles are positioning the enjoyment of game play in terms of kinaesthetic experiences rather than disembodied ones.[46] Different gaming contexts shape the types of choices a player makes about how they create and play with or as their character/avatar.

Avatar–player relationships can be quite powerful and self-referential in massively multiplayer online role-playing games (MMORPGs), as numerous studies have demonstrated.[47] These relationships and online performances can be so powerful that players sometimes form communities that traverse online play spaces, as Celia Pearce describes in her ethnography of the *Uru* diaspora in *Second Life* and *There.com*.[48] The meaning of belonging to an online community also shapes geographically copresent experiences of identity. In her ethnography of *EverQuest* players, Taylor found that her identity as a member of a particular server[49] became relevant during a real-life *EverQuest* convention: "I never really thought of myself as specifically a 'Bailerbents player' until this moment where, in a huge hall filled with people, it becomes a shared identity and easy point of connection."[50] Likewise, real-world identities can be made relevant in online play, as Bonnie Nardi demonstrates, when players link their online avatar to pictures of the player behind the character, use voice chat, choose to disclose personal information in chat, or employ grammar that bespeaks social-class, geographic, or racial identities.[51] In addition, as Celia Pearce, T. L. Taylor, and Bonnie Nardi each discuss, the online space itself, including both the social space of the game and the structure of the software object provided by the server company, shapes how players perform their identities as players and as their avatar.

Persistent virtual worlds are different from the environments of solitary play, as Klevjer theorizes.[52] Moreover, it is important to remember that not all online games are social, in the sense that they cause players to talk to and make friends with others. During her gaming interview, Amy played a series of short games from an online site where players were ranked based on their performance in solo games. She never interacted with other players through the site; it was simply a free portal to quick games she could play at work. Similarly, not all offline games are solitary, as many can be played with others in the same room, like *Rock Band,* as discussed later.

Many of the arguments made about how online gaming shapes players' choices, in contrast to offline gaming, implicitly reference online, social play. Online, social games rely on complex interrelations between online and offline identities in both the playing of the game and the development of social relationships with other players. There are some similarities to the limits posed by both social games and solitary games, of course. Devon described this in terms of playing *World of Warcraft*:

> My character collects the minipets that are available in the game. . . . And then whenever we're like gathered in a group, I'll just bring out the pets. . . . I'm not saying anything, just seeing if anyone notices. I'm just [*makes hand gesture*], I'm just dropping them out. So in that sense, I try to make him kind of personalized. You know, everyone plays this game, but I'm the guy that collects the pets.

In this online, social game, how Devon represented himself to other people playing the game was of more interest to him than who his character was in a narrativized sense. In offline, solitary games, however, he felt more strongly identified with characters with backstories.

Playing as an avatar that is like or unlike you in some way is different from performing as oneself (or another) in a social space. Unlike offline, solitary games, "in online games, one's avatar becomes a persistent, representation of self; one that often remains immutable once it has been chosen."[53] Cody said of *World of Warcraft*, "On the one hand, that person is a reflection of me, but on the other hand, I'm talking to you as [Cody], not the character." That identification with avatars in online and offline spaces is different may answer Francis Steen et al.'s and Mia Consalvo's questions about "what went wrong" and "what happened" when *The Sims* went online.[54] Beyond the technical changes to the game that both articles outline, the shift from offline to online play changed the context in which players interacted with their avatars. In their analysis of *The Sims Online,* Steen et al. found that participants disassociated from the game partially because they did not feel connected to their avatar.[55] Social contexts can shift players' attention from their relationship with their character to their relationship with other people and, in turn, shape their feelings about the game itself. I would not go so far as to assert, as Torill Mortensen does, that "avatars in a multiuser game . . . have a much stronger connection to the players than a ready-made figure . . . and the sense of identification is, of course, stronger."[56] Mortensen does not define identification but points to the *different* types of connection available in online and offline play rather than to a clear-cut hierarchy of identification by type of game or game play. Context of consumption, moreover, shapes the experience of different forms of sociality available in game play and in media consumption more generally.

Media consumption is not inherently social or solitary—it is contextually so. In Pouncy's first interview, they described the act of reading with a friend:

> Yeah, like my best friend and I would go get *Dragonlance* books at the bookstore, and then we'd hang out like lying on her bed reading them. Like each of us reading our own book, and her brother would come in and be like, "What the hell are you doing? You could do that by yourself." And we're like, "Shut up!"

Pouncy articulated here that certain types of sociality could be seen as "less than," at least in the friend's brother's young eyes. He insisted that activities that could be done alone should be. There is pleasure to be gained in passive social interactions, however, as Pouncy and their friend found in sharing reading time. A single medium is not inherently more or less social, as all media are embedded in social practices. As John Storey describes in terms of television:

> Watching television is always so much more than a series of acts of interpretations; it is above all else a social practice. That is, it can be a means both to isolate oneself (Don't talk to me, I'm watching this), or to make contact with other family members (watching a programme you are indifferent about, or worse, in order to make contact with a particular member of the family or the family as a whole). . . . In these ways, the cultural consumption of television is as much about social relationships as it is about interpretations of individual programmes.[57]

Most game studies work analyzing sociality and games focuses on massively multiplayer online games (MMOGs) or on people playing together. Even those who want to expand this focus often end up reproducing it. For example, Juul reviews different social aspects of gaming by focusing on multiple people playing the same game at once.[58] Though he is careful to explicate the different social interactions this may entail, his account obscures other ways in which people might play together. In this scholarship alternative socialities of gaming are rarely acknowledged. However, games can be played alone, together, alone together, or together alone, as I describe below. Here, "alternative" does not refer to something special about certain types of gaming but rather signals that there are forms of social interaction that are involved in playing video games that are different from online, social play or offline, colocated play. These are all social aspects of gaming that rarely get addressed in the literature, though they make up an integral part of the experience of gaming.

There are many different social arrangements in which one can play games. At the most simplistic level, games can be played alone or with others, and the latter is not inherently more social than the former. An interviewee from a previous project argued that video games were "the most social way to be antisocial that I know of." In her example of *Dance Dance Revolution,* she said, "You can be dancing with someone else, not looking at each other, just moving to some arrows." Actively playing a game cooperatively or competitively with others does not necessarily result in the personal connections often attributed to sociality (though it can). Similarly, one can play an offline, one-player game while talking to a partner sitting on the same couch the entire time. Solo gaming is not inherently antisocial.

Moving beyond this simple dichotomy, games can be played alone together. One might play an MMOG while sitting alone in their apartment while interacting with people online. This game play might even be considered more social than offline cogaming, as an MMOG usually requires explicit verbal communication with others, whereas physical copresence can be enough in offline cogaming, as in the *Dance Dance Revolution* example. Playing together does not always imply playing *together* in a social sense, even while in the same room or while playing the same game, as Bjorn Sjöblom similarly argues.[59] Games can be played together alone if two partners sit in the same room playing on their respective computers, handheld devices, or separate televisions. During my gaming interview with Zahriel, her partner sat on the floor near us playing his Nintendo DS while I watched her play *Halo* on an Xbox 360. Later, while waiting out a sudden thunderstorm, I played on my cell phone while she played on her DS and her roommate played on the Xbox. We spoke to each other, but were engaged in very different forms of play.

Similarly, that a given game is designed to be multiplayer or single player does not determine with whom players do or do not play. Studying online play and community formation obscures the other, perhaps more mundane, socialities of gaming. For example, Sasha recounted game nights from her childhood:

> We used to have little powwows, me, my brother, and stepsister. And we used to make homemade Rice Krispie treats in the bowl—just in the microwave. Used to eat it out of the bowl and play *Super Mario Bros.* and *Duck Hunt* on Nintendo. Every Friday. [My stepsister] would beat us because she was like twelve and I was like five, but that was fun nevertheless.

The games she described were primarily single-player games, so ostensibly Sasha and her siblings took turns, her stepsister winning by virtue of getting farther or a higher score than the others. The context of play, the way they used the game, defined the sociality much more than the game objects themselves.

Many different forms of sociality are made available in different gaming contexts. Players often interact with others in ways unaccounted for in most game studies literature. While playing a solo game, my interviewee Janet texted a friend for advice on a particularly difficult puzzle. Cody recounted that when he was younger, in the days before networked consoles, he and his friends would call each other on the phone while playing the same game in their separate homes. Additionally, during her gaming interview, Kat created a series of Miis based on her friends because, she said, "I think it's more fun to play when you, like, know who you are playing with, and so I played with people who I was familiar with." Game researchers and other media scholars tend to overlook these types of interactions because they detract from immersion or incorporation into the text. Melanie Green, Timothy Brock, and Geoff Kaufman assert that detracting factors limit enjoyment of media by inhibiting transportation.[60] To use one of their examples, many annoyances (crying babies, talking, etc.) can detract from enjoyment in movie theaters because they pull viewers out of being entirely absorbed by the story and image on-screen. Following this logic, making fun of aspects of a video game, discussing choices made during play, or even making jokes while cowatching a movie with friends would be considered forms of media enjoyment that precluded transportation into the narrative. Yet as my interviewees' stories demonstrate, transportation may certainly be enjoyable, but enjoyment of media is amorphous: it shifts in relation to different types of texts and contexts. The pleasures interviewees found in games were often *dependent on* rather than threatened by these "detracting" practices, and these social contexts often superseded identification with on-screen characters.

Although there are pleasures to be found in social aspects of gaming, it is important to note that solitary gaming is desirable in and of itself, as well. In terms of identification, several interviewees said that playing alone could make them feel closer to their character or avatar. Tala said of *Eternal Darkness* and its insanity effects, "Playing in the dark, it does freak you out. I do follow what the character is going through."[61] Tala was quick to note the pleasures involved in being freaked out, an experience she would not have had playing in a room with others. Several interviewees said that playing with other people around them made them more detached from the game and less likely to identify with the characters. There was more self-reflection involved when other people were watching. Evan noted that the gaming interview made him feel self-conscious: "Because you do get into it. You're like she [referring to me] knows that I'm not killing enough Nazis." Most often, interviewees said that it was in online, social play that context most significantly shaped identification. Specifically, playing online made them the most reflexive about how they were perceived through their avatars/characters. This was identification as sameness more than empathic identification, however.

Context similarly shapes when and how players choose to dance along the moral spectrum. There is a great deal of popular and academic worry about players identifying closely with the violent aspects of many games.[62] Lieutenant Colonel Dave Grossman has often argued, for example, that video games give players the "will and the skill to kill."[63] As shown thus far, however, players connect with game texts in ways that are too varied for such stark pronouncements. Many interviewees asserted that identifying with media characters entailed deciding whether they would make the same decisions as the characters and weighing the effect of context on those decisions.

Morality is one way viewers/readers interact with a text that could engender identification.[64] Caine defined identification as "saying, you know, why yes that is a horrible decision to make. I'm not sure what I would do, but given the choices, I would go with choice A." Caine, like other interviewees, recognized the game system had a limited number of options and, when faced with moral dilemmas, chose as best he could under the circumstances. In one study Elly Konijn and Johan Hoorn found that although their participants felt more distanced from "bad" characters, their appreciation of those characters was not significantly different from theirs of "good" characters.[65] They assert that players can make judgments about characters' ethics, aesthetics, and epistemics without necessarily identifying with those characters. Both my interviewees and this scholarly argument suggest that media do not necessarily *directly* shape how we think of ourselves and how we think of others. Rather, researchers can draw on Noël Carroll's clarification thesis regarding media and morality to understand the complex interaction that takes place between audiences and texts:

Clarificationism does not claim that, in the typical case, we acquire new propositional knowledge from artworks, but rather that the artworks in question can deepen our moral understanding by encouraging us to apply our moral knowledge and emotions to specific cases. For in being prompted to engage our antecedent moral judgment we may come to augment them.[66]

Moral clarification, like identification in Stuart Hall's formulation, requires active processing of difference and sameness and of individual's recognition of aspects of themselves within or absent from the text.[67] Identity, if not identification, becomes relevant if the player feels uncomfortable, or comfortable, choosing to be "bad."

I explored this issue in great detail during my gaming interview with Bryan. On a cold winter's night he introduced me to his new fiancée and dog before taking me to the converted back porch that housed his game room. One wall was covered with a large flat-screen television and several generations' worth of Sony PlayStation consoles and peripherals, while a large leather couch took up the other. In the center of the room, he had a leather-covered footlocker that was specially built to contain his *Rock Band* instruments and extra controllers. He offered me a beer, grabbing one for himself, as he waited for the system to start up. He was excited to show me *Disgaea,* which he described as "the crack that got him back into gaming."[68] The game narrative followed Laharl, the prince of the underworld, and included both preset characters and avatars that players could create themselves. The player could pick from the set and created characters in order to make a team for each level (or board).

Bryan played and showed me the many parts of the game he found interesting. He had already clocked hundreds of hours playing based on the internal game clock. The entire game was about demons in the underworld, and Bryan noticed that one of the things that appealed to him about it was playing as an evil character. At the same time, however, good and evil were not mutually exclusive in the game. Describing the protagonist Laharl, he said: "That's another big theme, is that he's very undemon-like. He sees beauty in the world, and you're not supposed to talk about stuff like that. And he uses, he likes poetry and describes the stuff that he sees that way. Whereas, you know, the demon way is to be a megalomaniac warrior and kill everything you see." Following this train of thought, he asked if I would like to see *The Bard's Tale,* a game he had talked about during our first meeting.

In *The Bard's Tale,* Bryan said that he identified as the main character primarily because the game allowed him to choose nice or snarky responses to non-player characters.[69] When we first spoke, he said he typically chose the nice option: "I pick nice more often, and that definitely mimics how I view myself." When he played through a section of it during the gaming interview, however, he asked me whether he should choose the nice or the snarky responses. We went back and forth between nice and mean choices, laughing at the results. We both used the research context as an excuse to explore optional "badness" that we would not have taken normally in our own game play.[70] Eventually, we came to the dog in the game, a computer-controlled sidekick who would follow the player throughout the game if the player was nice to it. Bryan had told me before that he could never bring himself to hurt the dog. When the time came, neither could I. Bryan told me afterward that he had hoped that I would go for the snarky option, giving him an excuse to see what would happen. I found, however, that I did not want to make a choice that would reflect negatively on my own morality in front of him. Clearly, for both of us, kicking a dog was a line we were not willing to cross, even playfully.

Whereas the games Bryan played were offline and, thus, his choices were viewable only to himself and me in the interview, other interviewees felt that their actions in online games more directly reflected the kind of people they were, and thus, they were less comfortable "being bad" in public. This tendency is distinct from Taylor's discussion of the importance of reputation in online, social games like *EverQuest*.[71] Taylor refers mainly to a player's abilities and good standing as guild members. Choosing the morally ambiguous route in online games was a related but distinct issue. As Cody pointed out, in games like *World of Warcraft* and *EverQuest*: "You are that person, essentially. . . . The character isn't talking for you; you're talking for it. . . . You know there's another real person on the other end. . . . You're going to have real-life conflicts [*chuckles*]." Another interviewee, Malcolm, was willing to take the "less noble option" in a closed game like *Dragon Age* but not when he played *World of Warcraft*: "The fact that it doesn't impact other people, that is a significant difference between the two instances." Devon asserted that in MMORPGs, "Your character is in that case more an avatar than in any other situation, because that is how you interact with other people that you've never met before, that's their first impression of you is through your character. So that influences things." This is not to say that there are not people who behave in antisocial ways in online worlds. Indeed, as discussed in the introduction, there is a great deal of bigotry in online gaming. The implications of bad behavior online are very different from those in offline play and, perhaps, say even more about a player's personality.

Clearly, online, social game play changes players' relationship to and performance of their avatar. But many of the concerns my interviewees recounted about identifying with their avatar in online spaces were still relevant in offline, social gaming. In an online, social gaming space, the avatar is, in the most direct way, a representative for the player in a social space. In offline gaming the avatar or player character might be an index for the player on the screen but often is not necessarily invested with the same aura of avatar-as-player that MMORPG research has demonstrated. When playing offline, social games, we might say that the experience of being a physical body in the space, be it a living room or an arcade, might supersede any identification the player has with the avatar. In sum, social context shapes reflexivity and identification as sameness as well as empathic identification.

Playing in different contexts shifted whether interviewees performed their own personalities or were willing to explore different options. Some interviewees said they could never choose to be bad when given the option. Devon said, "Whenever there are games that have a lot of moral choices that you are supposed to make, I always do the goody-goody type, because I just can't, I can't do the bad things." His partner Ephram said, however, that he could be bad. A similar exchange occurred when I spoke with Carol and Chuck. Chuck, like Devon, said he could not bring himself to be the bad guy, though Carol said she could. Sasha said it could depend on timing and context: "I'm sporadic. Just because somebody might pick the hero, I'll just be the bad guy. It depends on who I'm playing!" Some interviewees were perfectly willing to be the bad guy in games to see different storylines, to role-play as a certain type of character, or simply to see what would happen if they were mean. Interviewees discussed this ambivalence only in relation to games where their actions had no impact on other people. Social context more than game text shaped their choices. In addition to different types of sociality and context, different experiences of embodiment shaped interviewees' feelings of identification with their character or avatar.

Embodied Play

One might conceive of the avatar as the key site of embodiment in the virtual game world, whether the player is working through a solo game or playing an MMORPG. Rune Klevjer speaks of the avatar as a form of prosthetic and fictional embodiment.[72] Timothy Crick states that "in most video games, the player controls the game through the exclusive intermediary of another: the avatar."[73] In this section I am interested in another form of embodiment: the physical reaction to playing. As Crick argues, playing video games involves a great deal of physical response, including jumping at moments of excitement and heart palpitations.[74] Players control the game through the input device, not just the avatar. This type of embodiment is approached very differently by different scholars. What might this mean for discussions of identification and representation?

Several authors emphasize the importance of looking at the body in video game play.[75] Indeed, the body has been the focus of many social theorists' working on identity.[76] The body of the player is deeply involved in the act of playing, and games are firmly situated in embodied social life—whether one actively plays with others or not. Sjöblom looks at embodiment as part of the social, collaborative space of Internet cafes, demonstrating the importance of activity that occurs both on-screen and off.[77] The physicality and sociality of play are increasingly evident in platforms with motion-sensitive controllers, which tend to be marketed via party games (Nintendo's Wii being the most famous), as well as games with atypical or what Juul calls mimetic input devices (such as *Dance Dance Revolution*, *Rock Band*, and *Guitar Hero*).[78] Simon argues that these games appeal to nostalgia for a particular form of familial play and focus our attention on the body rather than the screen, both of which disrupt the full-immersion potential of game play.[79]

Using the example of *Dance Dance Revolution*, a game played with a dance pad on the floor as players mimic dance steps shown on-screen, Bryan Behrenshausen argues that game studies should look at games not just in terms of visual representation but also in terms of physical performance by players.[80] He writes, "Video games are not something players look at; video games are something players do."[81] Behrenshausen draws on phenomenologist Maurice Merleau-Ponty, who asserts that we should "go back to the working, actual body—not the body as a chunk of space or a bundle of functions but that body which is an intertwining of vision and movement."[82] Focusing on how the body of the player is represented in game art, Thomas Apperley argues, "Game art implicitly acknowledges the body of the gamer as a key site in the everyday experience of gameplay by exposing digital game play as a laborious process and the labour that goes into producing the game worlds."[83] Game interactivity hinges upon a body that makes the system respond and, in turn, upon a body that responds to the system. This body does not simply interact with the software and hardware that make up games but is embedded within social context, as can be seen in my gaming interview with Sasha.

I arrived late to Sasha's house for our second interview. When she welcomed me, she seemed unwell, from what I later learned was a migraine, though she insisted on going through with the interview. She sipped a Coke slowly and wore an outfit significantly more casual than the work attire she wore during my first visit. We sat on a futon covered in an orange comforter in the converted porch game room at the front of the house and discussed game options. She had decided on *Marvel vs. Capcom* on the PlayStation 3 (PS3), as it was one of her go-to games.[84] She set it up and asked if I wanted to play. I said yes . . . and lost. Then, I lost again. She offered me some tips, and I started to do marginally better. After the fourth loss, where I didn't lose quite as badly, my hands ached, and I suggested she play against the computer instead. She defeated the computer soundly for several rounds. She tended to use the same characters, Juggernaut and Ruby Heart, in some combination with various other characters, telling me later that she knew their special combos (action combinations) best. When she finally lost to the computer, she tossed the controller onto the futon in disgust. "Oh! Not . . . what did I just do!" she exclaimed as some of her earlier glumness lifted. She played several times, with different combinations of characters, before she finally beat the level. At that point she cheered, I clapped, and we high-fived her victory. Her mother, taking a distance-learning class in the next room, laughed.

Throughout the gaming interview with Sasha, embodied experience was directly implicated in all levels of play. Her ability to beat me, for example, was not simply an intellectual matter. She was more attuned to the PS3's controls and game combos than I was; her reflexes, faster; her hand and wrist muscles, more able to withstand round after round of play. Her body expressed her disappointment and her joy in a way that was extratextual to the game itself, and success in the game helped her forget the painful ache in her head. More than that, in the space that included her mother and me, the implications of her success were more directly social and, in turn, made her more self-reflexive than if she had been playing alone, as she often did. If identification operated in this space at all, it was her identifying as a *Marvel vs. Capcom* expert in a room of people who were not. She was more self-aware than she was identified with the on-screen characters.

In nearly all of the gaming interviews, participants got quite animated while playing. Evan made fun of the fact that when his brother played, his whole body "got into it," even though his body's actions did not directly mimic the on-screen actions. As I watched him play, however, Evan did this, as well. In our second gaming interview, as he navigated James Bond through the snowy Austrian landscape to get into the castle, he ever-so-slightly shifted his body using the controller to make his character dodge bullets and look around corners.[85] Christine used her body to urge her Wii bowling ball in the right direction as she watched it roll down the lane. This embodied relation to actions in space is not unique to video games. I have seen many people try the same telepathic technique in bowling alleys, leaning their bodies in the direction they wished the ball to roll. My sister and I both duck, "making the car shorter" we jokingly say, when we drive into a parking garage with a low ceiling. Several interviewees made me fear they would break the television in the room with their over-the-top punches or golf swings while playing *Wii Sports*. In many of these instances, embodied reactions to the game were sources of embarrassment. Participants apologized for getting "too into" the game. Again, this type of embodied experience in the social space made them more self-aware than connected with their avatar/character.

In a different form of bodily response, several interviewees mentioned feeling their heart pound as they played particularly intense portions of games. This is not unique to games, as many people jump during scary movies or cry during tragedies. I have met three people, separately, who have acknowledged that long sessions of playing games like *Grand Theft Auto* (in which player characters run over pedestrians with their cars) have caused their bodies to either want to run down pedestrians while driving or, conversely, want to avoid motorists (rightly, so it seems). One might interpret this type of physical engagement as an emotional or intellectual engagement with games that translates into identification. This is perhaps because, as Giddens argues, awareness of the self is intimately tied to the body.[86] Yet what game technologies also do is lessen the distance between player and text, and as I argue, distance is a fundamental requirement for identification. I must understand myself as distinct from an on-screen character in order to identify with the character—particularly, given interviewees' definitions of identification, as discussed in chapter 2. Thus, when game scholars suggest that a lessening of distance makes players more closely identified with their on-screen characters, they are significantly misreading the embodied reception process. In games that diminish distance, identification is thwarted.

A shift occurs when we think about video game audiences as active in this physical sense. Michel de Certeau argues that the withdrawal of the body from the experience of reading (specifically, the shift from reading aloud to reading in silence) alters the relationship between reader and text.[87] This distancing frees the reader from the predeterminedness of the text: "Because the body withdraws itself from the text in order henceforth to come into contact with it only through the mobility of the eye, the geographical configuration of the text organizes the activity of the reader less and less."[88] Video games may represent a shift in the opposite direction. Indeed, as Larry Grossberg argues, "The most powerful effects of video games may be determined less by ideological dimensions than by certain forms of embodiment, by the way in which the player controls/ produces the sounds and lights that engulf, produce, and define a 'rhythmic body.'"[89] A game that entails full bodily involvement like *Dance Dance Revolution* does perhaps discipline the body, in Foucault's sense, in a way that a game like *Minesweeper* does not. Players can extract themselves from this type of commandeering of their bodies, however, by disengaging their bodies from play. Though some interviewees made floors shake with their exuberance, others like Sara could play Wii games with a barely noticeable movement of the wrist. Level of embodiment, regardless, was not the same as the level of identification. Similarly, social context played a key role in whether and how participants identified with game characters.

We might think of this relationship between identification, interactivity of game texts, embodiment, and social activity surrounding games in terms of Jennifer Stromer-Galley's discussion of the dual meanings of the term *interactivity*.[90] For Stromer-Galley interactivity-as-process refers to social interaction between people, which can occur in a variety of forms. Interactivity-as-product references the technological aspects of a text that allow users to interface with a system, be that a digital game or a website. She argues that conflating the two is problematic for many reasons, especially as it "occludes an ability to see that product interacts with process; that is, it is possible that the degree or features of medium interactivity might affect outcome variables of human interaction."[91] Repeatedly, Thomas Malaby argues that we must look at games as both products and processes.[92] My gaming interview with Carol and Chuck Faygo illustrates the way both types of interactivity can intersect.[93] For the interview we played *Rock Band,* a game that came with a full set of band equipment (electronic drum set, microphone, guitar) to be used as input devices while players matched button combinations on-screen in order to play along with popular songs.[94]

On a rainy winter night, I went over to the Faygos' house, following two separate initial interviews with each of them. Zahriel, who knew the couple and whom I had interviewed a few months prior, joined us, as well, so we could have a full band. We had dinner after they settled in from a long day of work. While Chuck cleaned up in the kitchen, Carol showed me the various rock stars they had created for the game. Some were fantasy creations. Others were based on their friends or people they once knew. One was a "dream Carol," which Carol let me play for the rock session. We spent nearly twenty minutes playing dress up with "dream Carol." When we were done, she said, "It's an honor to have you play my character and trick her out so nicely."

The four of us each chose a character and began to play. We went through song after song, switching instruments so that everyone could have a turn on each. The on-screen characters remained with the initial instrument chosen, so by the end everyone had been represented on-screen by each rocker. Over the course of several hours, we played songs by Queen, No Doubt, Sleater-Kinney, the Jackson 5, the Beastie Boys, and many other bands. I found it hard to pick songs when it was my turn, both because some songs were not as fun to play on certain instruments or to sing and because there was a certain level of intimidation involved in choosing music in front of people who were self-described music geeks.

The fun was in play rather than in mastery, I think, but mastery was involved, as well. In playing the game, it was not about the individual score as much as the overall experience. We would high-five if someone achieved a "flawless" performance and laugh when someone got "most gutsy" as an achievement because of a low score. We giggled at songs with lyrics that struck us as funny, like "Fat Bottomed Girls." Zahriel and Carol could sing well enough that they could change words as they sang and still maintain the pitch required for the song to progress. They used this talent to critique the implied rape in one song's lyrics and to add "when we 69ed" to the lyrics of a famous Bryan Adams song. Play in this way transcended the game mechanic or the game as the primary object. The social setting was playful in a way that was not determined by or reliant upon the game.

Rock Band is interactive on multiple levels. First, as a product it allows players to design their own characters (within limits) and select and buy an array of music (within limits). Players can create rockers that are similar to them, totally different from them, or randomly generated. The game is narratively interactive only if players create rocker and band narratives on their own outside the game. It is inherently interactive at a ludic level, though, because players must perform the appropriate input to navigate each song successfully and because designing characters and subverting song texts can be playful. It is bodily engaging whether one is singing or playing the various instruments. Some players perform stoically; others rock out to a greater extent.

When we were done with *Rock Band,* Chuck and I played *Left 4 Dead* as Zahriel watched and Carol did some work before driving me home. Zahriel backseat-gamed while Chuck and I played the split-screen game. Again, in this game and this context, the identities of the on-screen characters were not particularly important, and neither Chuck nor I identified with the them per se, as we were too busy interacting with the group in the room to think of the characters on-screen. The game served as a point of departure for other social interaction.

Both *Left 4 Dead* and *Rock Band* can but do not have to be social activities. Moreover, playing the games with others in the game room or online are not the only ways the games can be made social. Rather, the games can be made social through how players use the game texts as the basis of social interaction. Sociality in *Rock Band* can include the display of shared stylistic tastes, musical tastes, or senses of humor. Sociality can also include discussions of the games by those not actively playing it. The *process* of interactivity benefitted from but was not defined by the *product's* interactivity, to use Stromer-Galley's formulation.[95] For this reason Malaby argues that researchers should look at games as processes, not merely as products. Games can "change through the unintended consequences of practice."[96] Some of these changes also negate the close connection between players and avatars. Even though Chuck and Carol put a lot of thought into their characters, we did not actually play *as* or identify *with* those characters while playing the game. Instruments were switched; individual players did well or poorly in the game; and the on-screen characters were watched rather than inhabited.

Types of Player Character/Avatar Relationships

Building on the ludic, narrative, contextual, and embodied components of game play, we can begin to index the variety of relationships between player and avatar/player character made available in different types of games.[97] Rather than focus on different players' approaches to the same game text or a textual analysis of different game texts, I address these relationships by analyzing how each interviewee described identification in relation to a variety of different types of games they had played. This allows me to parse empathic identification and identification as sameness, as Tronstad describes.[98] Caine demonstrated the nuances such an approach reveals:

> The more direct options you have to choose exactly what your character says, and I guess the less defined personality they have going in, then the more I can identify as that character. I guess *Baldur's Gate*, another role-playing game, is the best initial example

for me, where you create your own character. They start out as very much a blank slate, and you choose precisely what they say, and that helps a lot in identification. But in a game where it's more mixed is *The Witcher,* another role-playing game, where you choose exactly what the character says. But he's got a predefined personality, because it's a licensed work based off an author's writing, and the character you play is the hero of those stories. So he's already got a personality built up before hand. So there, it's more zoomed out, like in *Mass Effect.* And then there's some games where, specifically strategy games, where you see the entire picture writ large, and so you're ordering individual personalities around, but you're also doing the same with the grunt troops, and it feels more like you're just watching the entire thing play out.[99]

Later, he elaborated that when he said the blank-slate *Baldur's Gate* avatar helped in identification, he meant identification as sameness. Caine described identifying *as* a blank-slate character as a form of connection different from identifying *with* a character who has a fleshed out storyline. The former places more agency in the hands and minds of players; the character or avatar acts on behalf of the player. In *The Witcher,* as it is more "zoomed out," the player is acting through the character. In other games, like strategy games, the player interacts with the system rather than the characters.

We can look more closely at these different types of identification in digital games by comparing identification in games with set characters, player-chosen characters, and self-created avatars. This book does not argue that a specific type of game promotes a singular type of identification or avatar–player relationship. Nor does it claim that certain types of players always identify with media characters. My interview data do demonstrate, however, that certain types of games promote particular types of relationships between the player and their proxy. What I present here is not a taxonomy of identification in games but rather a parsing of the types of relationships made available in game texts between players and their characters/avatars.

Set Characters

As Klevjer describes, we can distinguish between games that have characters with personas and those in which the character is little more than a tool through which the player engages with the game world.[100] In games with personas, there are further distinctions to be made, as well. In some of these persona games, one might play as a specific character throughout the game, like Lara Croft from *Tomb Raider* or Kratos in *God of War*. Other persona games have players play as several characters. For example, in her gaming interview Tala played *Eternal Darkness: Sanity's Requiem,* in which the player switches between twelve different characters from different historical periods. In most of these kinds of games, as Devon put it, "Basically you're playing a character that somebody else has already created. And in that case you can really understand where he's coming from, understand the choices he's making, even though maybe it's not the choices that you'll make." Other games incorporate preset and player-created characters, like *Disgaea,* which Bryan played during his gaming interview.

Set characters can have varying degrees of depth. As Newman describes, the identity of game characters is often relevant only in cut scenes and not in the action of the game, a fact that some of my interviewees noted, as well.[101] Furthermore, Julia's claim, "He could be a bunny rabbit for all I care!" reveals the ways character identities can be largely irrelevant to players and to the game action itself. Andrew Burn's analysis of Cloud from *Final Fantasy VII* notes a similar dual nature to that character—Cloud is narratively developed, but his personality is ludologically irrelevant.[102] In yet another example, Espen Aarseth states of Lara Croft in *Tomb Raider,* "When I play, I don't even see her body, but see through it and past it."[103] Frans Mäyrä similarly states that Lara "is, in a way, a beautifully animated cursor for the player to use while solving puzzles and exploring the game world."[104] Due to this shallowness, set characters were often described by my interviewees as puppets, chess pieces, or dolls, not characters with which they could identify. This reveals some interesting differences between games and other media forms. Although films, novels, and television shows often have stock characters without psychological depth or backstories, as Devon put it, "In movies there's never that type of situation where you have someone that is so a blank slate that you could write yourself into it." Stock characters are not blank slates, even if they are undeveloped, whereas set characters in games often are.

Matthew Barton argues that this shallowness makes it easier for players to place themselves into the character's shoes.[105] In making this claim, he draws on comic artist Scott McCloud's assertion that it is easier for comics' readers to put themselves in the place of iconic characters.[106] Ian Bogost states, in fact, that Will Wright, creator of *The Sims,* used McCloud's principles of comic design as the basis for his famous franchise.[107] Specifically, Wright drew on the idea that, as McCloud puts it, "The cartoon is a vacuum into which our identity and awareness are pulled. . . . We don't just observe the cartoon, we *become* it!"[108] Following this logic, digital games without well-developed characters would encourage players to put themselves in the place of the characters more readily than games with detailed and clearly developed characters. McCloud's claim is not based on any empirical evidence, however, for which he has been criticized by some scholars.[109] In the case of my interviewees, this lack of detail actually caused them to be more self-aware than engaged in character identification. They were themselves, not the character, particularly in games that relied on caricatures. As Carol described, it is difficult to connect with or see oneself in caricatures:

When I play zombie shoot-'em-ups, there's already preset characters . . . just the like [unclear] Asian guy, the feisty, loudmouth black cop, and then like, you know, a stripper type that's avenging her brother's death and she's got, you know—she's a badass and she's cool, but she's also got like enormous boobs [*laughs*]. On the one hand, they named her Varla, which is the name of the super badass in *Faster, Pussy Cat! Kill! Kill!,* so that's cool. But not so easy to relate to.

It is important to recognize that McCloud bases his theory primarily on visual information (e.g., sketches versus detailed drawings), and when extrapolated to narrative character development, the theory falls short. Games that leave characters too empty lose out on the chance that players will identify with the characters. This is particularly the case in games that rely on caricatures of minorities, as Carol describes.

A lack of depth does not necessarily mean that players cannot get into the heads of the on-screen characters, of course. Rather, it just requires more work for them. Even when there was no real character development or identifiable character to speak of, interviewees said they could create a sense of their character's personality and what they might be thinking. Gregory was able to explain the mind-set of the spaceship icon's pilot in *Space Invaders* although the game had no human characters to speak of: "Everything rests on him, and he has to save the world from the aliens."[110] Despite the fact that the game depicted only inanimate objects (spaceships that shoot, etc.), Gregory conjured a human pilot. This imagining did not necessarily entail creating a full backstory, but as Devon said, "Since they don't give you much, you can really write whatever you want into the character." Character depth, when it exists, is usually narrated within a game, but if it is not, some players can make the leap to creating their own backstories.

Intertextual or paratextual associations related to the game, like ads, books, films, comics, websites, fan fiction, etc., can also help develop depth.[111] In our current convergence media culture, characters appear across texts and provide added layers to players' reception practices.[112] Sasha said she could get a sense of the players in her sports video games because she knew about the atheletes in real life. Similarly, Evan felt he had a good sense of James Bond in *007: Nightfire* because the character was more fully developed in other texts. Cody could identify with the wrestlers in his game because he watched wrestling when he was younger. Zahriel did not pay much attention to *Halo's* narrative when she originally played the game but later found texts that broadened her understanding of the game: "It wasn't until later on. I really wasn't playing much anymore, but I was bored and had the resources here, the books and stuff, that I really started getting, like understanding the philosophy and the whole myth, the whole storyline." Returning to Lara Croft, in many ways the *Tomb Raider* paratexts, including its marketing and the films, have overdetermined player interactions with the game, according to some authors.[113] These paratexts build up the character's narrative, which interviewees defined as crucial to the identification process, particularly in games with set characters.

Choosing or Customizing Characters

Choosing characters is an interesting middle ground between set characters and customized avatars. In some games the chosen characters have narratives or backstories that make them like set characters, and choosing them may or may not impact game-play options (e.g., the powers available, storylines, etc). In other games character options offer different game-play experiences or possibilities, but the characters themselves do not have developed personas. In other games, as Newman describes, character choice often has more to do with in-game advantages.[114] Finally, in some games choice of character has no significant impact on the game, is largely aesthetic, and is inconsequential to game success. Although choosing characters can be done for strategic reasons, if it makes no difference, a player might default to characters with which they connect the most or that represent some aspect of their personality.

Strategic choices have been used to make sense of players choosing characters/avatars of a gender different from theirs. When men choose female avatars, as Esther MacCallum-Stewart states, "They often chose these for ludic, rather than gendered reasons. . . . Thus, man playing woman has become a normal practice, and not one that is seen as either aberrant or subversive."[115] Marsha Kinder points out that choosing a certain character, like when a male-identified player selects Princess Peach from *Super Mario Bros.*, can sometimes have more to do with the ability advantages, which may in turn downplay "the risk of transgender identification."[116] Newman points out, as does Henry Jenkins, that researchers need to reconsider if and how players actually identify with these characters.[117]

Christine was not usually invested in game characters, except when she played *The Sims*: "I do feel more invested in them because I control their lives, basically. I don't feel emotionally connected with them, but I care more about what they are going through in the game."[118] It was not an individual character Christine invested in but rather the game itself. This was true for other interviewees, as well, even when they did not re-create themselves or even make realistic, humanoid avatars. Connie played a racing game during her second interview and said that she typically felt more ownership over cars she could customize and "own" in the game world. In the gaming interview she chose a car that was the same make and model as a car she used to own because, she said, it made her feel more connected to the game. As these examples show, interviewees did not necessarily create characters who were "like them," but some did feel invested in what they had created. This was most often the case when interviewees created narratives for their character in excess of the game text. When making a character, as Tracey stated, "You start figuring out what the person's character or personality's going to be like, you know because you're creating them." Extratextual work like this helps to blur the line between empathic identification and identification as sameness. Caine reported, for example, "When you have a blank character that you're creating, you start telling their own stories, whereas in other cases . . . it's someone else's story that you're helping along."

Sometimes, interviewees' choices reflected a balance of both self-representation and what made sense for a specific text. When Caine played *Mass Effect* for his gaming interview, he showed me the version of the game's protagonist, Commander Shepard, he had created. It looked somewhat like Caine, though tailored for the game space: "I went with the same sort of skin tone and beard, but there wasn't really a glasses option, and since this guy is a ground forces marine, that made sense. And then I gave him a scar just because it looked cool." I also noticed that his Commander Shepard was heavily built, in comparison to Caine, who was tall and skinny. He said the decision to make the avatar look similar to him was a random one. In many of the other games he played, he created avatars that looked very different. Indeed, several interviewees said that sometimes they made their avatars look as much like them as a game allowed simply because it was easier than creating something totally from scratch. When given an open buffet of representational options, sometimes it is simply easier to stick to the face you see every day in the mirror. Caine moved back and forth in *Mass Effect* between identifying the avatar as him and seeing the avatar as separate from himself:

> In this case, it's sort of a mix. Because as you might have noticed, the way the dialogue options are structured you choose a general phrase, and the character will say something more specific. Of course, sometimes you choose a general phrase intending one thing, and the writers thought you meant something completely different. And so Shepard says a line, and it's like, "No, no Shepard! What are you doing? I didn't mean that! Don't be a jerk Shepard, stop it!" So it's sort of a fluctuating middle ground between the two.

This is similar to the projective[119] or hybrid identity[120] that game scholars describe. Caine played this avatar as a specific type of character but also put a bit of himself into the avatar. In many ways it is

this interplay that makes some games exemplars for how identification works, if we think of identification as a process of connecting
with sameness and recognizing difference. It is crucial to note, however, that this is not what game studies literature often calls the blur-
ring of difference between player and character/avatar, but rather,
it is the continual reminder of that difference.

Avatar Creation

In terms of identification for my interviewees, choosing characters
was only slightly different from playing set characters in that narratives helped engender feelings of sameness while maintaining a
sense of the character as other. Designing one's own character was,
however, another matter. My interviewees described being much
more attached to avatars they created themselves than to preset
characters. Indeed, as Waggoner demonstrates, players put something of themselves into choices they make in games.[121] Investment
in the character was not, however, always synonymous with identification. In fact, sometimes identification named the relation between
an interviewee and the *game* (not a character/avatar) or between an
interviewee and the type of objects or beings in a given game.

As with choosing characters, if it influenced success in the game,
interviewees based their avatar design on strategic choices. Beyond
those tactical choices, aesthetic judgments shaped the way they created or dressed their avatars or characters, as MacCallum-Stewart
finds in her study.[122] It is important to note that context shaped those
aesthetic decisions in online, social games. In one interview Malcolm told me that he used to play *EverQuest* with a man who had
a female character for which he "had a set of equipment he would
wear on his female character when she was in town and a different set when he was off adventuring, just based on the aesthetics."
Lisbeth Klastrup and Susana Tosca observe that at least in online,
social games, the "way our character looks is important to us, even
in cases where appearance plays no role whatsoever in the reward
system of the game."[123] They use ethnographic methods, surveys,
and interviews to analyze the role of fashion in *World of Warcraft*.
They find that aesthetic choices play the dual role of differentiating
avatars from everyone else and displaying status and group belonging within a normative social hierarchy. When engaging in battle,

players choose the gear best suited for fighting, but not all game interactions require this strategic equipment.

Rather than viewing such choices as mere idiosyncrasies or actions that reveal some inner truth of individual self, I want to emphasize how social contexts, as well as game systems, shape these choices. As Murphy describes, "Within the 'closed' virtual worlds of most video games, occupying an avatar is a different experience from going online and representing one's identity as a different race or gender."[124] For my interviewees the relative importance of avatars differed with respect to whether they played with others or alone, online or offline. In the offline game *Diablo II,* which Malcolm played during the gaming interview, each class of character came in only one gender: "If you choose one class, you're playing a male character; if you choose another class, you're playing a female character."[125] He played as both a male and a female character during the gaming interview.[126] When he played the online avatar-based game *World of Warcraft,* he would not play as a female avatar:

> Picking a female avatar just has way too many random issues associated with it. . . . There's always fourteen-year-old boys playing out there, and they see the avatar as female, and even if they know psychologically that 90 percent of the people that play these games are male, they are still going to, you know, hope that that's a female and try to interact with you in that way.[127]

Here, Malcolm's choices were not solely shaped by his own desire to create an avatar with which he could best identify but rather by the structural misogyny of the online game space in which female avatars were often sexually harassed. Playing in an online environment with other people (versus playing in an offline environment by oneself) changes the types and implications of player choices. In online spaces people represent themselves to an audience that will make assumptions about them based on their aesthetic and ludic choices. The interpretation of those choices is shaped by the way those games spaces are designed. If everyone in *World of Warcraft* had to play as an androgynous or female character or if there was not a distinct difference between the appearances of different genders, the implications of playing as a female toon (the term for the player's avatar in *World of Warcraft*) would be altered.

Sometimes, there is a sexual component to playing the "other," according to MacCallum-Stewart. She claims that when some players choose differently gendered avatars, it is because those "avatars [are] deliberately and consciously objectified by players . . . in order to negate claims of deviance or atypical responses about their adoption of differently gendered avatars."[128] According to this logic, male players that choose female avatars do so not out of gender identification with those avatars but rather out of sexual desire for them. As her participants were heterosexual, it makes sense that this would be her reading of their choices. What about when queer players choose avatars of another gender, however? Significantly, not all players who share a sexual orientation and/or gender identity make the same character/avatar choices, and we should not assume that they would. For example, Ephram, who identified as male and gay, said he always played as female characters, whereas his male partner, Devon, who identified as gay, said that he did not like playing female characters:

EPHRAM: I don't know. I like the idea of a female character kicking ass kind of thing. I think it's mainly like the *Xena* effect [*both laugh*]. Like, I'd watch *Hercules* and be like, eh? But I watch *Xena*, and it's the same thing.

DEVON: Just as bad, but it's so much better.

EPHRAM: So I guess that's the only way I can think of it.

For Ephram this was perhaps an aesthetic choice rather than a sexualized one. In MacCallum-Stewart's study players argue that they "choose women avatars because they like to look at them."[129] Similarly, Devon sometimes created or chose male characters based on attractiveness: "I'm going to be playing this character forever, you know, if I'm going to be staring at their face or their butt or whatever, I want it to be sexy [*chuckles*]." Ephram said that Devon always played as the character Lewis in *Left 4 Dead* because he was "the only attractive guy." When creating or choosing characters/avatars on the basis of aesthetic or sexualized reasons, players are not so much creating avatars that represent their own gender identities as creating objects of desire. Tracing the nuanced differences between gender identity and sexual desire here is vital, as one does not necessarily lead to or even inform the other, as Devon's and Ephram's examples make clear. Studies that collapse the two do a disservice to the complex ways audiences engage with video game texts and the complex ways we all build our sexual and gender identities throughout our lives. This is another form of interactivity with game texts, one that is perhaps simultaneously ludic, embodied, and social and that does not result in identifying with or even as the created character/avatar. In these examples the players' constructed characters were created for objectification purposes, not for functional or identificatory purposes.

It is important to separate online, social and offline, solo play as two distinct contexts in which cross-identity character/avatar choices take place. In turn, the implications of cross-gender role-play are contextually specific. Lisa Nakamura defines "identity tourism" as a type of playing as "other" that draws heavily on stereotyped notions of gender and race.[130] This happens largely in online spaces, where the goal of stereotyped performances of racial and gendered identities is to pass for a member of that group. This is, I would argue, distinct from what David Leonard describes as "high-tech blackface," which he explains is the way games tap into the pleasure of playing as "other," particularly in offline games like *NBA Street* and *NFL Street*.[131] The two contexts foster very different types of identification. Particularly when offline gaming, my interviewees did not automatically take on the role of avatars or characters. In turn, playing as a character who was ostensibly "other" to them (in terms of gender, race, or sexuality) was not necessarily or always oppressive, transgressive, or even perspective altering, especially in offline gaming. The relationship between player and character/avatar is complex, contextual, and malleable.

Some interviewees' feelings toward creating characters who looked like them varied regardless of context. Some people made avatars completely unlike them, based them on other people they knew, or modeled them on celebrities, regardless of the game they played. Amy said she created characters who looked how she wanted to look or who looked nothing like her, rather than creating characters who looked as she thought she did. On their Wii both Tanner and Rusty had created Miis. Tanner's looked mostly like her, and she even mentioned needing to edit it, as she had recently changed her hairstyle. Rusty had created a short, dark-skinned character with a named modified by the adjective *lil'*.[132] As a white male who was "six-one, two hundred pounds," he said, "lil' [screen name] sounds better." He enjoyed the incongruity between the Mii's appearance and his own, as well as the discrepancy between the moniker *lil'* and his actual physical size. Rusty later explained that he rarely created characters who looked like him, because he used games for escapism. When I ran into him a few months later, however, he told me he had recently started playing *Star Trek Online* and created an avatar that was more similar to him, just to see what it would be like.

Context can also shape how others read one's avatar. Some interviewees created representations of themselves that were not viewed as accurate by others who knew them in "real life." Renee described this in reference to her Mii:

> My sister came over, and she was like, "Oh, who's that," and I'm like, "That's me!" And she was like, "When was the last time you wore those glasses?" I'm like, "I have them. I wear them like daily. I just usually wear them later." And she's like, "Yeah, but why would you make your thing with the glasses?" I'm like, "'Cause I'm someone who wears glasses. Shut up" [*laughs*]. "When was the last time you wore your hair in pigtails?" "Would you shut up?!" [*laughs*]. So it looks like the me I think of.

Renee was "someone who wore glasses," and so the Mii she wanted to represent her wore glasses, as well. Her sister did not think of Renee in that way and thus noted a discrepancy between daily-contacts-wearing Renee and her on-screen proxy. In online gaming, where one does not know or meet or see other players' real-life bodies, such accusations are unlikely to occur. Of course, online players do often meet up in person or know each other offline, but even in those instances one might suspect—though more research is required to demonstrate this—that incongruity is seen as part of the experience, given the long history of people playing as other selves online, as Sherry Turkle famously describes.[133] In games played primarily offline, where if you do play with others they might be more likely to compare the you on the screen with the you on the couch, these discrepancies take on new meaning, particularly if the avatar is supposed to be a mimetic representation.

As discussed, the distance between player and avatar complicates how we think about identification. For my interviewees, creating self-representative avatars generally resulted in identifying *as* that avatar. Avatars not meant to be self-representative did not result in a type of identification that was the same as identification *with* a set character, except to the extent that players were able to role-play as the non-self-representative avatar. In *Mass Effect,* for example, players select one of three preset backstories for their Commander Shepard. Caine tried to play his character in a manner that reflected that narrative. Role-play, as Tronstad argues, lends itself to identification in a way that other avatar play does not.[134] When interviewees created narratives for these non-self-representative avatars, they saw them as distinct from themselves but with a level of player authorship higher than that experienced in games with set or chosen characters.

For my interviewees narrative was central to their identification with avatars, just as it was for set characters, but the context of play greatly shaped their avatar design choices. Context moreover shaped how others interpreted those creations. Given the significance of context and the varied reasons interviewees gave for their avatar creation choices, researchers must be careful to not leap too quickly to the assumption that how players create avatars necessarily reflects how they view themselves.

Conclusion

As discussed in chapter 1, focusing on texts when studying identification in many media has its drawbacks, but video games compound these issues. Many scholars' accounts of identification in video games do not necessarily articulate what is meant by *identification.* These accounts also fail to engage with the question of whether and why the process of identification in video games is different from those in other media. As my analysis shows, the act of playing obscures and often supersedes the process of identification with characters in some games. Identification *as* and identification *with* characters are blurred by the interactive aspects of games. For my interviewees much of their game play involved too much self-reflexivity for them to feel the distanced connection required for identification. Researchers must also consider that different types of relationships between players and characters/avatars are available in different types of game texts.

Despite shelves of books and articles suggesting that game studies needs its own understanding of identification separate from those in other media studies and while games as texts are experienced as qualitatively different from other media, identification as a process is not as medium specific as we might suspect. Interviewees' understandings of identification, their experience of the process, was too embedded within other media-reception practices for new definitions to be useful. As demonstrated in this chapter, these players' understandings of identification were similar to descriptions of identification in nonergodic media. At the same time, game scholars need to deal with the fact that interactivity and involvement with the game as a system are distinct from identification with characters as narrativized subjects in their own right. In some cases, I suspect, it may turn out that researchers are not interested in identification at all. Identification as presently used by some scholars may be standing in for other types of game engagement, something that a clearer articulation of identification, recognizing it as an experience that exists across media reception, would help elucidate. There is one area of game studies, however, in which understanding the nuances of identification with game characters is of crucial importance: arguments for diversity in representation.

One argument for the representation of marginalized groups in digital games is that representation is important so that members of those groups can play games without feeling excluded.[135] Another argument focuses on the fact that marginalized groups should be represented *well* so that those who are members of dominant identity groups can see accurate representations of those marginalized groups rather than oppressive stereotypes.[136] In either case, an assumption exists that inhabiting a specific identity category will determine how people approach texts (i.e., identification), as well as an assumption that players see, care about, and always engage with representational aspects of games.

If players do not think that much about the character on the screen, then can we still talk about the way representation is important in games? Aarseth argues in relation to *Tomb Raider*'s Lara Croft that "a different looking body would not make me play differently."[137] Although it may be true that the game play itself would not change radically for Aarseth, he sidesteps the question of whether his views about women more broadly would be changed by seeing a different body type. I argue that the relative unimportance of character/ avatar identity to player experiences is a strong argument for diversity in game texts. I assert, much like Stuart Moultrop, that even if it is true that players do not care about what their on-screen proxy looks like, these texts exist within a system of cultural norms where, for example, sexualized images of female characters are common.[138] In other words, it is not game play that stands to benefit from, or even be dramatically transformed by, more diverse representations but rather culture more broadly.

We need to be critical of the fact that games with the greatest potential diversity in representation (i.e., games that entail creating or choosing one's own character/avatar) are also the games in which players do not tend to identify *with* the character/avatar on-screen, even though they might have strong investments in them. These types of characters/avatars do not often have narratives with which players can identify. Players identify with narratives above and beyond the physical characteristics of characters or avatars. As Waggoner demonstrates, these games do not appeal to all players, and game literacy plays a strong role in whether players can even engage with a game well enough to identify with their avatar/character.[139]

Alexander Galloway argues that "the more emancipating games seem to be as a medium, substituting activity for passivity or a branching of narrative for a linear one, the more they are in fact hiding the fundamental social transformation into informatics that has affected the globe during recent decades."[140] A similar turn takes place when the issue of diversity in representation is pushed increasingly onto the player. Beyond simply creating the "menu-driven identities" that Nakamura describes, there is a logic at work that makes the "problem" of representation an issue only for those players willing to design their own avatars.[141] Even more broadly, the push toward insisting on representation via demonstrating a group's viability as a market requires marginalized groups to articulate their representability to the industry.[142] As Nakamura asks, however, "Who can—or wants to—claim a perfectly pure, legible identity that can be fully expressed by a decision tree designed by a corporation?"[143] The goal in increasing representation in games is not expanding customization options but rather making more games that reflect more modes of being in the world.

Rather than look to games with self-created avatars as primary sites for increasing diversity (through, for example, increasing the number of hairstyle and clothing options available), I suggest that designers focus on games with set protagonists. Currently, these are the ones with less diversity and thus are rich sites for interrogation and intervention.[144] If my interviewees are right and what the on-screen proxy looks like does not matter to players, if it could really be a bunny rabbit and not matter (and I can imagine many a game in which that would be possible), then what logic remains for the majority of characters being normative along the axes of race, gender, sexuality, age, etc.? In other words, if the body on-screen could be gay, pansexual, genderqueer, Chicana, old, young, or disabled and players wouldn't care, let's make it so. If they do care, then we might actually be able to have a more nuanced discussion of why representation matters in games.

Certainly, the on-screen body may have mattered to interviewees more than they were willing to admit. Perhaps, interviewees just did not want to acknowledge that they liked seeing only normative identities or that they wanted more people like them on-screen and reported being fine with having a bunny rabbit represent them merely as an alibi. Game studies scholars have also questioned the importance of representation in these texts, however, suggesting it is not merely a research anomaly. As most interviewees were marginalized in some way, they may be more skilled at putting up with mis- and underrepresentation than those in the majority would be. If they learned to enjoy games that did not represent them, it is likely heterosexual, white, cisgendered men could too. Moreover, I want to take my interviewees at their word. They consume and play games, like games, and are important participants in gaming culture. Their takes on in-game representation are valid and deserve to be treated as such by researchers. Given their insistence that a wider diversity of characters would not interrupt their ability to play and enjoy the game, including those whose identities were more normative, I think that those who want to argue for the importance of representation can actually deploy the relative irrelevancy of player character/avatar representation more forcefully. If players do not care about what represents them on-screen, then part of the trouble of Lara Croft's visual design in *Tomb Raider* and the violent masculinity of Kratos in *God of War* is that they are so normative.

Games could and should play (pun intended) more with which identities are portrayed and what stories are told. It is, in sum, actually empowering that players do not always identify with characters in games, because that is the very reason there should be more diversity in this medium. When and how this representation comes to matter in video games is explored in the next chapter.

4

When and Why Representation Matters to Players

Realism versus Escapism

I began this book with the assertion that researchers must take a step back and interrogate whether and how representation is important. As discussed in chapter 1, the media representation of particular identities has often been addressed as either "good" or "bad" or as nonexistent. Researchers and theorists usually describe it as unquestionably important and argue that positive representation can lead to social benefits. We can think of representation as recognition in the sociopolitical sense, as does Charles Taylor.[1] He states that the politics of recognition rests on the following thesis:

> Our identity is partly shaped by recognition or its absence, often by the *mis*recognition of others, and so a person or group of people can suffer real damage, real distortion, if the people or society around them mirror back to them a confining or demeaning or contemptible picture of themselves.[2]

He goes on to say that the recognition of individuals can take into account particularities but that at the more social level, ironically, we are asked to recognize people in a difference-blind fashion.[3] The politics of recognition assert, he argues, that we must, paradoxically, see people as individuals but groups as not inherently disparate. This is the particular challenge faced by those who study the politics of representation. We face the dual task of seeing our research participants as nuanced individuals and making arguments for the recognition of entire groups in ways that value, without essentializing, the differences between groups.

Being represented in media demonstrates a public, often corporate or state, acknowledgment that differences exist, that "we" exist. Demands for representation are similarly tied to social-justice activist groups' aims to stand up and be counted. However, as Nancy Fraser famously critiques, "By equating the politics of recognition with identity politics, it encourages both the reification of group identities and the displacement of redistribution."[4] Representation in popular media does not correct the lived experiences of oppression, nor does it necessarily reorganize the structures of power that have maintained inequality.

Recognition is not the same as the redistribution of resources, and this difference requires that we critically address when and how marginalized groups are included in game texts. Take, for example, the time-management game *Diner Dash*.[5] In this game and its many sequels, players take the role of Flo, a white woman who has left the financial world to pursue her dream of running a restaurant. In each level players must learn to navigate the wants of various types of diners as Flo acts as hostess, takes orders, serves food, buses tables, and collects money (another character cooks the food). Diners must be kept happy, or they leave without paying. With each level there is the chance to earn new items to speed service and help Flo manage an ever-increasing stream of diners with special wants.

It is significant that nearly all of the customers, staff, and Flo herself are represented as white. There is only one man of color in the series, an Asian man who runs the sushi restaurant that Flo assists in revitalizing. Additionally, there are only two women of color represented in the entire game series: Barb, a businesswoman (a big tipper with a short temper), and Margarita, the other female culinary entrepreneur (who needs Flo's help when her landlord raises the rent on her restaurant).

As a businesswoman, Barb is one of the most socially elite characters in the game. The only other characters with an equal class position are celebrities, so there is a self-made woman quality to her. Both she and Margarita are displayed as women of color who are professionally successful. Given a long history of women of color being portrayed as servants and the lack of racial diversity in the game overall, these two characters are counterstereotypical with regard to class. As other stereotypes are deployed in their characterizations, however, they do not automatically call into question all larger racial disparities in society. Barb is represented as an angry black woman caricature—hotheaded, short-tempered, and likely to cause a ruckus (Figure 18).[6] Similarly, Margarita may own her own

Figure 18. Screenshot of introduction of Business Woman character, one of only a few people of color in the game series *Diner Dash* (taken from *Diner Dash 5*). When the customer type is introduced, the game warns, "Business Women are great tippers, but do NOT make them wait!"

restaurant but requires help from Flo to keep it going, playing on the common white-women-saving-brown-women trope critiqued by Gayatri Spivak.[7]

Although counterstereotypical representation is not the secret weapon to eliminating social inequality, recognition and, in turn, representation remain important, nevertheless. As Angharad Valdivia describes, lack of recognition is indicative of and helps to perpetuate social disparities.[8] It is also important to recognize that class differences are often overlooked in work that focuses on the representation of marginalized groups. As Lisa Henderson argues in *Love and Money,* treating recognition and redistribution as mutually exclusive goals ignores that class is also an identity and a site of community identification.[9] I argue that much of the work on video game representation exacerbates these inequalities, even if individual critics seek to challenge them. One key way this happens in the game industry and even in some game studies texts is by reducing identity to market logics. The pluralism that stems from market logic–based representation, which is focused on specific identifiers, in many ways creates separate-but-equal visibility. This is fundamentally distinct from the transformative goals of media diversity. True recognition of diversity, understanding what that means, could impact redistribution in fundamental ways.

One of the problems with conventional approaches to media representation is the focus on producers, texts, and audiences defined by specific identifiers. Much of the work on sexuality, race, and gender in video games tends to focus on specific groups, specific texts, and specific kinds of gaming. Game scholars Jennifer Jenson and Suzanne de Castell outline the way that much of the existing research on gender and games "encourages the further persistent conceptual misunderstanding, that somehow all girls/women and all boys/men will have similar approaches under similar conditions."[10] In chapter 1, I discuss the ways that marking specific audiences in this manner pushes already marginalized populations to the further peripheries of gaming. Additionally, as shown in chapters 2 and 3, people connect with media in much more complex ways than this approach allows.

This chapter addresses the issue of representation via audiences rather than texts. I do this to emphasize that the importance of representation (and, relatedly, identity) does not live in texts alone. As Néstor García Canclini argues, "Identity is a construct, but the artistic, folkloric, and media narratives that shape it are realized and transformed within socio-historical conditions that cannot be reduced to their *mise-en-scene*. Identity is theater *and* politics, performance *and* action."[11] Representation is part of a process of meaning making, but textual analyses tend to focus on the finished product. Here, I discuss why representation is and is not important to individual interviewees in order to reframe how researchers address this issue. Rather than focus on how identities affect media choices or how representation affects one group's knowledge of another, I use interviews to unpack *how* representation comes to matter to my participants in different media. In addition, in response to the common refrain that these are "just games" (and thus too frivolous to warrant serious academic analysis), I assert that game scholars, as well as media critics more generally, must grapple with the paradox of arguing for the seriousness of representation in games in a way that is not dismissive of play.

This book pushes back against a text-centered critique of representation for another reason: time. Studies that focus on fans of specific games, analyses of a circumscribed set of texts, or the current makeup of an industry cannot account for the ebbs and flows of media usage and the combined effect of transplatform and transtemporal consumption practices. My interviewees that identified as gamers continually demonstrated that gamer identity was mutable, shifted over time, and wove together complex relationships between media representation, consumption, and identification. Tanner and her husband Rusty had both played video games for about thirty years each. Rusty identified as a "full-on gamer," whereas Tanner said that she identified as a gamer at one time but currently went back and forth about identifying:

> I guess there were times when I would say yes and times when I would say not really. I guess overall, yeah, as someone who is maybe drawn to games more than the average person. . . . But not like a full-on gamer-gamer kind of person where it's a major part of what I do with my recreational time.

In another interview she concluded that she was "a gamer at heart," but that did not lead her to declare herself a gamer. The times she identified as a gamer were tied to gaming taking up large amounts of her recreation time, making gamer a relative rather than a descriptive category. Research studies that sought out gamers and made claims about those who played video games based on the results would miss Tanner entirely. Clearly, self-identified gamers are not the only ones who play video games or, even, play them a lot. Furthermore, the fact that gamer is an identity people take on and off at various times during their lives means that it may not be as stable as many studies presume.

Relatedly, the ebb and flow of media consumption is rarely acknowledged in media consumption and representation scholarship. It was, though, a common experience of gaming for my interviewees. As Evan said:

> Towards the end of high school, [playing video games] sort of dropped off. . . . And then, I don't think I picked it back up until, jeez, maybe, maybe five or six years ago. . . . I really don't play that

often. . . . Like, I'll pick it up, and I'll play every evening after work or school for two, three, four weeks, and then I'll put it down again for months.

In these binges Evan plays only one of two games: *Call of Duty 2: Big Red One* and *James Bond 007: Nightfire.*[12] Other interviewees similarly discussed replaying their favorite games, rewatching their favorite movies, and rereading their favorite books, over and over again. When scholars talk about representation, we often focus on what is currently permeating our many screens. Studies of representation, given their very text- and industry-centric approaches, do not take into account that as audiences we do not live in magical time bubbles into which only the media from the past few years can enter. Kat was born in 1988 but professed a love of early 1980s movies. I myself grew up watching *I Love Lucy* and *Bewitched* on television as much as I did *Seinfeld* and *Friends,* despite being born long after the first two had gone off the air. A focus on texts from the contemporary moment obscures many of these issues, which is why this book argues for recentering our understanding of the politics of representation on the *audience.* Media give us the tools to imagine what might be possible, regardless of when they were produced or what medium delivered them. Only by starting with audiences can researchers inform the macropolitics of our arguments for representation with the micropolitics of meaning making.

To Whom It Matters

To whom is representation important? Arguments focused on the influence of media portrayals tend to emphasize the educational and political importance of media representation. As discussed in chapter 1, the assumption that representation is important to and desired by marginalized audiences is also a prominent theme in this literature—this is part of the market-logic argument for media representation. Both cases assume that those who are marginalized care about the representation of those identifiers that contribute to their marginalization (e.g., LGBTQ people wishing to see LGBTQ characters and storylines foregrounding sexual and gender identity). Conversely, the market-logic argument seems to presume that dominant audiences do not wish to see people unlike them in their media (e.g., white audiences having no desire to see characters of color or storylines foregrounding race). Contrasting two pairs of interviewees offers another perspective from which to view this issue.

Rusty identified as a heterosexual, white male in his late thirties who grew up in the suburbs of Chicago. He lived with his partner, Tanner, in a predominantly white, suburban, professional Philadelphia neighborhood.[13] On my first visit to their house in early fall, he made dinner, which we ate on their deck while discussing his annoyance at cutbacks on leaf pickup in their neighborhood. Gregory identified as a black, gay man in his early thirties and was born and raised in a Philadelphia working-class family.[14] Gregory lived with his mother and younger sister, whom he helped care for, in a predominantly African American neighborhood in North Philadelphia. During our interview Gregory mentioned that his neighborhood had been "hot" lately, as a number of police officers had been shot over the previous months. He told me that he played video games in part because spending time outside ran the risk of police harassment.[15] Indeed, I noted on my second visit to his house that a city no-loitering sign was hung, unironically, near the bus stop on his block.

Based on these racial, sexual, class, familial, and neighborhood differences, it would seem easy to contrast Rusty's comments to Gregory's. Rusty asserted that he did not think much about whether he identified with characters or about representation: "I just kind of know who I am, and that's the only thinking I do about that." In part, he tied this to the fact that he saw himself as boring and viewed games as a way to escape, rather than find, himself: "I'm white; I'm boring [*laughs*]. I want to be that Orc that could rip a car in half with my hands or, you know, blasting cities from orbit." Inhabiting often unmarked racial and gender categories (normative, white masculinity), Rusty could afford to be blasé about representation, particularly in a world where people like him were overrepresented in popular media. In contrast, representation was important to Gregory. He stated very specifically, "[Seeing people like me in media] shows that I'm being heard and seen and I'm being acknowledged and I'm here." Though it is rhetorically useful to contrast Rusty and Gregory based on their social demographics, to rely only on those factors to explain their differing opinions is overly simplistic. These two men are different in terms of their racial, sexual, familial, and class identifications. Their geographic locations, both former and current, separate them even more. More factors than these can explain their differing takes on the importance of representation, however, as demonstrated in a counterexample.

Kat identified as a white woman in her early twenties, did not disclose her sexuality, and was raised in what she called the "WASPy suburbs of Atlanta." I contrast her answers to Julia's, who identified as an African American, gay woman in her late thirties who grew up in Northwest Philadelphia. Julia did not feel strongly about representation. She argued that this was because she did not identify with the signifiers that typically signaled "blackness." Her partner, Elise,[16] who took part in the first interview, made a similar comment about queer identity and representation:

> JULIA: It's not important to me. I would think it's important to most other people because of what most other people do. You know, they tend to do what people like them do. So, I mean, OK [Julia and Elise both laugh], for instance, for me personally, I don't listen to R&B. I don't listen to rap. I don't watch BET. I don't have the weave. I'm not saying this to offend [both laugh].
>
> ELISE: Not to generalize! [laughs].
>
> JULIA: All I'm saying is that, not to generalize, if that's what you're into, but I don't. I'm not like that, so I don't look for that . . . because it's not what I'm into. I don't identify with those people, even though they are black. We have nothing in common whatsoever. So I don't, for me, [representation is] not important at all. . . .
>
> ELISE: Being gay is this much of my life [holds up thumb and forefinger slightly parted]. You know what I mean? . . . I mean, we tend to hang out with gay people, just I think by virtue of being into the same stuff, but I don't think I would specifically watch a show, like we never watched Queer Eye or The L Word or anything. It was sort of like we would, but it wasn't like, "Oh my god, there's a queer person!" You know what I mean?

For both women representation was not important, largely because they rarely felt their versions of those identifiers were represented. Julia also believed that the lack of representation in video games was not an issue, because they were "just games." At the same time, demonstrating the tension between realism and fantasy in discourse about representation, being represented was largely unimportant to Julia and Elise in part because representation of people like them was never "realistic" to their experiences. For Kat, however, representation was very important, even in video games. When she discussed the importance of seeing people like her in media, she felt not only as though that was important but that diversity in media in general was important, and this tempered her need to see people specifically "like her":

> It's important to me. I can think of, I don't know, beauty advertisements for me. I always get upset when it's like these picture-perfect people who I can't identify with at all because I'm never going to have like a twiggy body, or perfect lips, or a perfect complexion, or any of that. And it's frustrating to me that our advertisers try to paint this alternate reality that's just never possible. And they try to encourage people to, or they psychologically encourage people to, think that that is reality. And in movies I'm definitely more prone to go see a movie if I see someone who looks like me and who has encountered situations like me, rather than someone else. But at the same time, I definitely value diversity. I mean as a white, American girl, I wouldn't be offended if they put more diversity in there. Because I think that's beneficial. I don't think that our media needs more white, American girls, you know?

Like Gregory's, Kat's comments reflected the long history of media criticism and the politics of representation literature. Representation was, furthermore, important to them not only in terms of racial, gendered, and sexual identities. Like Kat, many interviewees stressed the lack of diversity of body types and physical appearances in media much more than they did the usual identifiers of race, gender, and sexuality. She valued diversity and actually wanted to see more people who were *not* like her in media because as she recognized, people who looked like her were often overrepresented. Moreover, diverse representation was important, Kat argued, because society was diverse. Lack of diversity is misrepresentation, an attempt by producers to present an alternate and unrealistic version of reality.

Tying these two comparisons together, we can see that the importance of representation is not simply tied to the often-marginalized identifiers most research tends to emphasize. Looking closely, we see that Rusty, Gregory, Kat, Julia, and Elise made very similar claims around the question of representation: *representation was important because it indicated what might be possible.* Rusty's escapist fantasies, Gregory's desire to be seen, Julia's and Elise's rejection of the limited way people "like them" were imagined and Kat's frustration at limited types of bodies all reflected a belief that media validated our sense of what is and what might be. When interviewees did not "care" about representation, it was often because they were pushing back against the way texts attempted to "hail" them, as those stereotyped or limited attempts often closed down the number of ways people "like them" were imaginable.

That is not to say that interviewees did not stress these marginalized identities when they described representation as important but that there was not an inherent correspondence between social marginalization and feeling that representation was important. Rather, these four interviewees offered an approach to media that could not be reduced to social demographics—despite sharing racial and class identifiers, Kat and Rusty did not have the same views on media representation, nor did Gregory and Julia. For one, some interviewees did not care about representation, since they viewed video games or other media as unserious. In addition, some were not invested in seeing representation of people like them, because they were all too conscious of the ways in which media representation could not encompass the diversity of those who shared an identifier. Certain types of texts and contexts also shape the way audiences interpret portrayals. My interviewees cared less about *whether* a group was represented than about the *function* of a specific representation, an issue discussed throughout Richard Dyer's work.[17] Representation of people "like them," for example, did not inherently make a text more appealing to interviewees.

These findings help us critique the fact that diverse representation options are available most often in the very games in which representation matters least to identification. If people are too invested in playing the songs to really think about their avatar in *Rock Band,* then representation in that game becomes purely aesthetic. In games with protagonists with developed backstories, however, most characters are white males.[18] In first-person shooters, where identity markers matter little in the actual playing of these games, "the white male is usually privileged by whatever markers of identity are supplied."[19] There are counterexamples, of course, like *Perfect Dark Zero,* featuring bounty hunter Joanna Dark.[20] We should be critical of the fact that game mechanics shape when atypical avatars or characters are offered to players. In both *Portal* and *Mirror's Edge,* the main characters are women of color.[21] Unlike most first-person games, *Portal* is a puzzle game, not a shooting or a fighting game, thus the choice to make the character a woman of color is perhaps slightly less transgressive, at least to the extent that the game as a whole is experimental and transgressive. Though *Mirror's Edge* is more of an action game than *Portal,* it is distinctly not a shooter and was heralded for its unique game play focused on free-running.[22] Although both games are valuable for breaking away from the norms of game design, it seems as though only games that are already thinking outside the box are interested in exploring nonhegemonic forms of representation.

Designers may not be able to assume how audiences will identify with texts, but they do shape, particularly via narrative, the potential for identification. Although not all interviewees said that representation was important, when they did say it was important it was in the social-political sense described by Charles Taylor.[23] The problem with arguments for minority representation diversity in video games is that they tend to focus on pluralism rather than diversity. They emphasize peripheral markets, targeted on the basis of specific identifiers. Such arguments celebrate texts that depend on active audiences to create their own diversity in games. Yet building on Nick Dyer-Witheford and Grieg de Peuter's critique that the game industry is increasingly built upon the immaterial labor of players, we can see the ways in which a neoliberal, do-it-yourself approach to representation has become increasingly central to how the industry conceptualizes representation.[24]

The findings in this book indicate that the marketing logic that focuses on marginalized groups as the target for diverse representation hinders the more political goals of media diversity. The marketing logic has resulted in a pluralistic version of representation, not diversity in a more general sense. In contrast to pluralistic representation, diversity addresses the way my interviewees described representation as important. Representation was important in a social sense, according to my interviewees, not the individualistic sense stressed by market logic. Whereas market logic suggests that diversified representation is important only because it is desired by individual players (who are potential exploitable customers), I argue that it is important because it has political and collective force. It can enforce but also expose social violences such as racism, heterosexism, misogyny, ableism, nationalism, and capitalism (the very ideology undergirding the market emphasis on individuals as customers). Too often, the argument for the importance of representation relies on realism as contrasted with fantasy. Interviewees' responses reflected this, as well. Representation was important to those players who wanted their media to be realistic; it was important to those who wanted their fiction to present the world in a manner that conformed to their expectations of that fictional world, as well as their real-life personal experiences. This raises the question, how does representation come to matter in a medium defined by play and fantasy?

Why It Matters

Why does representation matter? Arguments *for* the representation of marginalized populations tend to highlight making the games more realistic. Arguments *against* representation as a goal tend to emphasize games as fantasy. Either case assumes, however, that recognition requires a reference to reality but that fiction is immune to recognition requirements. In my past research I have seen industry workers argue on International Game Developers Association discussion boards, as have gamers on various game-discussion websites, that representation of marginalized groups is not an issue because some games do not include any characters (for instance, *Tetris* and *Minesweeper,* puzzle games with simple graphics).[25] Therefore, if a player wanted to avoid games with characters who were not like them, they could play the many games without characters. Such arguments are like saying that if audience members do not like watching movies with women being raped and tortured, then they should not watch those movies. If a particular type of movie—say, horror movies—often features that content, then there are plenty of other genres to watch. This assumption that it is audiences' responsibility to avoid offensive content builds on neoliberal logics and niche-marketing norms. It seems inconceivable to those who make these arguments that there is a social responsibility to think through who is always being excluded from particular genres and media. More than that, it refuses to acknowledge that critiques are not about personal consumption. They are about a world in which certain types of bodies are relegated to specific roles.

It is a common assertion in those venues, as echoed by some interviewees in this project, that games are fantasies and that discussions of realistic representation are therefore irrelevant. This position ignores the very realistic bases of many fantasy games.[26] Whether games are fantastical or realistic, the representation of certain identities and not others is telling of the assumptions made by game makers. As Geoff King and Tanya Krzywinska argue, "The moment any choices are made about what material to include, how to treat it and what kinds of activities are required of players in order to succeed, particular meanings—or the potential for such meanings—are created."[27] On the one hand, researchers must call out the unquestioned use in games of white, English-speaking, heterosexual males as normative and the use of other identities to mark difference. On the other hand, they must avoid assuming that these identity markers are the ones most significant to players and deal critically with the common dichotomy of realism versus fiction in how people make sense of if and how representation is important.

Arguments about both "good" and "bad" representation often rely upon realism. Bad representation is often justified using this frame. Dean Chan argues that makers of war games justify their problematic representation of groups with authenticity claims, particularly when games reference historical events.[28] For example, that Arabs, Nazis, or the Viet Cong are enemies in games is dismissed simply as a realistic representation of U.S. wars. Sports games are often similarly described. As she played a lot of *Madden NFL* football games, I asked Sasha if she thought it was a problem that the only games with large numbers of representations of African Americans were sports games.[29] I explained David Leonard's critique of the ideologically problematic aspects of this limited form of representation.[30] She responded, "Of course, there's going to be a lot of black characters, like, on *Madden* and *NBA Live,* because it's an *exact* replica of what is out there!"[31] Sasha was correct that these specific game texts provide mimetic versions of professional, American athletic organizations—the characters are based on real NFL and NBA players, large numbers of whom are African American. The problem researchers can investigate, however, is not the veracity of a given representation—for example, that sports games are not problematic, because they are realistic—but the particular deployment of realism in discussions of representations. We should be interrogating how structural racism in employment, education, and housing makes physical labor in the form of professional sports one of the few options that African American men have in the United States for economic advancement. Chan makes this argument in terms of texts and producers, but I think that those who wish to create change in representation in video games must look also at how audiences use the realism/fantasy dichotomy.[32] Moreover, that sports, urban crime, and war games are the *only* games in which people of color (usually men) are represented demonstrates a lack of imagination on the part of game designers. Racial diversity is present, it seems, only when game content makes it "matter."

Realism in video games is not a simple either/or concept. Alexander Galloway argues that games can be divided into two groups: "those that have as their central conceit the mimetic reconstruction of real life, and those resigned to fantasy worlds of various kinds."[33] One might amend this to add the placeless, characterless games Jesper Juul describes, like *Tetris*.[34] Galloway also distinguishes between two categories of representation: (1) whether groups are represented stereotypically or in depth and (2) whether the game's graphics are abstract or realistic. Critics must look, he argues, at both categories when they discuss representation in games. He goes on to assert that researchers must assess games in terms of realism of action. We cannot study games' "realistic-ness," he argues, without looking at the audience's interactions with each game.

Building on these ideas, researchers could look at audiences' expectations for realness, as well. Interviewees who said representation did not matter for them, explained this was so because they experienced game texts and media texts in general as forms of escape and fantasy. As discussed, both Rusty and Julia dismissed the importance of representation by stressing the fantastical aspects of games. Bryan made a similar point:

> If I'm playing *Rock Band* and I'm dressing up my rock character, I'm going to give him a green mohawk and leather pants, which is not something I would rock in real life. Do I identify more with a charac-

ter who is a short, brown-haired boy who's got plainish clothing or is wearing a monkey suit to go to his job [Bryan's appearance at the time of the interview]? No, probably not, because it doesn't make for a good game.

In the same way that identification with video game characters was not always important to them, interviewees did not always care how those characters were represented (even if they created those representations). That is, interviewees did not necessarily play video games to see a reflection of reality; indeed, many said that was definitely *not* the purpose of games. Some made a similar argument for media in general. Amy argued that she could easily separate fantasy from reality and thus did not think that media representation was important:

> I totally don't. I'm thinking about all the various articles about like there aren't enough people of various races and things like that. . . . Like, for example, *Friends*, New York City with very few black people, that sort of thing. I don't care. I have no problem distinguishing reality from fiction. So I don't think it's any issue.

Amy referenced Phil Chidester's argument that *Friends'* lack of characters of color reinforces whiteness as the norm.[35] Realism mattered differently to different interviewees and in different texts, however, which makes broad pronouncements on when and how representation matters in media consumption difficult to make. Countering Amy's point, Gregory declared in one interview, "It's just unrealistic, some of these shows. Like *Friends*. Are there no black people in New York City?!" Both saw it as unrealistic, but they differed on whether that mattered (returning to the earlier discussion of time, they also both used a show that had been off the air for six years as their point of reference). For Amy and several other interviewees, they knew that the world was more diverse than what was depicted on television, so what was on the screen did not matter. For others, like Gregory and Kat, they knew the world was more diverse and thought media should represent that diversity.

According to interviewees, the play element in games sometimes trumped the need for more realism. This argument is one commonly made against the importance of representation in video games. Many comments on online articles about diversity in games emphasize what game scholars call the "magic circle" of play—this magic circle is imagined to cordon off games from concerns about realistic representation. The magic circle is often used to define the ways in which play sits outside "normal" space and interaction and runs according to its own set of rules and norms that may not align with rules and norms outside the game. We can think of this in terms of a stadium, where the field of play is one in which the ritual of the game is played out. Any trash talk, name-calling, or violence on the field is considered part of the game and thus allowable in the game space, even if such behavior would not be sanctioned (indeed, would probably be criminalized) outside the stadium.

This notion of a magic circle of play as something distinctive and separate from reality draws from Johan Huizinga's work on play, though Roger Caillois argues that this concept may be a more accurate description of games than of playfulness generally.[36] It is also an issue that has been much debated in contemporary game studies.[37] In debates over representation in digital games, for example, it is a common theme.[38] Often, people who make excuses for not "dealing" with issues of representation insist that these are fantasy worlds and should not be encumbered with reality or that they represent the reality of the fictional worlds they create. Of course *Grand Theft Auto* is violent, misogynistic, and racist.[39] It is a gangster fantasy. How could it be otherwise? This argument curiously combines realism and fantasy as justifications for misogynist and racialized violence. The game is just a fantasy, so the violence does not count. It is realistic because violence exists in these worlds, so it is not offensive.

In *A Theory of Fun for Game Design,* game designer Raph Koster argues that the assertion "it's only a game" stems from the fact that the puzzle, the game mechanics behind the narrative, are what players really see when they play.[40] According to this logic, players are "really" seeing the structure of and requirements to complete missions in *Grand Theft Auto,* not the misogynistic and racist violence. This argument assumes, of course, that the violence being played out in this *particular* realistic/fantasy space is not also part of the appeal (something that is likely untrue). Koster goes on to contend, however, that the proper matching of narrative and game play reinforces the overall experience: "Players see through fiction to the underlying mechanics, but that does not mean the fiction is unimportant."[41] Caine discussed realism versus fantasy in relation to a pen-and-paper role-playing war game that he played, which involved painting models: "Because of the science-fiction nature, you have a bit more freedom and creativity in painting together a force. Eh, I want to make this guy blue. Whereas if it's a historical game, I would feel very guilty painting up a tank to be blue when that sort of tank was never blue." As a history major with a focus on military history, he was particularly attentive to historical realism in this regard. In games that he felt were meant to be realistic, representational issues were highly important to him. He was more flexible in fantasy texts, though he felt diversity in a broad political sense was important.

Devon discussed realism in terms of what constituted good gay representation in games and television:

> I guess when I see it and I believe it. . . . You got the token gay friend. They're fabulous. . . . I'm sure there are people like that, but they're not the only, not all gay people are like that. . . . You never see gay nerds; you just don't see them. . . . I think it's important that things seem realistic in that sense because a lot of times in cases like *Fable* and *The Sims* it makes sense that there isn't a difference, because in many ways there isn't. But then when you're watching things on TV, they're trying to—because there are differences but they are playing up the wrong differences. They're playing up the fact that if you're gay, you're fabulous instead of playing up, you know, like, if you're gay, there are a lot of challenges in life.[42]

Realism in and of itself was not a goal for Devon. The differences that made a difference to representation were, for him, the hardships experienced by those who were marginalized. Those are not the differences that typically make their way into games, where diversity tends to be more aesthetic than anything else. Moreover, that certain realities are always the ones validated in media representation shuts down the possible realities that could be, as well as the alternative realities that already exist.

Other interviewees attacked this lack of realism in representation, as well. Tala stated, "I would like to see people more naturally depicted." Tala went on to explain her distaste for reality television because it was, ironically, unrealistic. Conversely, Janet said she watched reality television "because it's got actual people represented, as opposed to a narrow subset that are considered OK to show on television." Her observation is similar to Larry Gross's argument that there is more representation of the LGBTQ community in reality television precisely because the presence of such individuals validates the shows' claims to present reality.[43] Granted, Janet and Tala described different types of reality television. Janet watched Discovery Channel–esque shows, which differed from the *Real World* progeny Tala castigated, yet in both examples the relation to reality was still a prominent issue. Devon described the importance of realism and representation in relation to documentaries: "I watch a lot of documentaries that have to do with sex or gender or sexuality. . . . You feel like you're not the only person if you watch a documentary about gays in the workplace or something like that." Similarly, Mary Gray's interviewees discussed the power of documentaries and online coming-out stories as evidence of "queer realness."[44] Reality shows and documentaries, with their assumed and constructed indexical relationships to lived experiences, offer the raw materials for identity building and knowledge about other ways of being.

Note that my interviewees did not discuss realism in the sense that media should be realistically accurate in a quantified or qualified sense. Rather, interviewees used realism as a way of making media producers responsible for what they portrayed. No one assumed that media should mirror reality. Many people made statements similar to Elizabeth Bird's argument that "we know that television does not mirror reality (nor do people want it to), but that it refracts back a sense of reality that speaks to people in different ways."[45] According to Alice Hall's research, audiences have many different ways of thinking about realism in media: plausibility, typicality, factuality, emotional involvement, narrative consistency, and perceptual persuasiveness.[46] David Machin and Usama Suleiman also found that "for many computer game players naturalism is experiential rather than perceptual."[47] Their interviewees engaged very different definitions of "realistic" when evaluating war games, definitions that were based on the player's identity, political ideology, and motivations for playing. For several of my interviewees, "good" representation was believable representation, and believable representation drew on the diversity interviewees saw in themselves and their world.

When researchers focus on representation, they often emphasize what is present in the text, but the absence of certain types of representation can be striking to researchers, as well, as it was for some of my interviewees. As Janet put it, "I mean, there is certainly no shortage of white women. But like, there's definitely an incredible dearth of people who are fat and just doing normal things that aren't specifically about being fat." As a white woman, she felt represented but that her body type and sexuality (she identified as gay in the interview and queer in the survey) rarely were. Caine, who grew up in Maryland after his parents emigrated from Pakistan when he was very young, discussed South Asian characters being absent from games and the negative representations of Muslims in most media:

> I can think of one video game where I recall a South Asian character having any sort of role. And it was a positively presented role, which made me happy. But even still, it was a passive rather than active role. . . . These days, it's more usual for it to happen and be in a negative light, which is rather frustrating. I look at shows like *24* where most of the Muslim characters who come on screen are complete antagonists and wind up getting killed off in various gruesome ways throughout the course of the show. That is frustrating. But every once in a while, there is positive representation, and I'm very glad to see that.

When interviewees expressed that representation was important to them, it was largely in the vein of critiquing which representations did or did not exist in relation to realism. In this and previous research, my interviewees did not say that they necessarily sought out representation. Moreover, they could rarely describe what type of representation they would like. As T. L. Taylor describes, "People may not know what they *could* enjoy."[48] Wanting representation, the act of desiring it, is different from critiquing portrayals that exist. The market-logic argument for representation glosses over this nuance. For many interviewees, representation was nice when it happened. In some ways, as explored in the conclusion, this sentiment pushes back against the assumption that audiences need to demand representation for it to exist. The reason representation mattered to some interviewees was that they saw the under- or misrepresentation of certain groups as unrealistic. This might lead, they hypothesized, to negative effects in the world at large. It was not, however, because they needed to see people "like them."

Why It Does Not Matter

My interviewees varied in their opinions about why representation mattered because the reasons individuals turn to media impact what matters to them in the texts they consume. For some people representation in games is just not important. As Sara said, "I like TV shows that make me think. Stories that make me think. The ironic thing is that I think a lot of the games I play aren't necessarily ones that make me think." Although uses and gratifications research is maligned by some scholars, an individual's reason for using a particular text or medium is directly related to how they interpret that text and, thus, the relative importance of representation in it.[49] Julia said, for example, "The things I look for in TV are different than things I look for in books." Similarly, the characterization of games as trivial in comparison with other media leads some people to view representation in video games as unimportant.

There also seems to be a relationship between how individuals describe their identities and the importance they give to seeing people "like them," though not in the way usually assumed. This is evident in the exchange between Julia and Elise discussed at the start of the chapter. For Julia and Elise, seeing people "like them" was largely immaterial to their media consumption. This was not because these identities were unimportant to them but because the typical articulation of these identifiers did not ring true to their experiences. Although both considered their racial, gender, and sexual identities important to their senses of self, they did not necessarily seek them out in media, because queer women and African Americans (and presumably African American queer women, though Julia did not say this) were not commonly represented well in media. Christine, an African American woman in her early twenties, discussed this in terms of both race and gender: "I guess it all, it has a lot to do with how you grow up, and I didn't really grow up in any one particular community, and I've never really viewed my being a woman as something—it's just too broad of a category for me, so it's not particularly meaningful." Malcolm was a graduate student who had lived in the United States for fifteen years but grew up in

Southeast Asia. Seeing people like him was not important because, he said, "I guess, I probably have less of a self-image than other people. . . . I never really had any particular, I don't know, mental frame." He also acknowledged that he very rarely saw people like himself in media, but he said that this did not bother him.

Related to this, some of the reasons interviewees cited when saying representation was not important to them indicated that they were cognizant of the problems of representation. That is, they were aware of the back-and-forth over what was positive and negative about various representations. Interviewees recognized that tokenization and stereotyping were the dangers of demanding diversity in representation. Chuck, a white, heterosexual man in his late twenties, felt representation was important but found it was often problematically done:

> When I think of diversity, how it's done in the media—do you remember when Burger King tried to have, like, the [Burger King Kids Club], where it would be, like, the kid in the wheelchair who's named Wheels and there's, like, the one black kid, the one Asian girl? That stuff always drives me insane.

Largely, these problems that Chuck identified stem from a focus on individual identifiers without the acknowledgment that identities are not reducible to individual signifiers. Yes, group differences exist, but the ways these differences are marked visually and narratively in media often oversimplify them. As Kat described, "I definitely don't think that we should overlook that different cultures have different ways that they've been raised and that has shaped their reality, but saying that you're born with an inherent value and capacity is not appropriate [*laughs*]." Here, we see that the antiessentialist claims (and anticonstructionist claims) of much contemporary theories of identity were evident in the ways interviewees discussed the topic.

Sometimes, always seeing characters who looked like them was a reason interviewees gave for representation not being important to them. This was particularly true of those who did not see themselves as marginalized. Chuck said, for instance, in response to whether seeing people "like him" was important, "No, because it is almost all me [*laughs*]. I'm a straight, white male who is twenty-nine. That's what 99 percent of media is for: me. I wouldn't mind it if it wasn't."

It was not, however, only those in the presumed majority of the gaming audience who said this. To Amy, who identified as a heterosexual, Asian American woman in her late twenties, having people who looked like her in games was not important because, as she said, "I consider myself fairly generic looking. And I think video games, to have memorable characters, would look more outrageous or something." The literature on representation asserts, as did some interviewees, that representation is only or most important to the marginalized. Pouncy said, for example, "I feel like that's only really important if you're not a white dude, because so much media representation is already aimed towards white dudes." This was not always the case, however.

Sometimes, interviewees said never seeing people "like them" was the reason they did not care about representation. Some described an apathy bred from resignation over never being portrayed. Others said it arose from the fact that the rare occasions in which they were represented did not resonate. Evan often disidentified with portrayals of transmen, and this led him to be uninterested in representation of people "like him." In another interview he referred to *Queer as Folk* and *The L Word* as texts that *should* have resonated with him as an early-thirties, white, middle-class, bisexual transman. He stated, "It was like queer content that was very specifically something that had to do with me and my lifestyle, and you want to talk about underrepresented—I had no interest." He did not watch these shows at all; even if they were supposedly shows with characters he could relate to. This latter point indicates that for some people seeing people "like them" is just not a driving factor for their media consumption.

As discussed in chapter 3, people are perfectly capable of enjoying media that does not necessarily represent them. As Bryan said:

I saw *The Hangover* recently . . . and yeah, ok, that could have been me. Goofy white guys, lost in Vegas. I've done that. Not to that extent, but I could see myself at someone's bachelor party and being in crazy situations. . . . But it doesn't make some other movie that has a character that has nothing to do with me—*Slumdog Millionaire*—nothing to do with me. It's some game show contestant, right. I've never been on a game show. But still a great story.[50]

Bryan's example of *Slumdog Millionaire,* a British film set in the slums of Mumbai that became a widely acclaimed global hit, points to the fact that many people in the world connect with texts that are not necessarily about people "like them."[51] As Hatshepsut described, the relative importance of representation is specific to a text. She reported that if she was watching a movie set in China, she was not going to see people like her—an early-thirties, African American/Native American, queer, female artist from California. She went on to say, however, "It's important to me in some cases, where if it's supposed to represent the people or the world in general, then I expect to see people that look like me, as well as other people." Again, she judged representation's importance in terms of realism. Realism for her, though, was contextual. The question we might then ask of games is, whose version of reality are games made to reflect? Rather than shoehorning in or tokenizing characters who are members of marginalized groups, how might the industry *as a whole* reimagine what settings, stories, and mechanics are made available to players?

Finally, my interviewees revealed that the way one was targeted was a reason for not caring about representation. Violet, a heterosexual, white woman in her early twenties said:

> I do not like watching shows where characters are like me. Like, I don't like dramas where the characters are my age—like, for example, *The Hills* is supposed to be for people like me, I think. I think it's marketed towards people my age. And I don't enjoy that show. . . . I think shows I like to watch are kind of like the video games I like. Almost an escape rather than a reflection.[52]

Again, we see escapism, the possible worlds, as more key to the experience of media consumption than realism of representation per se.

People argue that change will happen in the representation of minorities in games when marginalized groups are seen as plausible markets for games.[53] To assert one's presence in the marketplace does not ensure an equal place, however, in mainstream game texts. The girl games movement provides a salient example of what can be left out when marketplace logic shapes how marginalized groups are imagined and represented. In the 1990s an attempt was made by multiple game companies, including several founded by women, to get girls interested in what by then had become a very boy-centric gaming space.[54] The girl games movement did not result, however, in the creation of a place for female players in the hard-core gamer market. Rather, it made content designed "for girls" a peripheral interest.[55] This kind of targeting distances women from mainstream games. It also alienates women who do not connect with those appeals. As my interviewee Carol described: "The marketing for girls' games that I see is so atrocious. It's like everything has to be pink." An anecdotal example from an essay by Stephanie Bergman emphasizes this point. She describes a girl and some boys talking about video games on the New York subway: "The concept of 'girl games,' on its face, is detrimental to the little girls who game. It's because companies are creating games 'for girls' that the boys had such a hard time understanding how this girl could be playing something other than Barbie."[56] Marketing performatively constructs (not reflects) a group as a particular kind of audience and can shape a person's relationship with a medium, a genre, and an industry. If we are to think about how representation matters to games, then we must broaden our focus to how the entire medium is constructed as for (or not for) certain groups. That should not entail, however, trying to mark specific types of games as for specific types of groups.

In the context of discussing the possibility of marketing games to a gay audience, partners Devon and Ephram brought up the girl games example:

> EPHRAM: I think it can happen. I don't think it's really going to happen a lot. Like, it's happened with girl gamers already where they had these awful, awful . . .
>
> DEVON: Oh, those were awful . . .
>
> EPHRAM: Here's girl games, and everything is pink and has ponies and you can decorate stuff and cook . . .
>
> DEVON: And yeah, that's what girls want.

Some girls might want these games, so might some boys, not to mention men and women, but the marking of games as *for* specific audiences has ideological power. Similarly, since games are often assumed to be for children, the representation of sex and sexualities is highly curbed. As Devon and Ephram pointed out, gay or queer representation in games comes up against a great deal more resistance than the representation of gender and race.[57] The moralistic attacks on media portrayals of nonnormative sexualities compound the resistance to the display of these identities in video games.

Sometimes, interviewees accepted, if begrudgingly, the lack of representation of their identity groups in video games because they acknowledged that they were not part of the mainstream, adolescent, white, heterosexual, male gaming market. At times, this resulted in a sort of defeated apathy. Sasha stated, "[Representation is] not important, but it's nice! Even though it's not going to happen. They've been doing this shit for years, so it's not going to change." This notion that representation is "nice" when it happens is returned to in the book's conclusion.

At other times, interviewees argued that their group was a good market for video games or that not marketing to groups was not only discriminatory but illogical. Carol recounted a scene from the show *Mad Men* in which the character Pete tried to convince executives from a television company to sell to African American markets. The executives in this episode clearly allowed their racism to trump their desire for money, but as Carol pointed out, "It's stupid to not market to people who have money to spend on your product." In another interview Sasha made a similar point: "By excluding certain characters, you are more likely to exclude certain markets. . . . That's why they made a black Barbie." These comments mirror the capitalist market logic that if an industry could get beyond its myopic view of its market, they could make a lot more money by offering more diversity in their products.

This focus on market logic is used in arguments that some audiences make against the lack of diversity in media representation. These arguments also offer audiences a form of resistance to this lack of diversity: voting with their dollars. Such a tactic often gets appropriated by media industries, however, and the subsequent marketing to particular groups results in the same sort of marginalization as under- or misrepresentation. As David Morley and Kevin Robins assert, "The very celebration and recognition of 'difference' and 'Otherness' may itself conceal more subtle and insidious relations of power."[58] The issue for them is not so much how identities are constructed but rather "an understanding of who is being differentiated from whom."[59] Research that uses this kind of market logic repeats many oversimplifications, including the static notions of identity evident in the industry's construction of the audience. This argument can be used to justify pluralism but does not offer a strong case for diversity. Interpellation by cultural industries is not the only factor in whether people see themselves as part of the audience. Social structures such as gender, race, and sexuality also shape individuals' relationships with gaming culture.[60] Moreover, players' connections with media characters are constructed across, within, and beside their individual identities and relationships to social structures.

My interviewees' resistance to targeting is part of the constant tension between representation and exploitation—between being given a voice and being pandered to—that has been traced throughout media studies' discussions of the representation of marginal groups. According to Ioan Davies, writers are "conscious of the problems that any voice that was given would be appropriated by those who wished to traduce them for their own interests."[61] Some of my interviewees, recognizing this problem, rejected the targeting boxes media marketers tried to place them in. This resistance included rejecting the importance of representation itself, an assumed importance that often results from and contributes to that type of marketing. For some of my interviewees, representation did not matter, because it was not important to see people "like them" in their media. The plural version of representation supported by the market-logic argument was not why representation mattered. Rather, they said diversity in representation in general, not done only for the sake of targeting, was important.

When It Matters

Media portrayals, like marketing, flatten the real-world existences they reflect. As Plato famously laments, artistic representations imitate but offer incomplete knowledge of the world.[62] When audiences recognize this, they also observe that individual identities are extremely complex. No single media text can perfectly reflect an individual or a group in its multifaceted totality. Similarly, seeing certain forms of representation is not necessarily the driving factor in media choices. That is not to say that representation is unimportant, just that it is not *inherently* important. Representation is, rather, *relatively* important to an individual's identity, the text itself, and the context in which a text is used. Identity matters because how people understand their own identities shapes what types of representation are important to them. Textual properties matter because they can shape how audiences interpret a given representation. Finally, context matters because representation is important in the broad social relationships in which people find themselves, not in a single, isolated text.

Identity Matters

For some interviewees the representation of certain identifiers was extremely important, though not always. Devon said he went through phases in which he just needed to find movies with gay characters:

> And then I'm like, these movies are so bad. Why can't we have good directors? And I watch them anyway, and I do enjoy them because I can identify with the characters even though so many are lousy, absolutely lousy. During those little phases it's really important because I'm really craving something to identify with during that time.

Even though Devon could identify with a wide range of characters, there were times his need to see his sexuality represented was so strong that he could overlook poor writing, acting, directing, etc. We should not read this as a sign that such identifiers overdetermine how audiences connect with media texts. Gregory explicated the nuances and complications of representation, specifically in relation to his sexual and racial identities:

> I used to watch *Queer as Folk* all the time, and I was like, this is the only fucking town where there is no gay black people! [*laughs*]. . . . You ever see that show called *The Wire*? Everyone talks about it. My mom loves that show. I never watched it. But they said it's a good show. I don't know. I mean, that might depict something, but everybody in the hood ain't a drug dealer. You know what I'm saying? [*laughs*].

In discussing two television shows that purportedly included characters "like him," Gregory offered an exemplar for the very issue with which I begin this book. Focusing on single identifiers in discussing representation, even focusing on intersectional identities (*The Wire* addresses race, sexuality, and class, among other categories), has its limits. A similar sentiment was present in other interviews, as well. Zahriel said:

> I'm very much a feminist. I've always felt that women were misrepresented and underrepresented in most media. . . . I was always infuriated by my *Star Wars* action figures because the women looked like very bad drag queens. Leia looked like a duuude wearin' earmuffs. . . . There's a game called *Super Princess Peach* for the DS . . . just reading it infuriated the crap out of me. Because Princess Peach, who is finally able to try and save Mario and Luigi now they've gotten kidnapped, she's got like four basic powers which are tied to her emotions. Angry, sad, loving, and I forget what the other one is. But she basically gets PMS and breathes fire. When she's sad, she cries a river and makes trees grow so she can do the beanstalk shuffle and stuff. When she's all lovely dovey, they all fawn over her. And it's just, like, what century are we living in again?[63]

Zahriel discussed this in the context of feeling as though some of the positive strides she saw made with the representation of strong women when she was younger (e.g., *Wonder Woman* and *Charlie's Angels*) were reversed later (e.g., *Beverly Hills 90210* and the Bravo *Real Housewives* shows). Carol made a similar point in her interview: "I think with movies and TV and music, it's a little frustrating how retrograde everything is." In part, Zahriel's and Carol's frustration was tied to the ebb and flow of representation. This ebb and flow counters the progressive narrative often offered up by historical surveys of representation—media (like politics) has not comprehensively "gotten better." Their frustration also points to the fact that audiences judge representation in the context of the broad history of media, not simply in terms of what is available now.

Zahriel tied her feeling that representation was important to her identity as a feminist, not just as a woman. Though scholarship on the representation of women (as an identity) abounds, there is little discussion about the representation of feminists (as an identity). Games or other media that merely put women on-screen in a desire to expand their range of representations miss this entirely. Other interviewees described representation as important because they wanted media characters they could identify with, though not only in relation to identifiers like gender, race, and sexuality. Although those identifiers were important to some interviewees, they did not encompass all of the representation desires that interviewees voiced. Of the musicians she enjoys, Renee said, "I feel like they are the same kind of people. . . . It's not so much that they have the same skin color or the same hair color, but they dress similarly or I feel like I'm kind of quirky in some ways in the things that I choose to put on in my everyday life and they are quirky in that sense, in that style." Other interviewees, like Sara and Malcolm, made similar claims regarding their senses of humor. For some interviewees, then, it was important to their enjoyment of media to see people like them. What "like them" meant was not, however, necessarily or always tied to the identifiers typically used to analyze media representation in the context of sociopolitical recognition. Chuck described this, for instance, in relation to being a comic book geek: "I'm a huge comic book geek, but I hate the movies because it's shoved into my face, like, oh this is what I really like." He disidentified with major motion pictures' attempts to hail him as a fan, in much the same way many people I spoke to disidentified with the commercial construction of gamer identity.

My interviewees differed in their views on the importance of identifiers to choices people made in games. When Connie played a Texas Hold'em (poker) game, for instance, she was annoyed when given only two character choices: a male or a female. The male character was a cardshark, whereas, she said, "They describe the girl, and it's like [in whiny voice], 'Made some bad choices in life and wants to buy a house for her mom and is really trying to go out on a limb and play poker.'" Connie ended up picking the woman because the actual personality of the character did not matter in the context of playing. Given more choices, however, she would have chosen a male character with a personality like hers over a female character who was so different from her. Earlier approaches to representation were right to argue that identity can shape how people approach a text. Finding characters "like you" is important, but only if the reason you are going to the text is to seek out reflections of your identity. Those earlier approaches missed the fact that what "like you" means is variable and contextual.

A great deal of academic attention has been paid to playing as the "other" (typically, in terms of race and gender). Lisa Nakamura has explored the appropriation of racial identities in online spaces.[64] Addressing offline or nonsocial games, Leonard argues, "There has been little theoretical or ethnographic work regarding the allure of 'virtual cross-dressing.' ... What does it mean ... when virtual reality provides space and ability to transcend one's spatial confinement and one's own identity to enter foreign lands and othered bodies?"[65] This is an interesting question, but it is often used in a simplistic manner to make assumptions about how audiences engage with on-screen characters and game mechanics. When Christine, an African American woman, played *Wii Boxing,* for example, she used a white, male avatar to defeat an African American, male opponent.[66] Using a textual analysis methodology, a researcher might point out that Christine was engaged in cross-identity performance and might even suggest that she identified with the white, male avatar and thus sought him out in the game space. Such a reading would not take into account, however, the fact that Christine felt no connection with her avatar. She was more interested in beating the game than in the appearance of the avatar. She went with the first Mii that appeared on the starting screen, and the computer randomly selected the opponent.

In his work on disidentification, "Muñoz underlines that perhaps in cross-identity identifications individuals do not abandon their own identity as they 'step' into the other person's subjectivity."[67] Moreover, if individual identities are complex, dynamic, and contextual, then easy correlations between identities based on social demographic categories and avatar choice are almost impossible. Similarly, we must consider whether it is a strategic choice to play as one kind of character over another. The often cited "oddity" of cross-gender avatar selection in video games may not in fact be that remarkable if the ways in which people interact with video game characters do not necessarily require identification in the sense of matching identifiers with a character.[68]

Textual Matters

Usually, texts are the focus of representation studies. They are central to representational issues, after all. Just looking at texts in isolation does not shed light, however, on why representation is important. A "bad" representation is a problem only in a context where those are the only kinds of representations. Leonard's and Chan's critiques of the representation of African American athletes in games resonate only in a mediascape in which, as Stuart Hall describes, this kind of exploitative representation of black athletic bodies is prominent.[69] Social history is partly why the representation of one group as the "baddies," versus another group, has meaning. As Alice Hall describes, "Media interpretation . . . is inherently a social activity. Even when audiences are watching a TV program or movie alone, they are interpreting it through criteria they have developed through interactions with others."[70] In sum, texts must be put into social context.

We can see these dynamics at play in the uproar over the representation of African zombies in *Resident Evil 5*.[71] In the original 2007 game trailer, the scene is set with various images from a nonspecific African village, showing off hyperrealistic graphics (Figure 19). The camera pans over dilapidated buildings and lingers over animals standing in alleys, a butcher chopping away at an open-air stand, and villagers lazily walking about their day. Tension builds as the camera focuses on what seem to be protestors screaming in response to a man standing on a makeshift stage and talking into a megaphone. We cannot hear what is being said, as a voiceover from the game's protagonist Chris Redfield declares, "Casualties have continued to mount over the long years I have struggled. More and more I find myself wondering if it's all worth fighting for. Perhaps not." Redfield is slowly revealed to the audience as a muscular white man who walks purposely through the village. Soon, he is alone on the streets, squinting in the harsh sun. He walks into a dark shed where we see a villager being infected with the zombifying virus. The villager quickly turns into a zombie and attacks Redfield. There is a quick transition into a montage of scenes in which Redfield is swarmed by hordes of villagers-turned-zombies.

Journalist Stephen Totilo critiques the trailer, writing that it "looks like it's an advertisement to virtually shoot poor people."[72] As André Brock argues in his analysis of *Resident Evil 5*, "Race stands in for cultural evil. Even before becoming infected, the Africans are depicted as malevolent and savage."[73] The game in isolation is not the problem. Rather, it taps into a long, racialized colonial history

Figure 19. Screenshot from opening of *Resident Evil 5* showing African-coded mob in early zombie transformation stage. Image by Emil Lundedal Hammar, November 11, 2013.

and a racialized representation of zombies, which makes the choice of a generalized African setting controversial.[74] The game comes from a Japanese developer, Capcom, and as anthropologist John Russell details, Japanese popular culture often draws upon Western imagery of blacks. This imagery serves the double task of preserving blackness's "alienness" while serving "the reflexive function of allowing Japanese to meditate on their racial and cultural identity in the face of challenges by Western modernity, cultural authority, and power."[75] Many online comments about the controversy insist that it is hypocritical to critique this version of the game but not its earlier iterations, which feature infected zombies in Spain, among other countries. As Brock goes on to argue, however, these attempts to shut down claims of racism express their own racist logic: "Repeated references to racism as individual aberrance points to a common misunderstanding of the structural efficacy of racism as well as the power of White privilege to disavow complicity with institutional structures while benefiting from them."[76] There are historical reasons that a game with a white protagonist shooting African zombie hordes is offensive that cheap comparisons to other games in the series ignore.

Despite many dismissals of the claims of racism, Capcom released a new trailer in 2008 in which the African setting was downplayed, the female sidekick was made more prominent (who was of African origin, though educated in Europe and lighter than those Africans depicted in the village), and the zombies were displayed as monstrous nonhumans with no ties to a specific country of origin. Although the game was not changed, clearly marketers in the company recognized that there was a way to sell the product that did not draw on histories of racism and oppression quite as transparently. Still, a thorough analysis of the game by Hanli Geyser and Pippa Tshabalala demonstrates:

> Focusing on the representations of the African zombies, through the eyes of a Western protagonist, and produced by a Japanese gaming company, *Resident Evil 5* depicts the decaying African state characterized by the ruins of colonialism. The subaltern of African are already seen as zombies in many ways in that they are not only regarded but also depicted as disenfranchised mobs viewed in the West only in the context of footage protests, and civil war.[77]

Resident Evil 5 relies on and promotes a history of exploitative and denigrating imagery of Africanness to lend an air of authenticity to its game environment. Further, it presents Africa as a monolith, thus collapsing a continent larger than the combined mass of the United States, much of Europe, China, and India into a single state.

As Dyer describes, how stereotypes are used matters more than that they are used.[78] In turn, how they are used is made meaningful through consumption. In games, however, in order to understand how meaning is made from representation, we must take into account the interplay between the narrative and the play aspects of games, as well as the broader cultural logics in which games are played.[79] In *Resident Evil 5*, for example, representation is intertwined directly with game play, as those marked as decidedly "other" are the enemy. We can unpack representation in games more thoroughly by making sense of why representation matters in this medium. More specifically, in order for representation to be important in a sociopolitical sense, it needs to matter within a text. Hatshepsut described this well:

> With certain games where the characters are stereotypical. It's, like, you like to see characters that are a certain way, that are different

representations. But at the same time, it can be offensive because it's stereotypical. . . . They have to actually have some purpose, value in there. Not just entertainment, I guess.

Diversity in games is great, but producers must walk a fine line between stereotype and archetype. How identities are signaled is important, but *why* they are signaled is crucial. Representations of identifiers, like identities, become relevant in relation to specific moments of articulation.

The significance of a given representation is also related to an individual's reason for engaging with the text. As Janet pointed out, "I guess it depends on what I'm getting out of it, how important that is to me." Moving to a nongame example, she discussed the types of people and bodies represented in the yoga DVDs she got from Netflix: "I'm, like, oh man, they should totally make a yoga DVD with somebody who's like kinda old and has bad knees like me. That would be great." In the context of other kinds of shows, however, that kind of representation was less important: "I don't require, like, somebody on a cooking show to be old and have bad knees, because that's not really relevant to the product that I'm consuming." Turning to games, she made a similar argument:

I guess it would depend on how important that was in the game. Like if I'm playing *The Sims*, I want to play someone who looks like me because why should I have to play a character who doesn't look anything like me? . . . If I was playing a fighting game, I wouldn't want a character who looked like me [*laughs*] because I would be terrible at it. I understand that I'm not particularly suited for some modes [*laughs*].

Certain game texts make representation matter more than others. Games that promise players the option of domestic realism, like *The Sims,* feel restrictive when the available options are limited. In games that were more fantastical, particularly when actions in the games were not ones they felt their own bodies could accomplish, interviewees were more willing to play as characters who were unlike themselves. *When* representation matters is as interesting a question as *if* it matters, and as Janet pointed out, some of that mattering is tied to the mechanics of the game.

In chapter 3, I discuss the relative importance of identification in different types of games. Similarly, representation is relatively important. Specifically, sometimes the mechanical, ludic elements of games matter more than representation to players. James Newman argues that play is more kinesthetic than visual, and thus, appearance does not necessarily matter when it comes to playing video games.[80] Diane Carr suggests, "Non-players . . . tend to overestimate the importance of representational factors in games . . . but seasoned gamers routinely distinguish between the 'look' of a game and its gameplay."[81] Certainly, interviewees discussed graphics and visuals of games as a deciding factor in their purchase, but the look of the game was certainly not everything. Overall, though, interviewees, like game scholars, described the relationship *between* play and representation as important.

In my previous research players often asserted that representation must matter, either to the mechanics or to the narrative of a game, in order for its inclusion to be valued.[82] In this project interviewees stressed that there was a relationship between whether they cared about the appearance of their avatar/character and a game's mechanics. Representation, which interviewees tended to describe in terms of how they went about choosing an avatar/character, mattered differently in different games. Cody, who identified as a heterosexual, African American male in his midtwenties, said that how he chose a character depended on the type of game. When he played *EverQuest* or *World of Warcraft,* he did not care what his character looked like.[83] He picked the one that had the abilities he needed to do well in the game. When playing a skateboarding game like *Tony Hawk,* which was more realistic, he would pick the African American avatar if available, because, "Why not?"[84] When he played sports games, he picked the athletes he most identified with, being an athlete himself. Cody showed me the avatar he created to play through the storyline option in a wrestling game. It did not look like him, as the wrestler had dreadlocks (which Cody did not), had lots of tattoos (which Cody did not visibly have), and wore a gas mask and a leather cape (which Cody did not seem likely to wear). The avatar did have Cody's skin tone, however, and a similar name. According to Cody, "I just wanted to make the guy as nuts as I could. No real reflection of me. That was fun. I didn't ever think to make my own guy would be fun, but it kind of was." Granted, we can read the similarities between Cody and his customized wrestler as part and parcel of the attempt to make the avatar "as nuts as [he] could." It was only by making the avatar somewhat like him that he could in turn make it so very different from him. When we recognize that mimetic representation is not the only goal of avatar customization, representational options in games take on a new level of significance. Not only do they allow people to represent themselves, but they also shape players' ability to play with their own representation. That is, I can make a goth-punk version of myself only if I am first able to create an avatar that looks somewhat like me.

In contrast to these contexts, when creating an avatar on Xbox Live that was supposed to be a representation of him, he made it look like him as much as possible. He stated later that this was because he played with friends online and off who would expect this avatar to be him. In contrast, however, he said his *World of Warcraft* avatars ran the gamut of appearances, none of which were similar to him (or even as similar as the fantastical avatars could be). In an interactive medium like games, the relative importance of representation can be traced through the ways players make decisions about their characters, not because researchers can somehow decipher a player's identity from their avatar design but because the process of making those decisions illuminates when, how, and if self-representation is important to players. This allows researchers to focus on the way game designers limit players' choices in some game texts but expand upon them in others.

Game mechanics can make representation matter or not. When Sasha played *Marvel vs. Capcom* for her gaming interview, she said she picked characters only for their abilities: "I find that I win more when I play with the Juggernaut. Like, you have to have somebody that's bulky, a bigger person, on your team, and you're more likely to win."[85] Hatshepsut similarly described the ways playing strategies trumped representation choices for her:

> Mercenaries has three characters to choose from—a typical tiny, busty woman, an average-sized man "of color," . . . and a brawny, kick-ass white dude. My first instinct would be to choose the female, but the weapons are so big compared to her that she looks like she'll tip over. I'm going with dude who looks like he's indestructible.

I don't care where he came from, what school he went to, or what his nickname is. I just want him to get the job done.[86]

Both of these women were aware of the importance of representation in a broad political sense and consumed media that appealed to their identities. When it came to playing these games, however, the structure of the game dictated the choices they made. Whereas Rachael Hutchinson analyzes the various types of identity play and resistance make available in fighting games like these, it is important to consider that the identity of characters matters little to some players.[87] In turn, we can critique the fact that the choices are structured in a way that makes the woman and man of color less viable choices. The critique of game texts is empowered by a better understanding of how players interact with the choices made available to them.

Some interviewees stressed that representation was less of an issue in games than in other media. As Janet described, "In gaming I guess it's not nearly as important, because it is a lot more about what can this character do. . . . Like in *Wii Golf*, I don't really care. I just sort of make the icon look like me because I think it's funny, but not because, like, I would feel uncomfortable swinging a golf club if I knew that, like, I was playing as a male character. I don't really care [*laughs*]." Connie chose the female avatar in *Lee Trevino's Golf* because she had balanced abilities and thus allowed Connie to "beat the pants off of just about anyone who challenged" her: "I didn't pick her for her gender. I picked her because I liked the fact that she was balanced in all the abilities." Researchers can look critically at when and how games make certain options available to players, as my interviewees did.

Players often work with and within the game world because they have to if they want to play.[88] As Elizabeth Hayes describes in her findings, players' use of a game involves an interplay between their own dispositions and the game's mechanics.[89] That is, they balance what they enjoy doing in the game with what will make them successful in the game. Researchers can interrogate representation by taking into account how players interact with these texts and how representation is tied to game mechanics. In light of this, researchers should be critical of the way certain identities matter in some games and not in others. For many players representation is important because they want *other* people to see people like them, not because they themselves need to see their reflection all of the time.

Most games present difference as optional and pluralistic, particularly with regard to gender, race, and sexuality. There are a number of problems with this approach. First, this means that players see people "like them" only if they make the effort to create those representations. Second, the political goals of diversity are not realized, because dominant group members do not have to see people unlike them. Some interviewees discussed video games as a medium uniquely suited to maximizing market segmentation in this regard, because they can give people the option of playing as people "like them" via avatar-creation tools. Carol discussed this specifically in terms of games like *Rock Band* and the ability to create Miis on the Nintendo Wii. Sasha said that avatar customization allowed players more choices: "Like Nintendo Wii, they have, like, all shades. You can, like, customize a shade. Because everybody comes in different colors. You know, all black people aren't dark skinned. All Caucasian people aren't pale." What was fascinating in Carol's and Sasha's articulations was that video games were assumed to overcome many of the essentializing problems of representation. Specifically, through avatar creation and character choice, games were assumed to offer nuances not available in other media.

I argue that these are purely aesthetic nuances, however. Avatar creation tools and character options make video games more readily suited than other media to providing audiences with the opportunity to create more diverse visual representations. Yet these are limited options. Speaking of bodies in *EverQuest,* for example, T. L. Taylor points out that "some bodies are ascribed legitimacy and some are not."[90] Avatar options, like bodies, "not only become places in which we express our identities but, because they are socially constructed, they offer or deny particular formulations."[91] A few interviewees discussed this in relation to being forced to create avatars that were skinnier than themselves, as avatar creation tools did not include a variety of body-type options. Kat pointed out, while making Miis during her gaming interview, "It was interesting to see the things that weren't there. Like there were no dreadlocks; there were no weaves. I don't know. It was interesting." Similarly, a friend of mine, an African American woman in her early forties with short salt-and-pepper hair, expressed annoyance that she could not find *her* hair when making a Mii to play *Wii Sports* at a friend's house.

Even the presumed freedom of representation in games that allow the option for customization is limited. In his analysis of sixty MMORPGs and ten tabletop role-playing games, David Dietrich found that the majority of games did not allow for nonwhite racial appearance, including skin tone, facial features, and hair options.[92] That should not discount the options that are made available. T. L. Taylor notes, "While we must consider critically how much freedom people have in reconstructing themselves online, virtual environments without a doubt remain a space in which users are constantly creating and performing a variety of identities."[93] Still, we can be critical of the fact that only certain game genres allow for customized avatars/characters at all.

Of course, making exact replicas of oneself is not always the goal in using these tools. Several interviewees described making characters who were attractive or created aspirational versions of themselves. Certain types of game spaces and texts encourage self-representation, however, and even of the ones that do not, researchers can still be critical of the limits placed on avatar creation. When the choices included in those spaces limit the types of "selves" that can be represented, audiences notice the absence.

In addition, this focus on self-representation, like market logic, places the burden of representation on audiences. It also marks diversity as the exception to the norm of heterosexual, white, and male, as several interviewees pointed out. Janet remarked:

I guess I'm really aware of that on a racial level. The fact that there's such an intense level of tokenization. I guess I'm very aware of the extent to which white male is seen as, like, the default, and so, like, these are all regular people plus one black person—black people aren't regular people? Or like, these are all regular drivers, but we'll show one female driver. She's not a regular driver. She's a female driver.

Researchers can critique representation in games by looking at which options are made available, but they should also pay attention to *when* they are made available. As discussed in the previous chapter, options are often available only in games where identification *with* characters is less likely. The choices made available also demonstrate the industry's very limited construction of its audience. As Sasha described in relation to gender:

> Even when it comes to car games, they never have, like, one pink car. They always have, like, monster truck, tank, motorcycle, but it's all manly motorcycles, manly trucks. They never had anything, like, geared towards females. . . . If it was geared towards girls, it was, like, oh, this is the Bratz video game. I don't want to play that [*laughs*]. I want to play an adventure game with a female. Make her good looking but not too, like, manly. . . . They never had, like, a medium. Except for, like, *Tomb Raider* [and Princess Peach from *Mario Bros*.]. But when you are playing *Super Mario Bros.*, you can't choose to be the princess in the beginning. You got to be Mario.

We can see here that Sasha was well aware of which types of games included female characters or feminized representations and under what conditions. Gender representation in particular tended to rely on extremes in her experience. Zahriel similarly discussed how in some games, like *Zelda* (one of her favorite games) and *Halo* (which she played in the gaming interview), gender did not matter to the game and yet the protagonists were still male: "Where it's painfully obvious that they could have used a woman if they wanted to, that really annoys me . . . or you could make the character gender neutral. . . . You could just make a person who is very androgynous, who could go either way, and leave it at that. But they just default to men." She noted that even in games that allowed choices of characters, binary gender options were the only ones given. The problem is not just the lack of choice but the resistance to designing a default character who is female or androgynous.

Games are not closed off from all progressive potential, of course. Video games have the potential for much more creativity in representation. As yet, however, explorations of that promise remain a bit underwhelming, particularly in commercial games. According to Sherry Turkle, online environments (though perhaps offline ones, as well) allow us to view "identity as a set of roles that can be mixed and matched, whose diverse demands need to be negotiated."[94] We must question the freedom of identity and identification some video game theorists and marketers assert are available in these spaces, however. Mirosław Filiciak argues that video games provide new ways of constructing identity outside "oppressive" structures:

> The possibility to negotiate our "self" minimizes the control that social institutions wield over human beings. . . . Avatars are not an escape from our "self," they are, rather, a longed-for chance of expressing ourselves beyond physical limitations, they are a post-modern dream being materialized.[95]

This freedom is, however, potentially much more like the freedom Nikolas Rose describes: "Freedom is the name we give today to a kind of power one brings to bear upon themselves."[96] Alec Charles argues that games provide only the illusion of agency and that "in appearing to satisfy [their] audience's desire for agency, in fact sublimates and dilutes this desire."[97] Similarly, games tend to provide diversity in a way that is marketable but not necessarily socially transformative. Indeed, games more than many other media manage to profit from making a single text pluralistic without having to face the potential backlash of making it actually diverse.

Context Matters

Video games do not offer players infinite options in character customization, but play spaces are also not inherently welcoming to all bodies. Games encourage and value certain types of play over others, which Thomas Malaby describes as the contingencies of play.[98] In terms of representation, different identities "make sense" in some games in ways they do not in others. Even online games, which purport to allow players to create new social selves, tend to promote what Dietrich calls a "habitus of whiteness" and are spaces where hate speech is an everyday experience for marginalized players.[99] In this way, gaming spaces are like nongaming spaces in the violences that marginalized players experience.

How representation matters in games is, likewise, structured by context. We can and do identify ourselves in a variety of ways structured by our social context. Certain types of identity are relevant at different moments and in different social configurations. Judith Butler famously points out that gender is performative—produced in particular social contexts to serve different purposes and reliant upon cultural recognition for coherence.[100] We are not, however, free to perform gender in any way we wish. There are norms that structure the enactment of gender and make it intelligible; performing gender otherwise runs the risk of not being recognized and having one's body and identity rendered unintelligible and potentially unviable. Such performances signify differently in different contexts. Similarly, where people play and with whom influence the self-representation choices they make. Ephram discussed this in relation to playing online with his partner Devon:

> Definitely, when I'm playing with my partner, we kind of create the characters to kind of mimic our relationship. Like, in *Final Fantasy XI* he would always pick the larger character, and I would always pick a smaller character, because that's just how we are in stature. . . . And we kind of base our characters around our personalities. . . . If we're playing together, we'll build it with each other in mind.

Researchers rarely consider that when audiences create content, they, like other media producers, are creating these representations for specific audiences.[101] Online self-representation is not just the performance of one's identity, nor does it necessarily entail role-playing. That space can, however, shape individual choices and, thus, the relative importance of the options made available.

Lisa Nakamura and Tanner Higgin describe the importance of identity and performance in online spaces. In virtual spaces it is often assumed that embodied identities, like gender and race, no longer matter.[102] Because of this, these identities actually become all the more relevant. Like the famous *New Yorker* cartoon by Peter Steiner states, "On the internet, nobody knows you're a dog."[103] This cartoon emphasizes the potential distancing of "real" and "virtual" identities. Analyses of how people use the Internet find, though, that offline identities are emphasized in some online spaces.[104] Perhaps nobody *knows* you are a dog on the Internet, but if you are the only dog you know and you want to know if there are others like you out there, proclaiming your dogness becomes an important part of how you present yourself online. This is particularly true for marginalized groups who are forced to interact in digital spaces where white and male are often the unmarked norm. When gender, race, and sexuality are considered unimportant in online spaces, it is through the pretense that everyone is the same. Usually, the assumption is that everyone is heterosexual, white, and cisgendered male—gender, race, and sexuality are considered unimportant only to those people who have the privilege of never being confronted with violence based on them. In other words, those who carry gender, racial, and sexuality privilege are the only ones who can afford to think they do not matter. People of color, queer people, women, genderqueer people, transgender people, and others never have this privilege. Pouncy described this in terms of the online version of *Settlers of Catan* they played during the gaming interview: "Unless someone has an overtly feminine-sounding name in their screen name, everyone assumes that everyone is male. Well, I don't [*laughs*], but most people." Pouncy discussed at various points in their interviews that many other players used homophobic language. Pouncy also said that they did not play with people who had overtly religious screen names and icons. Social context affected both their experience and interactions with games.

In a previous study I asserted that the reason the LGBTQ gamers I interviewed did not care about representation was attributable to a distinction between online and offline play.[105] I pointed out that online homophobia was, for that group of online gamers, a much more important concern than representation in game texts. At the time, I posited that because my interviewees played primarily online, interactions with others were more central to their experience than the content of the games themselves. Putting this earlier research together with chapter 3 of this book, we can see how the context in which a text is consumed shapes players' experiences of representation. Pouncy's gaming interview demonstrates this quite clearly.

As previously discussed, *Settlers of Catan,* which Pouncy played for the second interview, does not have characters. One might argue, then, that we cannot talk about this game in terms of representation. This argument significantly oversimplifies representation, however. We can relate this to a debate over *Tetris,* reviewed by Ian Bogost, that is often used to encapsulate the ludology/narratology divide.[106] Janet Murray argues that you can read a "story" in *Tetris.*[107] Specifically, she interprets it as an allegory for contemporary American life. This interpretation is resoundingly dismissed by Markku Eskelinen, who focuses on the properties of participation made available in the game.[108] Bogost goes on to conclude that "in both interpretations, something is lacking," as both game play and meaning making are intertwined.[109] I argue, moreover, that beyond the play and narrative aspects of a text, researchers must look at the way players approach it. As Pouncy described, one could certainly read a game like *Settlers of Catan* in terms of its representational elements: "I used to play with a friend of mine who refused to call the little houses settlements [*laughs*]. She's, like, why don't we just hang a fucking Israeli flag over them if we are going to call them settlements! But, no, I don't really think about that so much." This was because, as Pouncy stated later, "I think part of the pleasure of playing the game is not thinking about the overt political undertones that you can dig out of the story." That is to say, it is not just that the ludic aspects overtake the narrative but that the purpose of interacting with the text shapes the relative importance of representational issues. Often, this purpose is playful; those who wish to argue for the importance of representation in games must contend with this more directly. More than that, much of the discourse has so far placed the burden of caring about representation on the shoulders of marginalized groups. Some of the resignation, ambivalence, and apathy about media portrayals expressed by my interviewees must be read in the context of being members of groups that have for so long been made responsible for doing all of the emotional labor around representation.

Social Matters

Popular and academic constructions assert that media representation affects how other people see us as members of social groups and not just in relation to identifiers like race, gender, and sexuality. Violet described this in terms of the reality show *The Biggest Loser* and body types:

> It offers people a chance, whether you are really obese or normal, to see people who are like you or not like you. And I think it inspires the people who may be overweight to be healthy or it's not some problem with who they are. It's not that they are a bad person; other people are going through the same thing. And for people who aren't overweight, when they watch the show it's kind of like . . . this is

going to sound horrible, but it allows you to see past what you would
see on the street. . . . It reminds you that they are not just the fat.

Violet acknowledged that her own assumptions about people who
were not within the bounds of normatively proscribed body types
and weights were problematic, and part of how she came to acknowledge that was via media representation. Her language was still
problematic in some ways (e.g., "obese or normal"), but she recognized that media images had power in shaping her language and
perception. Pouncy, during one interview, wondered if a game that
subverted heteronormativity could produce a similar effect: "So
you're on a quest and you have to, like, have this great prince help
you out, and he's like, we have to rescue my true love. And he's just,
like, some random prince, but the thing is his true love turns out to
be another random prince." A few other interviewees brought up
similar hypothetical scenarios for games. These types of representation would confront out-groups with representation, which is the
demand of diversity that cannot be fulfilled through pluralism alone.

Typically, when people write about the importance of representation in video games, they try to convince marketers it is more
financially lucrative to appeal to diverse audiences. In contrast to
this capitalist argument, a political argument for representation
would emphasize the effect of representation on those who are not
members of these marginalized groups. I argue that representation
is important in the context of the entire mediasphere, not only niche
marketing. Devon posted about one of his gay-film binges to his
Facebook page, and it resulted in a bit of an uproar from his social
network:

> They're like, "I don't know why it's so important to have a gay
> movie." And I'm like, "That's because you're not gay [laughs], and
> that's why you don't realize how important it is that everywhere you
> go." You know, I think they would be offended if everywhere they go
> everything was a gay movie.

People often cite this type of articulation when asserting that
representation matters because marginalized groups want to see
themselves in media. Ultimately, however, interviewees said that
representation was *socially* important, not important to them as

individuals. They wanted *others* to see diverse experiences and identities on-screen. It was not merely important for individuals to see themselves reflected in a mediated mirror. When Tracey said, "Everybody wants to see themselves," it was in reference to a sentiment Sasha explained: "It's uncomfortable to be the minority anywhere. Even if it's in real life. If you're a six-year-old, you don't want to go in the three-year-olds' class." People do not want to feel alone and unseen. Representation is important because it is an external acknowledgment of one's existence. This is intertwined with Gregory's assertion that people want to see themselves in media texts because they want people like them to be seen.

My interviewees who felt they were "mainstream" (regardless of whether they were marginalized in some way on the basis of demographic categorization) did not think they needed or, in some cases, had the right to say that representation of their group was important. Relatedly, representation does not matter if you can find yourself in the media in some way, as discussed in chapter 2. In an increasingly pluralistic and alternative-channel-filled media environment, it is possible that many people feel that they can find media that speaks to them. In some ways, this may be why my current and previous interviewees felt more ambivalent about representation than did participants in earlier media research. When one is not accustomed to seeing representation of oneself, any representation becomes noticeable. As Evan described, "[Representation is not] important to me, but it happens so infrequently that it certainly sticks out when it does happen and it's very noticeable." Overall, however, as discussed in this book's conclusion, interviewees described representation as "nice when it happened." This is distinct from actively desiring representation of people like them.

Regardless of whether interviewees felt it was important to see people like them in media, everyone said that it was important for other people. In some cases they displayed what communication scholars call a third-person effect, based on the assumption that "those" people did not usually get to see themselves and thus representation was important to them.[110] As Renee said:

> That's funny. That's really funny because I don't really think it's important to me. But I think it's important to other people, to see

people that look like them. Like, I see people that look like me all the time, and so I don't think of it as that important, but I think that if I didn't see people that looked like me all the time, I would think that I would think that it's important. But that's a lot of "I would thinks."

Renee acknowledged that because she recognized her own consumption practices and was able to find herself in media, she did not feel representation was important or missing. Other interviewees expressed that they also got to see some aspects of their identity represented. Pouncy made this point, for example:

I feel like the media is full of representations of people who look like me in terms of skin color and—well, I don't feel like my gender is represented very often in terms of gender not being a binary, which is not a way that a lot of people look at that. But more in terms of characters that think like me and have my values.

People often think of themselves and their groups in a nuanced and inclusive manner. When they talk about other groups, however, they tend to view them as static and cohesive. This is in fact the trouble with representation. We can see correlations between this and Elizabeth Bird's study of focus groups' attempts to create television shows featuring a white character, an American Indian character, and a female character.[111] She found that participants relied on stereotypes of characters of other racial identities when in the homogenous focus groups. People see other groups as defined entities, whereas they see themselves and their groups as multifaceted and complex. In turn, part of the problem in saying that media makers *should* offer diverse representations is that when producers try to represent groups, they tend to think narrowly about what membership in those groups entails.

Several of my interviewees described the lack of representation of marginalized groups as a problem for young people in particular. As Pouncy stated:

Just because representations in our media of people who aren't white dudes oftentimes suck. And they are unrealistic or just really don't represent the broad range of people who aren't straight, white dudes out there. And yeah, it would be great if all the people who aren't straight white dudes growing up were able to see heroes that represented themselves doing awesome shit.

Many interviewees said young people needed positive reinforcement of their identities. Carol stated, "I mean, if you aren't represented and you're marginalized and you're young and you are sort of forming your sense of self, then it's easy to think, 'What's wrong with me? How come I'm not in this game?' I think that's really simplifying it, but yeah, absolutely." Similarly, Sasha asserted, "It's nice to show kids that they have a variety, and just to be a hero you don't have to be a guy. There could be girl superheroes, and you can choose them to play." She went on to compare this with President Barack Obama, who offers "children of any other race besides white children hope that they can be president." Janet had a mixed-race niece and was worried about her exposure to certain types of representation: "My niece has darker skin and very, very curly hair, and like, all the dolls she wants to play with have straight hair and light skin, and it does make me wonder, why don't you like those other dolls? We bought you some. Why don't you like them? Where are you getting that from?" Such worries are tied to the compelling and disturbing findings of Kenneth and Mamie Clark's famous doll study, recently re-created in the documentary *A Girl Like Me,* in which African American children exhibit a marked preference for white dolls over African American dolls.[112] There is, moreover, a great deal of research on the importance of media representation for children and a tradition in cultural critique of worrying about children.[113] This is absorbed, it seems, into lay theories about media effects on children and is demonstrated in my interviewees' comments.[114]

Although confident that representation was important to them on behalf of children, interviewees were hesitant to say that representation *should* matter to other (adult) people. Janet qualified her worry about her niece by describing her own position as potentially proscriptive:

I don't always think it's a bad thing. If you're going into a gaming environment as a bespectacled Asian dude and you want to play a gigantic blond Amazon, like, it's no skin off my ass. I don't think you should have to sit down with a therapist and fill in a form, like, whether it's okay for you to do that [*chuckles*]. Whether it's culturally acceptable. Whether this panel of experts says it's okay.

There is a pathologizing of cross-identity play in some discussions (academic and popular) that Janet called into question here. Certainly, we can be critical of the power and fetishizing involved in some "identity tourism," to quote Nakamura, but many of those critiques presume a particular privileged identity as a starting point.[115] Moreover, as Anya pointed out, to some extent the emphasis on representation may be a form of hegemonic discourse:

> People definitely say that [representation is] important. . . . I want to say part of it is political correctness. Like, it's supposed to be important, and society and media tells you that it's supposed to be important, so that's why people argue for it. But I don't know how many people really stop and think about whether it's important.

The very notion that media representation is important is tied to assumptions about social power. Nick Couldry has discussed this in terms of the "myth of the mediated center," the assumption that "'the media' has a privileged relationship to that 'centre,' as a highly centralized system of symbolic production whose 'natural' role is to represent or frame that 'centre.'"[116] The media is assumed to be the primary site through which we can make sense of social reality. This is in turn why people think that media representation signals or is the path to social equality. Media become the target for treatment, when they are only a symptom of social ails.

This focus on media derives from assumptions about media effects. As Gregory points out, however, in an excerpt that seems to cover vast swaths of social and communication theory, "Some people are influenced in so many different ways. . . . You learn from all different places. You can learn from friends; you can learn from reading a magazine. . . . You could have ten people play this game, and they all take something different from it." Here, we see incidental references to active audiences a la John Fiske, polysemy, and theories of personal influence.[117] The assumption that representation matters is rarely disentangled from why it matters. It matters, as some scholars suggest, if media help shape our world views.[118] As Gregory suggests, however, this is not a deterministic process.

Arguments for the importance of representation cannot ignore the active meaning-making process conducted by audiences, nor can they focus too specifically on the individual, marginalized audience member as the primary target for media representation.

Concluding Matters

Most research on audiences and media representation assumes representation's importance at the onset and then examines how members of specific groups understand representations of that group or members of an opposing identity group (e.g., one race versus another race, one gender versus another gender). In contrast, this book focuses on if and how people understand representation to be important. As it turns out, representation was not necessarily important to members of a marginalized group simply because they were members of marginalized groups. Contrary to popular and scholarly opinion, many of my interviewees did not consider a specific identifier (e.g., female, African American, bisexual) to be central to their senses of self. For those people, seeing that identifier represented was not important to them. Audiences are also attuned to the many shortcomings of representation, including tokenization. Some interviewees, furthermore, were fed up with media or simply did not think it was as important as often claimed.

Following from all of this, it is overly simplistic to say that people want to see people like them in their media. The market-logic argument for representation is simply wrong. Both texts and audiences are impossible to pin down in terms of singular meanings and specific identities. One might ask, then, if identities are complex and audiences are active, can we still talk about the importance of representation? I argue yes. The representation of a specific group present in a given text is not important in isolation. The way in which representation matters exists, like identity and identification, at the nexus of several factors, including individual players'/viewers' reasons for using a text, how individual players/viewers understand their identities, how and if a representation is made relevant in a given text, the context in which texts are consumed, and the social sphere in which those texts are created and consumed. The revelation that representation does not always matter frees us to focus on those times in which it does matter. I argue throughout this book that it is important media offer a diverse view of the world, not simply a pluralistic and targeted version of representation.

Regardless of whether my interviewees said it was important for them to see people "like them," they believed other people did think that representation was important. In some cases, interviewees described this as a third-person effect. They assumed that more-vulnerable people, like children or those who were marginalized, *needed* to see representations of people "like them." In other cases, however, while some individual interviewees did not feel a strong need for representation, they were aware that other people did— that is, if public discourse discussed representation as important, then perhaps it was just important to everyone else and not to them. Related to this, if an interviewee felt representation was important, they assumed others felt likewise. Generally, though, there was not much evidence that representation was central to how they chose their media.

Media makers and scholars, as stakeholders whose livelihoods center on these texts, care more about the importance of media representation than did my interviewees. Media producers believe their products are important and effective. How else would they make money with them? Similarly, media scholars, particularly those who research marginalized media, are often in the position of articulating the importance of their chosen topic by relating it to well-established discourses about the effects of representation. In Williams et al.'s "census" of characters in top-selling video games, for example, the authors emphasize a possible cultivation effect on video game players when viewing such a narrow representation of the world.[119] Martins et al. analyze female bodies presented in 150 top-selling games in relation to anthropometric data from a sample of 3,000 American women, noting discrepancies in relation to specific game genres and making connections, again, with cultivation analysis.[120] King and Krzywinska similarly emphasize the ideological implications of the lack of diversity in video games.[121] My interviewees were aware of and hinted at all of these arguments, but there were many qualifiers in their discussion of why representation mattered.

Overall, my interviewees' assertions about the importance of representation were tied to their assessments of the importance of realism in a given text. They judged representation as accurate and, in turn, good in terms of realism. Conversely, bad representation was largely considered unrealistic. Interviewees also dubbed representation as unimportant in texts they used for escapism or which they viewed as primarily fantasy. For some interviewees representation in video games did not matter, because the medium was primarily unrealistic. If scholars rely too heavily on the dichotomy between reality (truth) and fantasy (in which truth does not always matter), the argument for representation sows the seeds of its own dismissal. Researchers and activists must deal with the fact that for those who think that video games' main purpose is not to reflect reality, the argument that games are misrepresenting reality holds little value. Again, the paradox those dealing with issues of representation in fiction must face is arguing for the seriousness of fantasy without diminishing enjoyment of the fictional.

This book has two main arguments. First, emphasizing that specific marginalized groups *could, would,* or *do* play games in a demand for representation appeals to pluralistic niche marketing, whereas the political goals of media representation require diversity across the mediasphere. Second, media researchers' focus on the "real" in analyses of representation dominates how audiences (and researchers) talk about diversity in representation. Together, they demonstrate that future researchers must be more attentive to the way they present and argue for representation. In chapter 1, I discuss how appeals to peripheral player markets (e.g., the focus on girl players in research and marketing) do not make the gaming audience more diverse. In fact, those targeted as a "different kind" of player often see themselves as excluded from both the primary gamer market and the targeted niche market. Similarly, the marginalization of gaming leads people to be less invested in claiming gamer identity. In chapters 2 and 3, I describe the ways misconceptions about how players identify with video game characters and avatars allow for glossing over the different types of identification and interaction made available by these texts. Researchers should be more critical of the fact that the games in which identification *with* a character matters least are also the games in which the representation of marginal groups is often player created/chosen. This is an example of pluralism, not diversity. In addition, the fact that some people use these texts purely for fantasy challenges the assumption that people always want to identify as or with media characters or that representation is always important to them. Finally, in this chapter I illustrate that diversity across media is what makes representation matter. At the same time, people see representation as important to realism, though not necessarily when they use texts for escapist reasons. In the conclusion I explore the implications all of this has for how researchers, activists, and producers approach the politics of representation in video games.

Conclusion

A Future Free of Dickwolves

We are in the midst of the most important and influen-
tial movement in video games in a decade, if not ever—
movement that is vital to the ongoing cultural relevancy
and maturation of our medium—and almost everyone
involved in the conversation is, intentionally or otherwise,
looking for ways to ignore everyone else. We can do better
than this, and we have to, in order to make progress.

—Adam Saltsman, "We Have an Empathy Problem"

The danger in writing a book about contemporary media and emerging media forms, in particular, is that they change so rapidly. New controversies over representation of marginalized groups enter my various newsfeeds daily. In the time since I conducted the interviews for this project, increased academic and popular attention has turned toward the questions of diversity in game texts, audiences, and industries. Indeed, as the chapter epigraph from game developer Adam Saltsman indicates, we seem to be situated in a cultural moment in which how digital games are thought of and spoken about is constantly changing. In the following few examples, we can see shifts (slow as they may be) in how the game industry is addressing the representation of marginalized groups in their industry, audience, and texts. Still, as much as things change, the core of the problematic discourses described throughout this book, as demonstrated in the *Tropes vs. Women in Video Games* example, remain the same. In other words, it is premature to jump on the bandwagon of "it has gotten better in the game industry." Some things have gotten better, but others will not get better unless researchers, activists, and designers change the way they talk about why and how representation matters.

On March 7, 2013, I took an early-morning bus to New York City to attend the LGBT Full Spectrum miniconference at the Ford Foundation cosponsored by Electronic Arts (EA) and the Human Rights Campaign (HRC). One catalyst for the event was the massive criticism EA and game developer Bioware received when they attempted to introduce same-sex relationships into the MMORPG *Star Wars: The Old Republic* (*SWTOR*). Bioware, the company behind the *Mass Effect* and *Dragon Age* series of games, has a long history of including same-sex relationship options in their offline role-playing games. Such relationships were always optional, and as Bioware had made them available only in offline games, there was no threat that other players online might witness a given player's relationships. Unlike in their offline games, in an MMORPG they could not rely on the optionality of gay content to protect them from the ire of homophobic players—because the game is networked, players can see other players' relationships. Fan message boards were set "ablaze with the fury of those Star Wars fans who feel that homosexuality has no place in the fictitious universe, calling for a return to intergalactic family values, albeit ones which are happy to allow inter-species coupling, genocide and the ruthless pursuit of absolute power at any cost."[1] As part of what was presumably a compromise by developers, same-sex relationships in *SWTOR* were limited to a single planet in the online game universe (Makreb) and were made available only to those accessing the paid version of the game. These compromises were seen as segregating and isolating same-sex content by fans who wanted or even simply appreciated the existence of this option in the game as a whole. In EA's press release announcing the miniconference, they expressed feeling as though they were between a rock and a hard place: "Whether it has been taking a stand against DOMA, introducing same-gender romance in our games, or participating in Pride events in our communities it seems we've always been met with some opposition and hateful comments. It got us thinking here that it was time to bring people together to talk about these issues."[2] Although the target of much of the discussion was homophobic players, throughout the event it felt as though they did not know what LGBTQ activists wanted from them, either.

The EA/HRC miniconference was their response to the Makreb

controversy. The miniconference was invitation only, leading some designers and academics on Twitter to note the irony of having an exclusionary event to talk about issues of inclusion. As it turned out, the event was not so much closed as EA did not actually know whom the stakeholders in such a conference would be. I managed to get an invitation, for example, after a short conversation with the staff member behind the EA Full Spectrum Twitter handle. The miniconference was organized in a week, and little was communicated about what it would entail. When I arrived at the Ford Foundation lobby, I showed my invitation and photo ID to the organizing staff before being directed to the elevators and the eleventh-floor conference room. This policing added to my sense that they did not quite know the politics of the audiences they seemed to be hailing, as some members of queer communities have IDs that do not match their presented gender identity or chosen name, if they have state-issued ID at all, making photo identification a structural constraint to who can attend such events. Over the EA-provided continental breakfast, I connected with the only other academic I recognized at the conference. None of the attendees I was sitting with knew what to expect from the event, though we chuckled among ourselves at the heavy-handed use of rainbows and gay-signifier music being played as attendees trickled in. We shared a good laugh, for example, as "We Are Family" by Sister Sledge came on, as it's a song that was once ubiquitous in Pride events throughout the United States and is perhaps most famous to the U.S. mainstream as the closing drag number in the U.S. adaptation of *The Birdcage*. What followed was a series of two panels made up of current and former EA employees and HRC representatives and an interview with Baltimore Ravens linebacker Brendon Ayanbadejo, an LGBT-rights advocate.

Games journalist Leigh Alexander pointed out that the miniconference felt "like a start."[3] Yet the event seemed like a public conversation among EA employees themselves much more than an actual conversation with attendees. Having spent many years studying, thinking, and teaching about queer media representations and games, I spent most of the event with a furrowed brow: not always angry but torn between feelings of "progress" and frustration that even as things change, things tend to stay the same. In 2007 I started conducting research on gay gamers.[4] Having gotten a sense of the audience side of the LGBT in-game representation question,

I decided to tackle the industry side.[5] I compiled a list of all the games I could find that had gay characters, queer themes, same-sex or same-gender relationship options, or gender-bending (fifty-six in all). I then emailed all of the publishers and developers still in operation. Most never responded. EA did respond to my email, nicely even, but told me they had no one available to speak to me due to a heavy production schedule. I ultimately used back channels, forums, and snowballing to obtain interviews for that project. Knowing from my research on LGBT representation in other media that activist groups played a huge role in portrayals of marginalized groups, I also emailed GLAAD to see what their take was. GLAAD responded that they just did not have the time or the resources to address video games proactively. They would respond to controversies as they arose, but they did not actively pursue digital games directly.

Given how hard it was to find anyone to talk to about gay content in games in 2007 and that a major mainstream LGBT organization saw games as peripheral to their interests, the 2013 EA/HRC event demonstrated a big shift in who could and would have these conversations. That EA was willing to issue invitations to me and to fellow researchers, activists, and designers for their exclusive conference was a nice change. Further, the fact that HRC and the Ford Foundation cosponsored the event indicated that mainstream political organizations saw games as mattering in a way that they had not five years ago. Of course, using HRC to signify a connection to gay politics demonstrated the corporation's very white, wealthy, cis-gendered, and homonormative conception of LGBT issues.[6] I was disappointed, moreover, that most of the problematic arguments I heard in 2007 still dominated the conversation at this industry event.

First among these was that LGBT representation was distinct from representations of race, gender, class, age, and other axes of difference. Panelists said things like, "Women have come so far" and "racial minorities have come so far" that we can now address "gay issues." Clearly, this presumed that women and racial minorities were somehow never a part of "gay issues," which of course implied that all gay people were white men and all women and people of color were straight. The statements about representation by EA and HRC representatives also presumed a static notion of how LGBT characters could and should be represented. This was inevitably exclusionary. Speakers cited the LGBT umbrella in a way that assumed transgender and bisexual politics had an easy relationship to mainstream (white, cisgendered, wealthy, male) gay politics. Indeed, that same-sex relationships were almost always cited as an example of how the industry had tried to be inclusive indicated that trans politics were not even on its radar.

Second, throughout the event there was an assumption that the video game industry could include representations of diversity only "when it mattered." This sort of discourse further marginalizes already marginalized groups. These industry employees seemed to think that diversity mattered only when marginalized players said it did. EA played a video of scenes from *The Sims*, *Dragon Age 2*, and *Mass Effect* to highlight their attempts to address issues of sexuality in games. All of these clips (and the games in their entireties) addressed sexuality solely through making same-sex relationships an option. I would argue, however, that sexuality is present and relevant in every single video game made, regardless of the sexual identities or relationships (or lack thereof) of the characters. For example, sexuality and sexual politics are present in every first-person shooter that employs sexual banter or "bro" humor (e.g., when game protagonist Duke Nukem hands money to strippers and asks them to "shake it, baby"). Similarly, the glimmers of backstory in *Left 4 Dead* are enough to provide a basic understanding of characters' lives and sexual identities. Both of these could be sites for intervention if game designers actually wanted to create sexual diversity in games. Sexuality and gender identity can be explored in all games, not just in role-playing games. Moreover, if there truly are places where representation "doesn't matter," then why not include marginalized groups more often? If the game's storyline and mechanics would work regardless of the character body on display, why not make that body Arab American, bisexual, genderqueer, femme, and/or disabled? Is it even true that the storyline and mechanics would not work were the protagonist different from the initial design? I want to be clear: this is not a demand that designers make a game specifically for and about a marginalized group (indeed, that is part of the problem). Rather, I am challenging designers to be cognizant of their own default choices (i.e., male, while, heterosexual) and task themselves to think outside those norms. Surely, such creative people can come up with something better. The comic book industry has worked hard to do this, with varying degrees of success, and in an arguably authentic way that game industry representatives often claim is difficult for them.[7] There is a history of this in-game diversity, in fact. If we go back to *The Sims*, the original introduction of gay relationship options was simply done by openly gay engineer Patrick J. Barrett III and allowed to stay in by the powers that be. According to David "Rez" Graham, no one questioned the new content largely because "they didn't think *The Sims* was going to do well at all."[8] What I think my audience research shows is that it might be worth risking such content in games that producers have faith in, as well. There are many examples of the integration of queer content, mechanics, and design into games on the part of indie game designers like Anna Anthropy, Robert Yang, Merrit Kopas, Mattie Brice, Liz Ryerson, Porepentine, Christine Love, Deirdra "Squinky" Kiai, and Zoe Quinn, to name but a few of an ever-growing list. Todd Harper/MIT's *A Closed World* project is yet another example and comes from the academic realm.[9] Moreover, the critically acclaimed *Gone Home* by the Fulbright Company, an indie game company founded by designers who previously worked on AAA games like *Bioshock 2*, demonstrates that one can create a game that according to scholar and games critic Samantha Allen, "closes the gap between queer and mainstream games."[10] Clearly, there are widely available models already in existence that game industry employees could learn from if they tried. If the industry wants to rethink representation, it should start by looking at work by people who already have.

Third, while targeting "the LGBT market" (a problematic construction itself) may seem easier by including same-sex relationship options in games that already have big audiences like *Sims, Fable, Mass Effect*, and *Dragon Age*, optional content does not address the social goals of representation. Luis A. Ubinas, president of the Ford Foundation, began the miniconference by making links between the popularity of the NBC television show *Will and Grace* and changing public opinion about gay marriage. Aside from the deeply troubling heralding of *Will and Grace* and the HRC-led campaign for gay marriage (both of which largely reflect and disproportionately serve the interests of white, wealthy, gay men), it is worth pointing out that optional representation will never be the *Will and Grace* of gaming.

If the video game industry is concerned about hate speech in online gaming, which dominated much of the conference discussion, inserting representation into games in a way that is integral to the game text is one avenue for change for which I think they should be held accountable.

The EA/HRC miniconference was but one recent event in which industry employees and corporations have begun to engage questions of representation and queerness that scholars, independent game designers, activists, and players have been wrestling with for decades. And as the EA/HRC event demonstrates, these industry attempts are uneven, sometimes feeling like one step forward and three steps back. We can see similar trends in the 2013 Game Developers Conference. Many attendees noted that questions of representation were central to the annual event's discussions.[11] During a panel Microsoft Studios narrative designer Tom Abernathy stated, "Women are the new core."[12] He also said, "There is no good justification for not featuring more nonwhite or female protagonists," as "morally it's 'the right thing to do.'"[13] The #1Reasonwhy and #1ReasonToBe panels at the conference featured a broad cross-section of women involved in the game industry and gave them space to discuss the hostility they experienced on a regular basis in the workplace and in gaming culture broadly.[14] Independent game development was highlighted at the event, with several designers earning top awards for boundary-challenging games.[15] In many ways, this event seemed a vast improvement on EA/HRC's, as it raised important questions of power, privilege, and violence that subtend any discussion of representation.

At that same conference, however, the International Game Developers Association threw a party featuring scantily clad female dancers. This conference party resulted in many people threatening to leave IGDA and in cochair of the Women in Games special interest group, Brenda Romero, resigning her office in protest.[16] While IGDA has argued that the event and the casting of said women were largely the doing of corporate cosponsor YetiZen, a social and mobile funding company, journalist Carol Pinchefsky still argues, "It makes IGDA look more like a frat house than the voice of an industry."[17] This type of event is not unique to IGDA, however. During the Penny Arcade Expo, a general gaming fan conference, Irrational Games creative director Ken Levine told a female audience member to accept that games needed to make money. According to Levine, instead of questioning the absence of the lead female character on the cover of the new game *Bioshock: Infinite,* she should just "play the fucking game."[18] He, like IGDA, later apologized. At PAX Prime in September 2013, the artist for the *Penny Arcade* webcomic, Mike Krahulic, said he thought it was a mistake that the site removed merchandise referencing the "dickwolves" controversy.[19] This controversy began when rape was used in a punch line in one of the series' comic strips. Feminists and antirape activists criticized the strip and were met with sarcastic responses from the strip's artists and rape threats from online commenters. *Penny Arcade* began selling "Penny Arcade Dickwolves" merchandise two months after the initial controversy, though after a great deal of protest the merchandise was removed from the site's store. Although Krahulic has since apologized for causing a controversy, his regret at the company's choice and continued defense of the "joke" demonstrate that he and his supporters fail to understand (or care) about what is at stake in representation.

At the 2014 Game Developers Conference, Manveer Heir, a Bioware Montréal game designer, gave a widely praised speech decrying the industry's overreliance on stereotypes. In his talk he discussed much of the research cited in this book about the under- and misrepresentation of marginalized groups in games. He critiqued the deployment of realism in discussions of representation and pushed for diversity in all forms of games. He ended by saying, "I want us, as an industry, to stop being so scared. . . . If we make them I am confident that the audience will come and accept them."[20] This was undoubtedly a powerful moment, perhaps even a turning point in the games industry, though it was not the first time Heir had pushed the industry to be more inclusive.[21] His conclusion is also quite similar to my own, though much of his argument rests on logics problematized throughout this book and overemphasizes the effects of negative stereotypes. Hopefully, the work presented in this book can push this conversation forward even further. It is worth noting that the coverage of his speech was clearly frustrating for the many women, in particular, who had been making similar pronouncements about game content for decades only to be dismissed or, even worse, threatened. In some ways my own response to Heir's speech is informed by comic artist Alison Bechdel's reaction to the use of the Bechdel Test as a rating system by a chain of Swedish movie theaters.[22] Bechdel has long felt ambivalent about having the test named after her because, as the strip itself acknowledges, it came from her friend Liz Wallace, who in turn probably adapted it from Virgina Woolf's *A Room of One's Own*.[23] The renewed interest is frustrating because what it really demonstrates is how long it has taken mainstream discourse about representation to acknowledge what has been so obvious to so many of us for so long. She writes, "I'm glad mainstream culture is starting to catch up to where lesbian-feminism was 30 years ago. But I just can't seem to rise to the occasion of talking about this fundamental principle over and over again, as if it's somehow new, or open to debate."[24] More and more game industry representatives are paying attention to diversity, but if it is always discussed as a new thing to be attentive to, I fear it will obscure the work many people have been doing in and around representation in digital games in the decades since they were first created. Instead, I think we can use this moment of attention to have a conversation about how we address representation.

Nice When It Happens

These examples of game industry events demonstrate a large disconnect between how industry employees and corporate models understand representation and how audiences do. The EA/HRC event in particular seemed premised on the assumption that representation of marginalized groups, in this case gay people, was of vital importance to media audiences and would determine whether audiences chose to engage with those media forms at all. As this book demonstrates, however, this is not the case. When asked if seeing people who looked like them or were similar to them in some way was important, most of my interviewees were actually indifferent or at least offered qualified responses. When I asked Carol if seeing people like her in video games was important, she said that it was a nice surprise but not expected:

> Nice when it happens. I never really expect to, at least not in video games. I mean, I expect to more with movies and TV because it feels more possible. I guess because I grew up during the dawn of the video game era and it wasn't until more recently that the

demographics of video gamers expanded and the types of games exploded, so my perspective is, oh, any character in a game being like me is not really a possibility. So I didn't really come to expect it. But it's a pleasant surprise when it happens.

Carol was conscious of how she had or had not been constructed as the intended target for games, and this influenced her expectations of representation. Most interviewees responded similarly to the question of whether identifying with characters in media texts was important to them.

Representation was "nice when it happened" and it was a "bonus," but my interviewees did not always have an active desire for it. They expressed a similar indifference about having characters to identify with in video games and other media. This was true regardless of whether interviewees thought that representation and identification were important. That is, people who thought representation was unimportant still said it was nice, and those who said it was important said likewise:

DEVON: I really like the *Fable* games, and I think it's great that you could play the character as a gay character, but that's just like *a bonus*. It's not like I got the game in this case because that's what it was.

TANNER: I think it is probably *nice to see*, but I don't think I seek it out.

CODY: I think it is *nice to see* people who look like you. But I don't know if it's a requirement.[25]

Many interviewees described the character-creation tools in games like *Rock Band* as a bonus. This "niceness" was articulated in three senses, in many cases simultaneously: (1) that media enjoyment was not inherently about identification; (2) that they appreciated diversity in a broad sense; and (3) that there was pleasure in the unexpected surprise of feeling hailed by a text. I suggest that thus far the power of market logic has been used to discipline this pleasure (in the Foucauldian sense). Media studies scholars should be more attentive to the ways that producers' attempts to define and appeal to particular kinds of pleasure ensnare it in systems of power.

First, people can enjoy media that does not include people "like them." Renee said, for example, "It's cool when it happens, but I don't seek out media or anything that does it." In part this is due to the fact that audiences are active and can "make do" with what texts provide them.[26] As explored in chapter 3, players can interact with video games in a variety of ways that may or may not necessitate identifying with avatars. Identification is not the only pleasure gained from media texts. Audiences have ways of connecting with media characters that are much more expansive than those for which research that focuses on specific identifiers accounts. Indeed, as Rusty described, individuals can identify themselves in ways marketers and researchers rarely think of: "I guess when you come down to it, identification, I don't identify with myself personally but more the things I belong to in real life: my family with Tanner, with our neighborhood, our house and how we belong to the community of this neighborhood." These types of identity/identification cannot necessarily be cultivated through representation. Representation is, likewise, not integral to enjoying all texts. Ephram said, "I guess it would be nice to see an Asian character or gay character that isn't a flaming homosexual or a huge stereotype of what an Asian person should be. . . . But again, it's nice when it happens, but I'm not too hung up on it." As described in chapter 4, the importance of representation is relative to the importance of realism in a given text, whether people identify as a member of the group represented, the function of the representation in a text, and the context in which they use a text.

Second, my interviewees valued diversity in a broad sense. As Carol put it, "It's always great to see things become less narrow-minded and a greater group of people acceptable." She noted, for example, that following their enjoyment of *Will and Grace,* her own parents seemed less overtly homophobic than they used to be. In some cases when people said that it was not important to see people "like them," it was because they wanted diversity in a more general sense in their media. Pouncy said:

I'd love to see more queers in science fiction, video games. I'd love to see more people who aren't male identified . . . but I'm not sure if that's because I would be able to identify with them more personally or just because I would be happy to see these institutions, video

games, and movies and TV shows branching out away from representing white dudes.

It was diversity, not representation of one's identifiers, that interviewees' described as nice. This was because they did not enjoy only
media that reflected their identities. Anya discussed this in terms of
representation following our discussion of identification:

> I think it's nice to see someone who's like you, but I don't think I have
> to see only people who are like me. Like I don't, the whole movie or
> the whole TV program doesn't have to be about a white woman in
> their late twenties. I think I can appreciate stuff about male versus
> female, old versus young, race-wise, and stuff like that. So, it's kind
> of like the previous question that you asked [about identification]. It's
> nice, but it's not something I look for. It's not super, super important.

Identification was, like representation, a pleasurable surprise but
not a driving factor in her media consumption. If diversity for the
sake of diversity is nice rather than imperative, then what might
this mean for how researchers and producers approach the issue of
representation?

Third, "nice" expressed pleasant surprise. Many of my interviewees did not expect to see themselves in media. As Sasha expressed,
"I've just become accustomed to not even caring or, like, thinking
about my preference, because I just automatically assume I don't
have any." Carol made a similar comment:

> But I don't consciously think when I'm watching TV, "There's nothing
> like me up there, and that makes me upset." . . . When something
> comes along that breaks that, I'm always very, very happy and
> encouraged. So it's important to some degree. I'll certainly tune
> out of the things that don't meet my expectations.

Previous research has argued that feeling excluded might cause marginalized audiences to not consume or to reject parts of particular
texts.[27] This book demonstrates, though, that such audiences might
also find ways of ignoring or engaging with a text differently. Evan,
who was earning a degree in gender and society studies at the time,
pointed out that just being aware of interlocking systems of oppres-

sion did not mean that he would stop watching offensive shows: "I might just watch it to see where this is going. But I don't know that it would make me stop doing that." Audiences can also find pleasure in media despite poor representation. In her study of *EverQuest*, T. L. Taylor finds that "women in *EQ* often struggle with conflicting meanings around their avatars, feeling they have to 'bracket' or ignore how they look. . . . In many ways, women play *despite* the game."[28] Players are capable, moreover, of a variety of interactions with characters and avatars, in terms of both identification and the activity of playing video games.

The trouble in talking about the pleasures in feeling represented or in playing despite not feeling represented is that pleasure is in many ways ephemeral. When we attempt to define what it is, we fix it in a way that belies embodied experience. Thus, when making games that appeal to particular submarkets of players, the industry overdefines membership in those groups as attached to certain desires. Similarly, when representation is reduced to character/avatar aesthetics, it cannot actually encompass the experience of inhabiting the world with a specific identity. As Foucault describes in *The History of Sexuality*, "So many pressing questions singularized the pleasures felt by the one who had to reply. They were fixed by a gaze, isolated and animated by the attention they received."[29] As pleasures are named, they are also created. Much of how we talk about the represented has helped define what audiences expect of representation. The pleasure of representation in games, as well as other media, has thus far been regulated through targeted marketing efforts and individualized content. Returning to Foucault, however, we see that pleasure can also disrupt or reject power. Referencing sexual pleasure, he writes, "Where sex and pleasure are concerned, power can 'do' nothing but say no to them."[30] That is not to say that pleasure exists outside power or in opposition to it. Rather, power is pleasure, and pleasure is power. There is a political agency in saying that representation is "nice when it happens" that acknowledges the pleasure of representation without succumbing to industry demands to make those pleasures definable and immutable.

"Nice when it happens" demonstrates a seeming ambivalence about representation, but such ambivalence can be explained in two different ways. First, in the contemporary media environment, audiences have access to relatively more diversity than was present in previous decades. Second, people often view video games as relatively trivial and, thus, in-game representation as inconsequential. What "nice when it happens" indicates is that individuals push back against the attempt to locate responsibility for representation in the audience. Market logic and the targeting it inspires place the impetus for representation on consumer demand. So too do character selection and creation tools. I have been arguing throughout this book that both emphasize pluralism, not diversity. Interviewees, because they did not personally need to see themselves constantly reflected in the media, rejected that responsibility of being the locus of demand. Instead, they argued that producers should imbue their texts with organic, realistic (i.e., not tokenistic) diversity. Realism need not, however, be the only lens we use to make sense of when and why representation matters in media.

Despite claims that representation matters only to realism, several interviewees discussed the fact that as texts that often rely upon fantasy, games are particularly suited to representing more diverse versions of the world. That is, the medium itself relies upon play and, in turn, can play with what reality means. Caine connected this to representation in science fiction:

> I would say, even in a setting where it's far future, aliens everywhere, in the best of media you've still seen efforts to try and present a more diverse perspective. I'm reminded of the original *Star Trek*, where Gene Roddenberry said, "No, we're going to have a black lady as a member of the bridge crew." Now point out that, even though he said that, poor Uhura didn't really get that much to do. But even still, it was so significant a step that at one point the actress who played Uhura, Nichelle Nichols, was considering leaving the show. She actually got—Martin Luther King Jr. said to her, "No. You can't do that, because you're presenting such a positive role model for black people everywhere."

What Caine points out here is that even in fantasy realms, like video games and science-fiction shows, the representation of marginalized groups is important to audiences. Why it matters is an important question that is rarely addressed in media analyses. Nichols's autobiographical account reveals an even more important detail about Dr. Martin Luther King Jr.'s insistence. According to Nichols, he said:

This is not a Black role, and this is not a female role. You have the first non-stereotypical role on television, male or female. You have broken ground. . . . Don't you see that you're not just a role model for little Black children? You're more important for people who *don't* look like us. . . . There will always be role models for Black children; you are a role model for everyone.[31]

This is the more expansive understanding of the importance of representation that this book is advocating. Fantasy and fiction allow us to imagine different worlds. Media representations are possible realities made material. Characters who are members of marginalized groups cannot be treated simply as lessons to out-group members or examples to in-group members. Their existence in media texts allow for more ways of being in the world, for all audiences.

Everyone, not just niche markets, must see diverse representations if they are to be politically and educationally valuable. My evidence suggests, moreover, that a focus on specific identifiers need not be the only way we think of representation. Critical identity theory can empower researchers, activists, and media makers alike to argue for diversity in representation in a way that does not focus on segmented identities. Media representation arguments can, in the words of Paul Gilroy, "build upon the contributions of cultural studies to dispose of the idea that identity is an absolute and to find the courage necessary to argue that identity formation—even body-coded ethnic and gender identity—is a chaotic process that can have no end."[32] I assert that researchers must be more conscious of the way they conceptualize the politics of representation. How we represent the importance of media representation is as important as media representation itself.

The goal of video game representation studies and, perhaps, media representation studies more generally should be to break away from this reification of groups that reemphasizes their marginalization. Marlon Riggs describes this in terms of the interactions of race and sexuality: "Our greatest challenge rests in finding a language, a way of communicating across our subjectivities, across difference, a way of negotiating the political and cultural borders between and within us so that we do not replicate the chauvinism and the reductive political agendas of the past."[33] A more nuanced understanding of identity, identification, and media representation lays the foundation

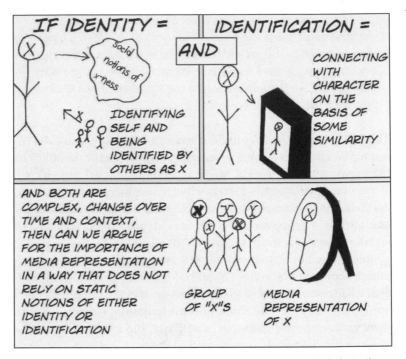

Figure 20. Author's comic, "Identity, Identification, and Representation," illustrating the connections between theories of identity and identification and arguments for media representation.

for understanding when and why media representation is important and what diverse representation might entail (Figure 20).

Some interviewees argued that producers must simultaneously recognize but not call attention to the diversity of experiences attached to inhabiting particular marked categories. The act of marking specific marginalized audiences through targeting shapes the relationships people hailed by such targeting have with video games. The video game industry cannot simply assume that all players are alike, but neither can they assume that identifiers like gender, race, and sexuality are differences that make a difference to how people play video games. Gender, sexuality, and race are inflected in but do not predetermine play preferences. Similarly, identifiers can provide one form of connection between players and characters, but that does not mean that those identifiers encompass the many other ways (e.g., emotional, experiential) people identify with fictional characters.

Interviewees were critical of representation that was used only to emphasize a group's difference to the assumed white, male, heterosexual norm, particularly if such representation downplayed the struggles involved in deviating from the norm. For these reasons, perhaps, interviewees in this and my past research did not necessarily demand representation. The act of demanding the representation of a group raises concerns about how that group should and will be portrayed. Rather, its importance was often seen as "nice when it happened," an articulation that expresses the importance of representation without developing proscriptive rules. It also reflects the emotional connection people have with media representation, for which the cold, hard logic of the market cannot account. "Nice when it happens" promotes diversity but rejects being the target of pluralism.

"Nice" may indicate a defense mechanism against constant marginalization. It may be a symptom of something akin to the "racial paranoia" John L. Jackson Jr. describes:

> The point isn't that race is less important now than it was before. It's just more schizophrenic, more paradoxical. We continue to commit to its social significance on many levels, but we seem to disavow that commitment at one and the same time. Race is real, but it isn't. It has value, but it doesn't. It explains social difference, but it couldn't possibly.[34]

The same might be said of gender and sexuality. "Nice" may be the result of hegemonic discourses, in the Gramscian sense, the result of power dynamics that leave audiences feeling powerless.[35] When market logic places the demand for representation in the hands of audiences, the audiences have that power only if cultural industries deem them valuable markets. Even in a medium like video games, which leaves a great deal of representational power (at least in certain texts) to the audience, researchers must consider that players must work within predefined norms. Moreover, the emphasis on player-created content allows for the illusion of diversity in game texts. Many of these games capitalize on pluralism without making the games diverse in a way that would actually matter in a socio-political sense. Anyone can play *The Sims* and create same-sex pairings, but not everyone who plays the game will be confronted with queer content.

As demonstrated throughout this book, we should be asking not whether people generally think representation is important but rather how the distinction between realism and fiction, between seriousness and play, forms the biggest divide between those who see diversity in media as a necessary goal and those who see it as relatively trivial. I argue that the way minority representation has been made to matter—through marketing and assumptions about audiences' interactions with texts—promotes pluralism in the sense that groups are represented only if they are targeted as a market. The defense of representation on the basis of marginalized groups' need to see people "like them" leads to niche marketing (pluralism). In contrast, diversity in video games should be promoted as valuable unto itself. This is feasible, in part, because players' relationships with in-game characters are complex and, in part, because interviewees stressed that they did not need to see only people like them in their media. Researchers should question the assumption that diversity requires a defense in the first place. Marginalized audiences are often called upon to demand representation, but media producers are not pressed to see diversity as an integral part of their products rather than a feature included only if the case for such inclusion can be made. In other words, we need to stop letting media producers off the hook, including game developers and game corporations. It is not the job of marginalized audiences to hold their hands. If media producers want to create culturally relevant and important media texts, they need to take the initiative, learn about cultural difference, and design texts that reflect it.

Where Do We Go from Here?

This need to simultaneously recognize difference without codifying it is a fundamental paradox of the politics of representation, as described by Julie D'Acci.[36] D'Acci asserts that studying the representation of "identity" in media, specifically gender in her example, puts researchers in a thorny position. On the one hand, we must interrogate how identities are produced through popular media and celebrate nontraditional representations of marginal identity groups. "But on the other hand, we face the importance of not replicating (even inadvertently) the gender binary while we demonstrate its cultural construction."[37] She goes on to say that researchers must not ignore the importance of identities and how they are created through and influence social interactions and media consumption. Thus, "We face the importance of recognizing the need for groups forged within the terms of the binary's inequalities . . . at the same time as we try to break the binary apart."[38] Even as studies of representation critique media portrayals of marginalized groups, they often reify, in some ways, the identity categories they interrogate. How the importance of representation is represented matters for the same political reasons authors have long argued representation matters.

In concluding, I offer two final suggestions. The first is practical. Rather than argue that video games should include more diversity because it matters, producers should include it precisely because representation *does not* matter to players in many games. This argument can contribute to the analysis and production of other media, as well. The second is paradoxical. The goal of those invested in diversity in games should not be to prove the importance of representation but rather to argue for the importance of representation in a way that does not dismiss the playfulness of gaming. This is not just a critique of representation in games but of how media researchers argue for representation in the contemporary media era.

Diversity without Defense

People cannot be appealed to only through specific identifiers, as the market-logic argument often implies. Similarly, the focus on specific identifiers in research on representation is not useful. Representation can become important in terms of these identifiers, but they are not the only ways people think about themselves, and thus, that focus is unnecessarily reductive. There is something problematic, moreover, in the way researchers argue for diversity. The act of defending diversity—by targeting specific kinds of players, for example—makes it exceptional rather than normative.

Chantal Mouffe says that "to construct a 'we' it is necessary to distinguish it from a 'them.'"[39] This is why both research and market approaches to diversity in video games have tended toward a pro-motion of pluralism rather than diversity. Focusing on who texts are of, by, and for tends to rely on a narrow view of "who" that results in an oversimplification of identity and its relationship to identification and media representation. Although it seems self-evident and useful to tie individual producers' or audience members' identities to the identities of media characters, this often results in a severe over-simplification of how individuals connect with media characters. My interviewees maintained that their identities were not reducible to simple identifiers. Christine synthesized this point:

> In terms of having a certain amount of black people, a certain amount of Asian people—I think it's important, but that's not the only aspect people should focus on. Those are really broad categories of humanity, and it really has to get much deeper than someone's race, someone's sex. Like, not all black people are the same, not all women are the same, not all black women are even the same. So I think they need to sort of look at personality traits, as well, and various other things that are much deeper than just skin color and even, like, the amount of money you have. Those are just too broad, I feel.

I argue that researchers and, indeed, anyone interested in encour-aging diversity in video games and other media texts must look at the power dynamics that are inflected in arguments about media representation. One of these dynamics is the emphasis on audience demand for representation. Another is the sense that diversity, not a lack of diversity, needs defense.

There is a wealth of literature that argues that diversity in media is politically and ethically important and should be demanded.[40] Such political and ethical demands do not sway corporations as much as financial arguments do (e.g., niche markets). Tying to-gether both positions, this book offers a compromise of sorts. We can think about representation's importance as "nice" rather than imperative. This presents an argument for the importance of repre-sentation that does not rely on effects or emphasize the representa-tion of specific groups. Rather, researchers can argue for diversity in media in a manner that takes into account the complexity of multi-faceted identities.

Granted, we cannot only look to the commercial sphere for equal-ity, much less liberation. At the same time, we cannot simply argue for the importance of media representation of marginalized groups without an eye toward commercial concerns. Inclinations toward diversity in media, whether political or artistic, are tempered by the demands of capitalistic enterprise. The possibility for represen-tation of women, people of color, queers, and transgender people in video games has been consistently tied to marketing concerns. To take a political stance as a scholar and argue for the importance of representation does not necessarily mean eschewing these commer-cial concerns. Likewise, arguing against and within a market-logic framework does not imply a bowing to the dominance of neoliberal capitalism in this current historical moment. Indeed, the market logic, whether promoting or preventing representation of marginal-ized groups, is not inherently at odds with more idealistic arguments for the importance of diversity in media. The insight this book offers is that idealism and pragmatism can be intertwined. Charles Tay-lor asks of recognition, "Perhaps we don't need to ask whether it's something that others can demand from us as a right. We might sim-ply ask whether this is the way we ought to approach others."[41] This is the question video game makers should ask themselves as they create texts—not questions of whom they should represent and how but more critically why they have represented whom they have and why they have ignored others. Additionally, I think there is plenty of evidence to suggest that there *could be* a paying market for indie game designers, though many have struggled to sell their work. It is dangerous to producers who are members of marginalized groups for scholars and critics to continually stress that nuanced, progres-sive representation is not financially viable. If that were the case, why would anyone invest in them?

In the conclusion of *Making Things Perfectly Queer*, Alexander Doty argues, "By publicly articulating our queer positions in and about mass culture, we reveal that capitalist cultural production need not exclusively and inevitably express straightness."[42] Queer-ness has been embedded in U.S. popular culture as long as there has been U.S. popular culture. Similarly, representation of margin-alized groups can be used to target mainstream markets. There are some telling examples of this in other media, specifically when it comes to the representation of sexuality. Ron Becker argues that the rise of gay content in 1990s television was done to target liberal, upper-middle-class heterosexuals.[43] *Yaoi* slash fiction, representations of gay male sexuality produced for the consumption of heterosexual teenage girls in Japan, is a somewhat similar example.[44] The representation of lesbian sexuality for the male gaze is another, exploitative example.[45] The edited volume *Everything but the Burden* analyzes a similar reappropriation of black culture by whites, a reappropriation that forms the basis of David Leonard's critiques of African American portrayals in video games.[46] These are certainly problematic examples, nor are they exemplars for what minority representation in games should look like. They do offer evidence, however, that belies claims that these groups can be represented only when they are the target market. The true claim is that industries attempt to represent groups *well* only when they are the target market. What Doty explains is that regardless of how texts are targeted to constructed audiences, people make do with the texts they are given. I argue we can more forcefully insist that the "mainstream" can (and already knows how to) "make do" with images of those different from them.

Some might argue that what I call for here amounts to dismantling the master's house with the master's tools. Those people would be calling upon Audre Lorde's oft-quoted castigation of second-wave feminism. In her famous essay, Lorde calls on white feminists to learn "how to take our differences and make them strengths. *For the master's tools will never dismantle the master's house.*"[47] What she discusses goes beyond the way the analogy is often used, however. She argues that oppressed groups are often called upon to educate their oppressors, further entrenching the oppressive hierarchy of labor. To assert that the marginalized must demand that the center acknowledge them is a displacement of responsibility. That displacement is the very core of the market-logic argument for representation. It is also the logic behind games that offer players the option to create their own avatars instead of integrating diversity into texts. Rather than call upon groups to demand representation or display their need to be heard, researchers, activists, and interested producers can argue that the impetus is on everyone to acknowledge and celebrate difference. Market logic is more precisely the master's tools, which "may allow us to temporarily beat him at his own game, but they will never enable us to bring about genuine change."[48] I concede that arguing representation can be included in video games because it does not matter and, thus, will not offend nonmarginalized audiences is in some ways a compromise. It is a compromise, however, that reimagines the "tools" in a way that might foster change.

According to my interviewees, if you do not always see yourself reflected in media, it is nice in the moments you do. Related to this, game designers often argue that their inability to develop rich descriptions of characters results in the lack of portrayals of marginalized groups.[49] That is to say exposition is necessary to explain the nonhegemonic (the homosexual, the African American, the female, etc.). "Others" must always be explained or must always explain themselves in ways that privileged subjects never have to. The rationale for including nondominant identities in media texts typically assumes that it must matter to the text or to marketing. This obscures the tacit market logic that goes into using heterosexual, white, and male as the default identity categories in these games. In response to the claim that nonhegemonic groups should be represented only when it matters, Caine pointed out, "If it doesn't matter, then how come all the protagonists wind up being white?" Individual audience members' interactions with texts are complex and not determined by specific identifiers, and thus, the reliance on a construction of specific markets to argue for media representation is unnecessary. T. L. Taylor makes a similar argument:

> If designers would rise to the challenge presented by a sociology of the body and a more complicated understanding (and rendering) of gender, the possibilities for evocative and immersive environments might begin to truly draw in a diverse gaming population and legitimize those already playing.[50]

Some evidence exists that this can be effective. For her master's thesis, Shaylyn Hamm designed female versions of two character classes, a Medic and a Heavy, for the Valve game *Team Fortress 2*.[51] She designed both female characters beyond the scantily clad, lithe female video game hero and aimed to have them maintain some level of similarity with their male counterparts.[52] Interestingly, returning to the previously discussed issue of realism versus fantasy in representation, she modeled one of the female fighters on images of World War II female Soviet snipers. The criticisms she received from respondents asked that the women have more realistic female shapes (e.g., curved hips, more realistic arms). After the design process, she fielded a survey asking video game players to assess the two characters. She found the following:

> The characters I created have body types, features, and ages that do not follow the ideal of what is typically marketed in the video game industry, yet they were well received by the majority of people who have reviewed them. My feedback also suggests that there is a desire among many gamers to see more varied female characters in games, and perhaps when more of such characters are introduced into mainstream games, the perception and role of females may become less limited.[53]

Though she made a relatively small study of a convenience sample, the fact that both male and female video game players responded well to these atypical representations of female characters is promising. It suggests that arguments for the importance of representation do not have to rely on the marketing of texts to marginalized groups.

Moreover, relying on the construction of particular kinds of audiences means that the only members of marginalized groups who are represented are those in the position to be "good" consumers. If Gregory were to say that it was important to see himself, for example, then that would be of interest only to those marketers who wished to target him as a consumer. As he was at the time of the interview an unemployed, gay, African American male in his early thirties who lived with his mother, he was unlikely to be a target market for many game makers, let alone other media industries. Rather, what I call for is a reflexive approach to production. As Gilroy describes, "We need to consider whether the scale upon which sameness and difference are calculated might be altered productively so that the strangeness of strangers goes out of focus and other dimensions of basic sameness can be acknowledged and made significant."[54] Market logic makes a social and political argument personal, as it stresses an appeal to individual consumers via an appeal to "groupness." The emphasis on consumer choice obscures the social and political importance of representation. In contrast, "nice when it happens" makes a personal argument into a social one. It admits the personal benefits of representation without accepting the responsibility for demanding representation. Rather, it insists that diversity is the social responsibility of cultural producers, not consumers.

Pluralism gives players the option of seeing marginalized groups represented only if a player so chooses, and therefore, it cannot fulfill the socially progressive goals of media representation. Diversity in video games necessitates that all audiences are confronted with different types of characters. Diversity is not the result of demand by audiences but the social responsibility of media producers. It requires that marginalized groups are represented not only because they are a profitable segment or because in a given text their representation matters but because the assumed normative categories of male, white, and heterosexual do not need to be viewed as defaults when a case for the representation of marginalized groups cannot be made. Media producers can take advantage of the fact that identities are complex, that identification does not require shared identifiers (particularly in video games), and that diversity in a nontokenistic sense can appeal to a much wider audience than pluralistic, niche marketing. In sum, diversity can address both the market-logic and the educative goals of media representation. While pluralism further differentiates between norm and other, diversity promotes difference without fetishizing it.

Just a Game?

Interviewees' assertions that diverse representation is nice rather than imperative may entail a feeling that representation in video games is frivolous, a guilty pleasure. Unless one feels that their identity and sense of self is actively under assault, seeking out representation is not necessarily required for one's continued well-being. Perhaps, then, we might foreground pleasure as Richard Dyer describes it: "Pleasure remains a forbidden term of reference, particularly on the left. Pleasure is something you can guiltily have, have after the important things, or get as a reward for doing other things. As itself a goal, it is still not, so to speak paradoxically, taken seriously."[55] There is pleasure involved in playing games and seeing oneself reflected in them. To some extent, "niceness" is a way for audiences to decline the assumption that it is their job to demand representation. In part, what the "nice when it happens" theme signals is that players are not interested in carrying the responsibility for *caring* about representation.

Researchers, as well as producers and players, must be cognizant of the ideologies encoded into video games: "Racial and gender stereotypes abound in the construction of these avatars and an outright dismissal of avatar representation leaves unchallenged the political dimension of these representations."[56] Yet these political dimensions cannot be articulated by dismissing the fun of games. The popularity of games is not, moreover, what makes representation in video games important. To say that representation in a medium is important in this way necessarily means being able to describe specific effects of interacting with those texts. In their "census" of video game characters, Williams et al. argue, for example, that consumption of these games can cultivate a particular world view within those individuals who have replaced most of their media consumption with video game play.[57] The problem with this assertion is twofold. First, video games' prominence in popular culture should not be the only reason researchers study them. Second, the effects are assumed to arise in those (few, if any) people who *only* play video games. One could argue in response to both that if games are a niche pastime and/or other media contain sufficient diversity, then representation in video games is not a problem.

Instead of focusing on whether a representation in a given game is realistic, researchers should focus on the availability of representation in different types of games. Certain games allow for or encourage some kinds of interactions with video game characters and not others. Indeed, in some games players do not identify with the in-game characters at all. This forces researchers to reconsider when and why both representation and identification are important. Certain texts and contexts alter how individuals connect with avatars, fictional characters, and media personalities. When representation is important, it relies on an appeal to realism that tokenism can never quite fulfill. Players do not identify with tokens, and thus, such representation cannot fulfill the market-logic or educative goals of minority representation. What this book also suggests is that for at least four reasons, cultural producers of any sort must be willing to risk a lack of identification in order to get at a deeper identification. First, people might connect but not deeply identify with people who are caricatures or abstract characters based on visual cues. Second, it is hard to predict why and how a person will identify with a character, so perhaps, specific identifiers should not be producers' primary focus. Third, my data demonstrate that identification is not always a goal for all individuals. Fourth, players' (and nonplayers') attitudes toward games shape whether they think representation in games is important. The marginalization of gaming must be dealt with more directly in the struggle for diversity in video games.

Although Jesper Juul argues that games have become normalized, several of my interviewees still felt like games held a distinct cultural place.[58] People often see gaming as something separate from other media. This, in turn, has implications for demands for representation. Juul claims that though not everyone plays video games, nothing "prevents this from happening. Video games are fast becoming games for *everyone*."[59] That there are games that appeal to mass audiences is not, however, the same as saying that games in a broader sense are *for* everyone. The fact that only about half of my interviewees identified as gamers, despite the fact that *all* of my interviewees played games, demonstrates this.[60] Usually, popular, academic, and industrial discourses describe the core gaming audience as heterosexual, white, and male. The primary way researchers and marketers challenge this construction is by focusing on female players. Such efforts focus on how female players identify with video game characters and seek the creation of female representations with which women and girls can identify. In many ways, this has actually made gender *more* of a barrier to inclusion in gaming culture or identifying oneself as a gamer.[61] The pluralism approach to representation in games does not lead to diversity in game texts or gaming in a broader sense. What those invested in the representation of marginalized groups in video games should do instead is focus on the way the medium is spoken of. Paradoxically, this entails making a case for the seriousness of representation in games in a way that does not ignore that play is part of what defines games.

Conclusion

Identities are neither wholly externally nor wholly internally defined. Market constructions and social relationships shape audiences' interactions with media. How people identify themselves does not define identification. Identification, in turn, does not necessarily drive media consumption. How producers create texts shapes the options for identification with characters in those texts. Researchers and players should be critical of the fact that the video game texts that preclude identification with characters (e.g., ones that make players more self-reflexive because of a lack of narrative and/or because players create their own characters) are the primary ones in which diversity is made available. Media representation is not only or even always important to marginalized groups. Moreover, the political goals of representation (recognition in a sociopolitical sense) necessitate that people who are not members of a particular marginalized group see representations of marginalized groups. Future research might even take these insights further to critique how hegemonic, white, heterosexual masculinities are presented in game texts.

In *Secrets of the Game Business,* François Laramée approaches the issue of representation through a discussion of the threat "shock value" violence and sex pose to the industry's legitimacy. Laramée quotes former International Game Developers Association president James Della Rocca about the pervasive fear of censorship if the game industry does not "play by the rules."[62] In a section where he distances commercial games from those created by "religious fundamentalist and racist fringe groups," Laramée writes:

> When game developers and publishers choose shock value for shock value sake . . . it smears us all with an aura of sleaze and, well, stupidity. It might even lend these gate games a modicum of legitimacy, because in the eye of the general public, they will not seem so different from what the official game industry does.[63]

The threat of government regulation is meant to drive aspiring game developers to practice due diligence in creating their products but not "preemptive censorship where it isn't warranted."[64] The examples Laramée gives are *Grand Theft Auto* and *Kingpin,* both of which have been widely critiqued for their reliance on racialized imagery in their depictions of urban gang cultures. In these cases, he argues, the casting is a legitimate design choice, whereas in hate games it is purely political and therefore out of bounds. This assumption that critique leads to censorship is fairly consistent throughout game industry (and some fan) rhetoric. In the *Games.net* video "Racism in Games," for example, journalists interview game industry representatives about questions of racism in *Grand Theft Auto* and the white supremacist game *Ethnic Cleansing*.[65] Interviewees in the video are ready to dismiss clearly racist political games but worry that equating commercial games with them will lead to censorship. Critiquing video game representation, they argue, might ultimately harm free speech because in the narrative they tell, critiques lead to regulation. There is no room in this framing of the issue to address personal responsibility of creators or systemic inequalities that lead their visions to represent a very narrow viewpoint.

A different narrative about representation in games exists, of course, as articulated in Sheri Graner Ray's *Gender Inclusive Game Design* and Justine Cassell and Henry Jenkins's often-cited *From Barbie to Mortal Kombat*.[66] In these and similar texts, authors argue that the North American game industry has largely hamstringed its own growth by appealing to a very narrow white, male demographic, making this critique via an analysis of game content. Graner Ray details in her book how to appeal to "female gamers" by relying largely on normative notions of gender-role behavior while noting the key role socialization plays in said norms. The authors of essays in Cassell and Jenkins's volume detail the many limits imposed by the gendering of game play and what games meant to appeal to girls might look like. Both books outline the important goal of expanding the gaming audience, but they reinforce norms of desire (what girls are supposed to like) while challenging norms of labor and consumption (who gets to make and play games).

Taken together, these two perspectives represent the majority of the current debate surrounding representation and video games, as highlighted by the *Tropes vs. Women* controversy. On the one hand, we see those at the margins of the game industry, of whom women are the most widely represented, attempting to crack open this medium and make it more widely available. On the other hand, unfortunately, they often do so by making the neoliberal argument that the market for games is wider than currently being reached and that broader representation is profitable. Indeed, Nick Dyer-Witheford and Greig de Peuter make the compelling case that games themselves, as an industry and as a medium, are structured heavily by the logics of neoliberalism and its emphasis on privatization, deregulation, globalized business, and the unwavering belief that the imperatives of capitalism can (and should) structure the whole of human life. The strong belief in neoliberalism is also what drives the industry to reject critiques of representation, arguing that if people don't like it, they will not buy it. Because of this, many makers and lovers of games take critique as a direct assault. Given decades of research and news programs highlighting fears about the effects of playing violent video games and subsequent bans on the sale of particular games, these might be understandable concerns. That is to say, it makes sense that the industry feels attacked, even if this reactionary approach itself bespeaks unrecognized white, male, heterosexual privilege. This fear, in turn, colors game makers' relationship to any critique of their product.

I argue for a third path, however, that gets us beyond both the effects question and the marketing justification for representation. Media representation creates what is and might be possible. Given this, diversity in games is a design imperative for this creative industry. This need not just be the role of independent game designers, though their place in the industry should not be discounted. Rather than see demand for representation as a limitation on creativity, it could be reframed as a checkpoint in design. Designers could look critically and ask themselves why they made the choices they did. What would it mean to flip the race, gender, sexuality, embodiment, and voice of a character they created? When creating avatar design choices, what shaped the options made available? What logic underlies the structure of options made, and what would happen if those logics were simply forgotten?

The issue of representation in games and, indeed, in all media industries is too often focused on what a "good" representation of a given group would look like. Such concerns are inevitably limiting. Races, genders, and sexualities are not fixable, knowable, static entities that can be described (at least not outside of the most problematic of ways). In my chapter in *Designing Games for Ethics,* I argue that in terms of ethics, recognition, hospitality, and truthfulness are key components of good game design practice.[67] In it I also assert that critical reflection on the creation process is key to representation. Good representation necessarily fails to encompass the totality of a group in a single body and recognizes its own failure to do so. Katie Salen and Eric Zimmerman similarly argue, "The cultural di-

mensions of games are exceedingly complex; your game should recognize this complexity and do it justice within its design."[68] This in
part requires substantially more diversity in games and in all media,
so that single characters do not bear the onus of standing for every
person that might share characteristics with them. In the end, it is
not about a single character in a single game but about all characters
in all games and all media.

Salen and Zimmerman contend, "It is possible for games to take
the concept of cultural rhetoric by the horns, not only representing
and challenging ideologies, but also changing them."[69] This can be
done through promoting critical play, as Mary Flanagan argues, or
simply by valuing the importance of "something new" in the game-
creation process.[70] In *Challenges for Game Designers,* for example,
Brenda Braithwaite (now Romero) and Ian Schreiber insist that designers think expansively about game character design:

> People play games because they provide an opportunity to explore
> a world that they would be unlikely to explore and play out an expe-
> rience they would be unlikely to have in real life. People want to play
> cool characters. They want to explore exciting destinations. Some-
> times, as in *The Sims,* they just want to experiment with everyday
> life and make their own stories.[71]

The trouble is education, however. Understanding how cultural
meanings are communicated and how identities are created takes
training. That can be academic training or self-education, but it is
not something one can wake up in the morning and know how to do.
Critical analysis of media is a rich field of study full of contested ideas
for a reason. This kind of work is hard, and it forces us to ask uncomfortable questions and face privileges that are easier to ignore. It is
work, however, that game designers, producers, players, researchers, and critics must take on. Additionally, I do not mean to suggest
that the commercial game industry is the only end goal. Indie game
designers have long questioned the norms of representation, and
audiences have at their disposal many tools, from mods to reading
against the grain of a game, to question normative representation.[72]

Defending games as part of how our culture makes meaning does
not necessitate that we have to "take them seriously." Games are fun.
Even when they are not "fun" in the typical sense of that word, as

frustration is an integral part of playing them, they are (for most) a freely chosen activity.[73] They draw us in for hours on end, and they fill short in-between moments in our day. They make us think, and they help us zone out. They bring people together, and they give us the chance to be alone. More people play games than realize they do, and yet gaming remains a cordoned-off fan space in many accounts. They are one of the first truly modern media forms that embodies all of the convergent, interactive possibilities of digital technologies, and yet the way they have approached the question of representation is incredibly outdated. They also present the exciting opportunity to challenge old modes of thought regarding audience reception, textual possibilities, and the politics of media representation more broadly. In particular, when we go out to the edges of play, we can see that what we know of games thus far is just the beginning, and in changing the conversations we have about games, we can begin to imagine a more inclusive future.

Acknowledgments

It would be impossible to thank everyone who helped make this book possible. It represents five years of work conducted across five different institutions and was discussed with hundreds of people. I am tempted to do as Allie Brosh, author of *Hyperbole and a Half,* did and just draw a giant "Thank You" dedicated to everyone. But she beat me to it. So instead, I shall do my best to include everyone here, and if you feel you should have been here, email me and I will send you a personal thank-you card later (yes, seriously).

First and foremost, I thank my participants for sharing their stories, their thoughts, their play, and, in some cases, their couches and dinner tables with me. Were it not for them, there would be no project. I also thank Twitter—yes, that Twitter. My editor, Jason Weidemann, originally contacted me because he was following a Twitter conversation between Mia Consalvo and Chris Paul about my presentation at a conference. Twitter has also connected me to an amazing community of game scholars, critics, and designers, and although I cannot name all of them here, the impact of their work can be seen throughout the book. Thanks to Twitter, I am also connected to Todd Harper and Emil Lundedal Hammar, who provided illustrations for this book (see Figures 15 and 19). Twitter did not make this book, but it certainly did enable it. I should also note that Angel Bourgoin took many photographs of her *Settlers of Catan* board to make Figure 12 possible. Thank you, Angel, Todd, and Emil for answering my pleas for help.

Friends and family throughout my life have shaped the ideas reflected in this book. I would be remiss not to single out Matthew and Rebecca Emerson, who got me back into gaming between college and graduate school. My entire academic career was shaped by this fact. I am grateful for a family who supports me, even when they aren't quite sure what it is that I do or why I do it. I am particularly thankful to my mother, first, for buying us that Nintendo back in 1987 and, more important, for helping me become the person I always wanted to be. I am where I am today entirely because of her.

The project in this book began as my dissertation at the Annenberg School for Communication at the University of Pennsylvania. It could not have happened without the resources, faculty, staff, and students there. I thank my graduate advisor, Katherine Sender, who has been amazingly supportive of all of my endeavors and is one of the best editors I have ever had. She is as good a teacher as she is a friend and by direction and example reminds me that working hard does not have to mean never taking time off. I am thankful to my other committee members, John L. Jackson Jr. and Marwan Kraidy, who have been as excited and interested in my work as I am. I could not have asked for a better group of scholars to work with, and I value their continued feedback.

Many other faculty members and visiting scholars at Penn shaped the scholarship contained herein. The nonexhaustive list includes Elizabeth Bird, Nick Couldry, Barbie Zelizer, Sharrona Pearl, Joseph Capella, Klaus Krippendorff, and Carolyn Marvin. The Annenberg staff was instrumental in the completion of this work. I am especially grateful to Brendan Keegan, Donna Edwards, Gavin McFeeters, Yogi Sukawa, and Joanne Murray for helping me navigate the nuts-and-bolts aspects of this project.

Support for the revision of the original project into this book was provided by the Mudra Institute for Communication–Ahmedabad, the University of Pittsburgh, Colorado State University, and Temple University. At Temple University, I am grateful to my graduate assistant Jaehyeon Jeong for collecting the many news stories about game representation controversies I needed to finish updating the manuscript.

Many friends and colleagues influenced this book. Thanks go to Harmony Siganporia, Rita Kothari, Jocelyn Buckner, Jennifer Stromer-Galley, Kate Kenski, Michael Serazio, Josh Lauer, Deb Lubken, Moira O'Keeffe, Seth Goldman, Angel Bourgoin, Mario Rodriguez, Piotr Szpunar, Cabral Bigman, Jason Tocci, Oren Livio, Keren Teneboim-Weinblatt, and Tara Liss-Marino. I offer special thanks to Shawnika Hull and Rosa Mikeal Martey, who listened to me explain this project over and over again until it started to make sense. My departmental and university colleagues at Temple provided me with the intellectual environment that made this book possible. My hockey team, the Philadelphia Freeze, also gave me much needed relief from working on this project at both the early and later stages (Go Freeze!).

Three game scholars first influenced my research with their work and then with their feedback. I admit that I was terribly star-struck the first time I met each of them and am grateful I got over it enough to really talk to them. Garry Crawford, thank you for making me feel like I did have something important to say that people wanted to hear. T. L. Taylor, thank you for your feedback, your kindness, and the "no lurkers" policy at the AoIR Singstar nights. Aphra Kerr, thank you for your work, your advice, and for introducing me to Ham Sandwich, whose CD was vital in the editing of this book. On that note, thanks to the following artists for providing the soundtrack for this book: The Shondes, Tegan and Sara, Deb Talen/The Weepies, Le Tigre, Rhianna, Ani DiFranco, The Dollyrots, Garbage, Dolly Parton, Tori Amos, Po' Girl, The Dixie Chicks, Girlyman, and the Broadway cast of *Joseph and the Amazing Technicolor Dreamcoat*.

Many thanks go to the University of Minnesota Press and Wendy Holdman Design for making this book into a book. I am grateful for an editor like Jason Weidemann, who spent a great deal of time talking me through how to make this book better. He understood and appreciated what I wanted it to do in a way that not many others did. Thanks as well go to Danielle Kasprzak for answering many questions about the nitty-gritty aspects of making this book ready for press; Mike Hanson for his excellent copyediting; and Rachel Moeller and Wendy Holdman for guiding this book through the publication process. I could not have found a better team.

Finally, there are not enough words to express how thankful I am for my wife, Cathy Hannabach. The home we have built with Ponty the Wondercat and Alot the Diva Dog gives me the energy I need to do the work I do. She edited every page of my manuscript (sometimes multiple times), fixed my errors, and forced me to make my points more clearly and more forcefully. She also created the book's index, which you should look at right now because it is pretty amazing (you too can hire her if you wish). More than that, she made me not work sometimes. Her brilliance, laughter, beauty, and kindness have made my work and my life infinitely better than I ever thought possible.

Notes

Preface

1. *Othello* (Kawada, 1986), video game; *Castlevania,* (Konami, 1987), video game.
2. *California Games* (Epyx, 1987), video game; *Tiny Toon Adventures* (Konami, 1991), video game; *Doom* (Sega, 1994), video game.
3. Worley, "Women Join Arcade Revolution," 30.
4. Frum, "Half of All Video-Gamers Are Women."
5. Worley, "Women Join Arcade Revolution," 32.
6. Shaw, "In-Gayme Representation?"
7. Shaw, "Peliharrastaja"; Shaw, "Beyond Comparison"; Shaw, "Gamer in Hindi."

Introduction

1. Sarkeesian, "Tropes vs. Women in Video Games."
2. Ibid.
3. Indeed, prior to the release of Sarkeesian's first video in the series on March 2, 2013, a parody Reddit thread was started to predict the kind of response she would receive. It unfortunately proved wholly accurate. "/R/gaming's Personal Hitler, Anita Sarkeesian, Is Releasing Her First Video Tomorrow," posted by Khiva, March 6, 2013, Reddit, http://www.reddit.com/r/circlebroke/comments/19thtd/rgamings_personal_hitler_anita_sarkeesian_is.
4. The phrase used repeatedly was, "Tits or get the fuck out." Sarkeesian, "Harassment, Misogyny and Silencing."
5. Lewis, "This Is What Online Harassment Looks Like."
6. Plunkett, "Awful Things Happen When."
7. Flash games are designed using Adobe Flash, a software program that allows digital games to be played through an Internet browser via a plug-in.
8. Lewis, "This Is What Online Harassment Looks Like."
9. Greenhouse, "Twitter's Free-Speech Problem."
10. Consalvo, "Confronting Toxic Gamer Culture"; Alexander, "In the Sexism Discussion."

11. Braithwaite, "'Seriously, Get Out.'"

12. For a critique of defining game culture as something specific, see Shaw, "What Is Video Game Culture?"

13. Although there were some negative reactions in various online forums to the video, opponents were not nearly as vocal as they were in response to Sarkeesian's project, though *Tropes vs. Women* may have simply received more press than *Gaming in Color*. See Gaming in Color, "Gaming in Color."

14. A full list of the book series' awards and select critics' quotes are available at Suzanne Collins's website, http://www.suzannecollinsbooks. com/the_hunger_games_69765.htm.

15. Suzanne Collins, *The Hunger Games.*

16. Bull, "*The Hunger Games* Hit by Racism"; Breslaw, "Another Racist Shitstorm Brews."

17. Caperton, "*Hunger Games*: What Do You Mean, the Black Girl Was Black?"

18. Bull, "*Hunger Games* Hit by Racism"; Breslaw, "Another Racist Shitstorm Brews."

19. Sieczkowski, "*Hunger Games* Movie's Rue Responds"; Peterman, "Opinion: Hysteria over *Hunger Games* Characters' Race Is Misguided"; Goldberg, "*Hunger Games* and Hollywood's Racial Casting Issue."

20. I use the term *video game* here in the sense articulated by Garry Crawford, as a widely recognized if often debated term. I use it interchangeably with the terms *games* or *digital games* as a way to refer to console, mobile, and PC games. When referring to board or other types of games, I use more specific terminology to indicate the shift. Crawford, *Video Gamers,* 3.

21. Sarkeesian, "Tropes vs. Women."

22. Chambers, "The All-Too-Familiar Harassment against Feminist Frequency"; O'Leary, "Fighting Harassment in Video Game World."

23. Empirical research would have to be done to assess whether the source of critique affects the response. Anecdotal evidence from women in game studies and game journalism suggests it does, but more research needs to be done.

24. This acronym refers to lesbian, gay, bisexual, transgender, and queer.

25. It is, of course, likely the documentary's goal in presenting a picture of this niche market and highlighting of producers is to lead to greater textual representation.

26. From the GIRL frequently-asked-questions page, https://www.soe .com/girl-qa.

27. This perspective is outlined and critiqued in Shaw, "Putting the Gay."

28. This phrase is attributed to Charlotte Bunch according to—and similarly deployed in—Abbate, *Recoding Gender,* 5.

29. Given the interactive nature of games, the term *audience* as conceptualized as a passive mass in classical media theories often seems inadequate

to describe game reception practices. At the same time, however, *audience* is useful as a term to describe the group as an industry construct. When referring to individual reception, I use the term *player*; for constructed audiences, I use the term *audience*; and when both are implicated, I use *player/ audience* to highlight that fact.

30. In invoking this term, I draw on Homi Bhabha's discussion of hybridity in relation to his concept of the "third space." This third space does not entail the hybridizing of two identity categories that are taken for granted. Instead, there is something specific about the experience of being in that third space, which is not the result of adding the experiences of two different identity categories together. "The notion of hybridity invokes the fusion of two (or more) components into a third term irreducible to the sum of its parts." Kraidy, *Hybridity, or the Cultural Logic of Globalization,* 14. Or as David Valentine discusses in relation to *transgender* as an identity category, "Age, race, class, and so on don't merely inflect or intersect with those experiences we call gender and sexuality but rather *shift the very boundaries of what 'gender' and sexuality can mean* in particular contexts." *Imagining Transgender,* 100; original emphasis. Elizabeth Spelman argues similarly that "far from distracting us from issues of gender, attention to race and class in fact help us to understand gender." *Inessential Woman,* 113.

31. This term is used as it was developed by Kimberlé Crenshaw to articulate "the intersection of racism and sexism factors into Black women's lives in ways that cannot be captured wholly by looking at the race or gender dimensions of those experiences separately." "Mapping the Margins," 1244.

32. Here, I draw on Bernice Johnson Reagon's notion of coalition politics in the essay "Coalition Politics." This concept is elaborated upon by Judith Butler in *Gender Trouble,* where she argues for political movements that are not contingent upon sameness but rather exist despite difference.

33. Identity politics refers to political organizing that presumes members of a specific group, women for example, share goals defined by that group membership. Intersectional politics, in contrast, looks at the way intersecting axes of difference and privilege impact people's life chances.

34. Irresistible-Revolution, "And WOC Are Invisble Yet Again."

35. Lewis, "Game Theory."

36. See, for example, Sender, *Business, Not Politics.*

37. This includes but is not limited to Michel Foucault, *The History of Sexuality*; Judith Butler, *Gender Trouble*; Stuart Hall, "Who Needs Identity?"; Paul Gilroy, *Between Camps*; Anthony Appiah, *The Ethics of Identity*; Gayatri Spivak, *In Other Worlds.*

38. The It Gets Better Project video campaign was began in September 2010 by columnist Dan Savage and his partner, Terry Miller. As described on the project's website, "In response to a number of students taking their own lives after being bullied in school, they wanted to create a personal way for supporters everywhere to tell LGBT youth that, yes, it does indeed get

better." "What Is the It Gets Better Project?," It Gets Better Project, http://
www.itgetsbetter.org/pages/about-it-gets-better-project.

39. Shaw, "Gay in Game."

40. Shaw, "Talking to Gaymers."

41. Representations of marginalized groups in games are of course designed in conversation with the mainstream representations of white heterosexual masculinity as the norm. It is not within the scope of this book to
address that particular intersection, but I am grateful to Garry Crawford for
reminding me of this point.

42. Jhally and Lewis, "Enlightened Racism"; Douglas, *Where the Girls
Are.*

43. Basil, "Identification as a Mediator"; Klimmt et al., "Identification
with Video Game Character."

44. Van Looy et al., "Player Identification in Online Games"; Li, Liau,
and Khoo, "Player-Avatar Identification"; Klimmt, Hefner, and Vorderer,
"'True' Identification."

45. *LA Noire* (Team Bondi, 2011), video game.

46. Many thanks to T. L. Taylor for her insightful comments regarding
this issue.

47. Bruns, *Blogs, Wikipedia, SecondLife, and Beyond*; Jenkins, *Convergence Culture.*

1. From *Custer's Revenge* and *Mario* to *Fable* and *Fallout*

1. Pouncy is an alias.

2. *They* and *their* are Pouncy's preferred pronouns.

3. *The Sims* is a life simulation game from Maxis/Electronic Arts.

4. Logo is a television channel directed towards an LGBTQ audience.

5. *The Gloaming* is a 1997 movie about a man who returns home
during the final months of his battle with AIDS-related illness, directed by
Christopher Reeves.

6. *Brokeback Mountain* is the 2005 Academy Award–winning movie
about a multidecade romance between two closeted, male ranch hands in
rural Wyoming, directed by Ang Lee.

7. *Settlers of Catan* is an online version of a strategy board game of
the same name created by Klaus Teuber where players form colonies by
collecting resources and establishing interconnected settlements.

8. Half of the interviewees who allowed me into their homes had cats.

9. Couldry, *Media, Society, World.*

10. For nuanced work on the game industries, audiences, and texts,
see Dyer-Witheford and de Peuter, *Games of Empire*; Kerr, *Business and
Culture*; Taylor, *Play between Worlds*; Consalvo, *Cheating*; Crawford, *Video
Gamers*; Bogost, *Persuasive Games*; and King and Krzywinska, *Tomb Raiders and Space Invaders.*

11. Cassell and Jenkins, *Barbie to Mortal Kombat*; Kafai et al., eds., *Beyond Barbie and Mortal Kombat*; Burrill, *Die Tryin'*.

12. Zimmerman, "Politics of Transliteration," 680.

13. Anderson, *Imagined Communities*.

14. Hall, "Question of Cultural Identity," 616.

15. Spivak, *In Other Worlds*.

16. Bernstein, "Celebration and Suppression."

17. Hall, "Question of Cultural Identity," 617.

18. Walker, *Like What You Are*, 207.

19. Ibid., 214.

20. hooks, "Postmodern Blackness."

21. Ibid., 421.

22. Jackson, "A Little Black Magic," 401.

23. Dornfeld, *Producing Public Television*; Henderson, "Storyline and the Multicultural Middlebrow"; D'Acci, *Defining Women*; Ewen, *Captains of Consciousness*; Sender, *Business, Not Politics*; Turow, *Breaking up America*.

24. Gitlin, *Inside Prime Time*, 330.

25. Adams, *Fundamentals of Game Design*.

26. Ochalla, "Are Video Games Getting Gayer?" Brenda Braithwaite now goes by Brenda Romero. I also want to emphasize that this is a quote that reflects a broader trend in how representation is discussed and is not meant as a critique of Romero personally. She is active in demands for greater diversity in games and has spent a great deal of energy in getting games taken seriously.

27. On terminology, *cisgendered* is used in this book to call attention to the presumption, invisible in many discussions of gender and gaming, that peoples' assigned gender and lived gender identity align. It refers to those whose gender identity conforms to the gender they were assigned at birth. Unless interviewees identify as cis- or transgendered, I do not refer to them as such here. The categories for gender on the recruitment survey were Female, Male, Transgender, Uncertain, Other (Please Specify), and Prefer Not to Say. Moreover, *white* is a long-contested and mutable category. In this study it refers to those who selected White on the survey but checked no other race/ethnicity/ancestry boxes. The complete list of categories was African-American/Black, Latino/Hispanic, Middle Eastern, Native American/Alaska Native, White, Arab/Arab American, Biracial, Multiracial, Other (Please Specify), and Prefer Not to Say. Similarly, sexual identity is discussed in terms of what participants indicated both on the recruitment survey and during interviews. The complete list of categories on the survey was Bisexual, Gay, Heterosexual, Lesbian, Queer, Uncertain, Other (Please Specify), and Prefer Not to Say.

28. Kafai et al., *Beyond Barbie and Mortal Kombat*; Cassell and Jenkins, *Barbie to Mortal Kombat*; Graner Ray, *Gender Inclusive Game Design*; Burrill, *Die Tryin'*.

29. Machin and Suleiman, "Arab and American Computer War Games"; Sisler, "Representation and Self-Representation"; Leonard, "High Tech Blackface"; Leonard, "Virtual Gangstas"; Leonard, "Not a Hater"; Chan, "Playing with Race"; Consalvo, "Hot Dates and Fairy-Tale Romances"; Consalvo, "It's a Queer World"; Shaw, "Gay in Game."

30. Tuchman, "Symbolic Annihilation of Women"; Gerbner and Gross, "Living with Television."

31. Hall, "What Is This 'Black.'"

32. Sender, *Business, Not Politics*.

33. Hall, "What Is This 'Black,'" 110.

34. Dyer, "Stereotyping."

35. Ibid., 298–99.

36. McRobbie, *Uses of Cultural Studies*, 109.

37. D'Acci, "Television, Representation and Gender."

38. *Custer's Revenge* (Mystique, 1982), video game.

39. Chalk, "Short History of Race"; Herz, *Joystick Nation*; Plunkett, "Rape, Racism and Repetition"; Sharam, "Native Americans in Video Games."

40. Sharam, "Native Americans in Video Games."

41. Pollack, "What's New in Video Games."

42. Freedman, "8-Bit Porn."

43. Bogost, "Atari Porn Games."

44. Smith, *Conquest*.

45. Couldry, *Inside Culture*, 2.

46. Kline, Dyer-Witheford, and de Peuter, *Digital Play*, 257.

47. Kerr, *Business and Culture*, 98.

48. Shaheen, *Reel Bad Arabs*, 32.

49. Gorriz and Medina, "Engaging Girls"; Cassell and Jenkins, *Barbie to Mortal Kombat*; Kafai et al., *Beyond Barbie and Mortal Kombat*.

50. Sender, *Business, Not Politics*.

51. Hall, "Encoding, Decoding."

52. Mortensen, *Perceiving Play*; King and Krzywinska, *Tomb Raiders and Space Invaders*.

53. *Super Mario Bros.* (Nintendo, 1985), video game.

54. Rao, "Shigeru Myamoto Talk"; "Nintendo's Shining Star"; Snider, "'Mario' Creator Shigeru Miyamoto."

55. *Sprite* refers to the two-dimensional animated image used to represent a game character against the static background scene.

56. Kent, *Ultimate History of Video Games*, 159.

57. Ibid.

58. Snider, "'Mario' Creator Shigeru Miyamoto."

59. Ibid.

60. Mark J. P. Wolf makes this argument in the introduction to *The Medium of the Video Game*.

61. Fiske, *Understanding Popular Culture*.

62. Jenkins, *Fans, Bloggers, and Gamers*; Butsch, *The Making of American Audiences*.

63. The combined term *avatar/character* is used to signify that not all player characters are best described as avatars and that ways of describing the relationship between players and their on-screen proxies can be similar in games with characters and avatars. A discussion of the difference between the two terms can be found in chapter 3.

64. As described by Frans Mäyrä, "Rather than just playing to 'win' the game, in role-playing games you were expected to become immersed in an alternative fantasy reality as characters living their lives in it." *An Introduction to Game Studies*, 78.

65. Barton, "Gay Characters in Video Games"; Consalvo, "Hot Dates and Fairy-Tale Romances"; Consalvo, "It's a Queer World"; Ochalla, "Boy on Boy Action; Thompson, "The Game of Wife"; Weeks, "Same-Sex Relationships"; Chalk, "*Dragon Age* Writer."

66. *Fable: The Lost Chapters* (Lionhead Studios, 2005), video game; *Fable II* (Lionhead Studios, 2008), video game; *Fable III* (Lionhead Studios, 2010), video game.

67. Throughout this explanation of the *Fable* games, I distinguish between choices I make and the experiences of or labels attached to my character. I use the term *character* rather than *avatar* because the backstory given to the player character in every game of the series makes it more than just an extension of the player in the game space. For an extended discussion of the difference between characters and avatars, see chapter 3.

68. Ochalla, "Boy on Boy Action."

69. That is the claim made in the article about the existence of same-sex options in the game, anyway. In playing the game, it does seem that female villagers are more likely than male villagers to reach that point where like turns to love.

70. In addition, when I marry any female villager, I receive a dowry and a cut scene of the marriage. When I marry a male villager, there is no dowry and no cut scene.

71. Throughout the game many ideological comments on sex are made, including the fact that any act of unprotected sex results in acquiring an STD or, if you are married, the chance of a baby.

72. I am indebted to Cathy Hannabach for pointing out the corollaries with real-life barriers to gender transition/confirmation. In her words, the game aligns with real life in that "life-saving identity documents, name changes, hormones, legal protection, and surgical interventions are similarly guarded by gatekeepers and only granted under select circumstances, based on folks' ability to perform subservience to the game." Cathy Hannabach, e-mail message to author, October 5, 2013.

73. Adding to the normative assumptions of the third installment of the series, the player character is supposed to be the child of the player

character from *Fable II*. Yet despite the gender options available in *Fable II*, not to mention the optional but irreversible Potion of Transmogrification, the parent in question is repeatedly referred to as the father of your character.

74. Quoted in Fitzgerald, "At San Francisco Convention."
75. *Indigo Prophecy (Fahrenheit)* (Quantic Dream, 2005), video game.
76. *NHL 2K5* (Kush Games, 2005), video game.
77. *Mass Effect* (Bioware, 2007), video game.
78. *Fallout 3* (Bethesda Game Studios, 2008), video game.
79. In Mia Consalvo's analysis of *The Sims,* she notes that "white" and "male" are the default options in the Sim-creation screen. "It's a Queer World after All," 40.
80. Higgin, "*Fallout 3*'s Curious System."
81. As Benshoff and Griffin describe in relation to film, "Queer audiences . . . learned how to read Hollywood films in unique ways—often by looking for possible queer characters and situations while ignoring the rest." *Queer Images,* 64.
82. Dyer-Witheford and de Peuter, *Games of Empire.*
83. Couldry, *Media, Society, World,* 57.
84. DeVane and Squire, "Meaning of Race and Violence."
85. Kalata, "Hardcore Gaming 101."
86. MacDonald, "A Gay History of Gaming."
87. Aarseth, *Cybertext,* 1.
88. Newman, "The Myth of the Ergodic"; emphasis added.
89. Taylor, *Raising the Stakes,* 182–83.
90. Apperley, "Genre and Game Studies"; Murray, *Hamlet on the Holodeck.*
91. Frasca, "Simulation versus Narrative"; Juul, *Half-Real.*
92. Mäyrä, *Introduction to Game Studies.*
93. Bogost, *Unit Operations*; King and Krzywinska, *Tomb Raiders and Space Invaders*; Voorhees, "The Character of Difference"; Mortensen, *Perceiving Play*; Crawford, *Video Gamers.*
94. Chan, "Playing with Race," 29.
95. Taylor, *Play between Worlds,* 96.
96. Burill, *Die Tryin',* 74.
97. Hall, "Encoding, Decoding."
98. Anthropy, *Videogame Zinesters,* 15.
99. No such text yet exists, though in *Gender Inclusive Game Design: Expanding the Market* Sheri Graner Ray has made strides in this direction for female representation. Similarly, Anna Anthropy summarizes the sentiment expressed by many a marginalized player: "As a queer transgendered woman in 2012 in a culture pervaded by videogames . . . I have to strain to find any game that is about a queer woman, to find any game that resembles my own experience." *Videogame Zinesters,* 1–2.

100. Dyer, *The Matter of Images*, 1; Morley and Robins, *Spaces of Identity*, 134.

101. D'Acci, "Television, Representation and Gender," 376.

102. Gross, *Up from Invisibility*; Johnston and Ettema, *Positive Images*; Oakes, Haslam, and Turner, *Stereotyping and Social Reality*.

103. Gross and Woods, *Reader on Lesbians and Gay Men*, 20.

104. Armstrong and Neunendorf, "TV Entertainment, News"; Dasgutpa and Asgari, "Seeing Is Believing."

105. Dayan, "Paticularistic Media, Diasporic Communications"; Gross, *Up from Invisibility*; Gross, "Minorities, Majorities and the Media."

106. Gross, *Up from Invisibility*, 13.

107. Beam, "Making Ourselves from Scratch"; Fung, "Looking for My Penis"; Walker, *Looking Like What You Are*; Mercer, "Dark and Lovely Too."

108. *Neurodiversity* is a term, first coined by sociologist Judy Singer, that conceives of learning and other cognitively related "disabilities" as normal variations of human development. Silberman, "Neurodiversity Rewires Conventional Thinking."

109. Oakes, Haslam, and Turner, *Stereotyping and Social Reality*.

110. Gerbner et al., "Growing Up with Television."

111. Gross, *Up from Invisibility*, 11.

112. Bobo, "*The Color Purple*"; Jhally and Lewis, "Enlightened Racism."

113. DeVane and Squire, "Meaning of Race and Violence," 279.

114. Couldry, *Media, Society, World*, 30.

115. Davis and Gandy Jr., "Racial Identity and Media Orientation," 367.

116. Bird, *Audience and Everyday Life*, 9.

117. In past research when I focused on specific groups of marginalized players, interviewees often rejected the responsibility of representing that group. In this project I wanted to talk to people without presuming a group identity.

118. Shaw, "Identify as a Gamer?"; Shaw, "On Not Becoming Gamers."

119. All names used to refer to interviewees are aliases, most chosen by interviewees themselves.

120. Appiah, *The Ethics of Identity*; Gilroy, *Between Camps*; Stuart Hall, "The Question of Cultural Identity"; Butler, *Gender Trouble*.

121. Valentine, *Imagining Transgender*; Gray, *Out in the Country*.

122. Means Coleman, *Say It Loud!*

123. Latour, *Reassembling the Social*.

124. Crenshaw, "Mapping the Margins."

125. Rutherford, *Identity*.

126. Radway, "Reception Study," 363.

127. Kerr, *Business and Culture of Digital Games*, 104; Consalvo, "Hardcore Casual"; Juul, *Casual Revolution*. As defined by Jesper Juul, the stereotypical casual player "has a preference for positive and pleasant fictions, has played few video games, is willing to commit small amounts of time and

resources toward playing video games, and dislikes difficult games" (29). A hard-core player stereotypically prefers "emotionally negative fictions . . . has played a large number of video games, will invest large amounts of time and resources toward playing video games, and enjoys difficult games" (29). He later acknowledges that players rarely fit easily into these stereotypes (146).

128. Allor, "Site of the Audience."

129. Ang, *Desperately Seeking.*

130. Allor, "Site of the Audience," 229.

131. Radway, *Reading the Romance,* 13.

132. Allor, "Site of the Audience," 230.

133. Giddings, "Events and Collusions."

134. Couldry, *Media, Society, World,* 44; emphasis in original.

135. Hall, "Encoding, Decoding."

136. Bird, "Travels in Nowhere Land," 251.

137. Stuart Hall, *Representation,* 1.

138. Ang, *Watching "Dallas"*; Bobo, *"The Color Purple"*; Hermes, *Reading Women's Magazines*; Manekekar, "National Texts and Gendered Lives"; Abu-Lughod, *Dramas of Nationhood*; Taylor, *Play between Worlds*; Bird, *Audience and Everyday Life*; Radway, *Reading the Romance*; Gray, *Out in the Country.*

139. "Thick description" is described in detail in Geertz, *Interpretation of Cultures*; Morley, *Television, Audiences and Cultural Studies.*

140. Ginsburg, "Culture/Media," 13.

141. In the interest of space, I will not delve into the debate on what ethnography is in a strict sense. This debate is outlined by other authors in much more detail, particularly with regard to the relationship between communication and media studies and ethnography. Murphy and Kraidy, "International Communication"; Jackson Jr., "Toward an Ethnographic."

142. The first interview was conducted at a convenient time and location for participants, including coffee shops, their homes, their offices, and meeting rooms in the building in which I work. Interviewees were asked to sign an informed consent form before the interview and, due to institutional regulations, asked to sign a payment voucher at the end of the interview. In the interviews I used a modified "life history" approach, as described in Langness and Frank, *Lives,* to get a sense of the interviewees and their media consumption over time. These were not life histories as such; it is "usually not advisable to attempt a life history until one has known the person and/or been in the field for some reasonable period of time" (39). I was, however, able to gain a surprising amount of detail from relatively limited interactions with participants. I began with questions about the interviewees' general backgrounds. I then asked them about their history with video games and other media tastes. During the second half of interviews, I focused on two things: (1) the interviewees' thoughts on media representa-

tion and (2) how and if they identified with media characters in general and video game characters in particular. I also wanted to get a sense of if/when representation and if/when identification was important to them. This approach does raise some ethical questions. As Langness and Frank point out, "The problem of privacy in life-history studies goes beyond the problem of disguising the identity of informants in other kinds of ethnographic research, for the reason that the individuality of the subject is precisely the object of detailed inquiry" (120). To temper the risk, I use aliases, chosen in most cases by the interviewees themselves, and my descriptions of their life details are deliberately vague.

143. Schott and Horrell, "Girl Gamers"; Shaw, "Rethinking Game Studies." Interviewees did not sign an additional consent form for these interviews but did have to sign another payment voucher. I had interviewees play a game that they had chosen ahead of time when possible or gave them a choice of games if necessary. Seven interviewees played on a Nintendo Wii; five played on a PlayStation 2 or 3; eight played on an Xbox; two played on both a Wii and an Xbox; one played on a PSP; and four played on laptops or PCs. While observing interviewees play, I talked with them about the game, what they were thinking during certain periods of play, and what they liked or did not like about the game. When they completed a level or reached a stopping point in the game, I asked more questions about the game in relation to their other playing experiences and other media. We also talked about identification and media consumption. By moving back and forth between talking and playing and by rephrasing questions from the first interview, I was able to get nuanced responses on these complex issues.

144. My position as a researcher must also be seen as a factor in the data analyzed. As a seemingly inconsequential example, I am allergic to cats—very allergic. This is rarely an impediment to my academic work. In planning this project, I was more occupied with the other potential dangers of doing home visits with strangers when making my research commitments than I was with participant pet ownership. That was, at least, until I noticed that many of my interviewees had cats. This was a "finding" many friends encouraged me to analyze. What it might "mean," however, is less important to me than is what it reflects about researcher perspective. A non–allergy afflicted person might never have noticed this trend at all. It is these minor shifts in attention that shape our findings. As researchers our predispositions to certain types of data factor into our analyses. As a white, queer woman who has played video games for most of her life and who studies the representation of marginalized groups in media for a living, I did not arrive at this topic of study by chance. The representation of marginal identities is of direct personal interest to me. These identity factors, in addition to age, class, and education markers, influenced my interactions with my participants, leading to easy rapport or differences to be overcome.

145. Fisherkiller, "Everday Learning"; Caughey, "Gina as Steven";

Barker, "Taking the Extreme Case"; Robins and Aksoy, "Whoever Looks Always Finds"; Steele and Brown, "Adolescent Room Culture"; Kerr et al., "New Media"; Hoover, Schofield Clark, and Alters, *Media, Home, and Family.*

146. Jackson Jr., "Toward an Ethnography."

147. Gray, *Out in the Country*; Abu-Lughod, *Dramas of Nationhood.*

148. Campbell, *Getting It On Online*; Bird, *Audience and Everyday Life*; Radway, *Reading the Romance*; Taylor, *Play between Worlds.*

149. Miller and Slater, *The Internet*; Morley and Robins, *Spaces of Identity.*

150. Crawford and Rutter, "Playing the Game"; Butsch, *Making of American Audiences*; Nasaw, *Going Out*; McCarthy, *Ambient Television.*

151. Sjöblom, "Gaming as a Situated"; Fine, "Frames and Games"; Taylor, *Raising the Stakes.*

152. Taylor, *Play between Worlds*; Boellstorff, "A Ludicrous Discipline?"; Nardi, *Life as a Night Elf Priest*; Pearce, "Productive Play."

153. Consalvo, *Cheating.*

154. Enevold and Hagstrom, "Mothers, Play and Everyday Life"; Shaw, "Rethinking Game Studies"; Hayes, "Gendered Identities at Play"; Waggoner, *My Avatar, My Self.*

155. When I distinguish between online and offline play, it is not in the sense used by James Newman to describe engagement with the game (online play) and passive watching of a game (offline play). Rather, the distinction here is made between online persistent worlds and more-closed game texts. "Myth of the Ergodic". For more on online persistent worlds, see Castronova, *Synthetic Worlds*; Taylor, *Play between Worlds*; Nardi, *Life as a Night Elf Priest*; Pearce, *Communities of Play.*

156. Fine, "Frames and Games."

157. Much of the research presented here is from my dissertation project, which I had only one year of funding to complete. Material and monetary support create real and important limits on research. This is something we should all be more aware of, particularly in the changing landscape of academic institutional structures. Projects are limited by our contexts, and our methodological decisions are (and should be) made in relation to our resources.

158. Most interviewees (seventeen) were from the Philadelphia–New Jersey area; three more, from other parts of Pennsylvania; and ten, from other states or countries. The majority (eighteen) grew up in suburban areas; six were from urban environments; and six were from rural areas.

159. Couldry, *Inside Culture*, 7.

160. Murphy and Kraidy, "International Communication," 315.

161. Taylor, *Raising the Stakes.*

162. I analyzed quantitative data from the survey with SPSS. Interviews were recorded digitally, and I personally transcribed them in full. The writ-

ten transcripts and field notes were then analyzed using a grounded theory approach. For more on this approach, see Glaser and Strauss, *Discovery of Grounded Theory*. Themes from the three primary research foci—identity, identification, and media representation—were analyzed separately, but I also found overarching themes that crossed all three areas during the course of analysis.

163. Bird, *Audience and Everyday Life*; Gauntlett, *Creative Explorations*.

164. Radway, "Reception Study."

165. Crawford, *Video Gamers*.

166. For a collection of *Brokeback Mountain* parodies, see hmillic, "A Cornucopia of *Brokeback Mountain* Movie Parodies!!," *The Adventure of a Lifetime* (blog), October 15, 2007, http://theadventureofalifetime.wordpress.com/2007/10/15/brokeback-mountain-movie-parodies.

167. Consalvo, "It's a Queer World after All."

168. Taylor, *Raising the Stakes*, 182–83.

2. Does Anyone Really Identify with Lara Croft?

1. *The Cosby Show* was a sitcom starting Bill Cosby that aired on NBC from 1984 to 1992. It earned top ratings for nearly its entire run. The show was remarkable and greatly critiqued for being one of the first network television shows to focus on an upper-middle-class African American family. Clair was played by actress Phylicia Rashād.

2. Schleiner, "Does Lara Croft Wear"; MacCallum-Stewart, "Real Boys Carry Girly Epics." These can include fictional characters; media personalities; virtual avatars; or set, chosen, or player-created video game characters.

3. Butler, "Collected and Fractured," 441.

4. Leonard, "High Tech Blackface"; Chan, "Playing with Race."

5. Chan, "Playing with Race," 29.

6. King and Krzywinska, *Tomb Raiders and Space Invaders*, 207.

7. Machin and Suleiman, "Arab and American Computer War"; Sisler, "Representation and Self-Representation." This perspective is critiqued in Shaw, "Beyond Comparison."

8. Hayes, "Gendered Identities at Play"; T. L. Taylor, "Multiple Pleasures."

9. Schleiner, "Does Lara Croft Wear," 223.

10. Mikula, "Gender and Videogames."

11. McLaughlin, "History of *Tomb Raider*."

12. Sayles, "*Rick Dangerous*."

13. McLaughlin, "History of *Tomb Raider*."

14. Not until the end of the original *Metroid* was player character Samus revealed as a woman. Throughout the game the character is encased in a Transformers-like space suit that obscures her gender but implies a male

commando. Once players beat Mother Brain in the final level, on the victory screen the space suit disappears, and Samus is revealed to be a buxom brunette clad only in a red bikini and boots. NowGamerTube, "Metroid Samus Reveal."

15. *Duke Nukem* (3D Realms, 1996), video game; *Tomb Raider* (Core Design, 1996), video game. Both games have a gendered difference in point of view. The former is in first-person perspective (all you see is Duke's hand at the bottom of the screen), whereas the latter is in third-person perspective so that Lara's body is always on display.

16. McLaughlin, "History of *Tomb Raider.*"

17. Ibid.

18. Salen and Zimmerman, *Rules of Play,* 524.

19. Graner Ray, *Gender Inclusive Game Design,* 33.

20. Kline, Dyer-Witheford, and de Peuter, *Digital Play,* 264.

21. Pinckard, "Gender Play."

22. Kennedy, "Lara Croft."

23. Mikula, "Gender and Videogames," 82.

24. Consalvo, "Paratexts of Lara Croft"; Rehak, "Mapping the Big Girl."

25. *Tomb Raider: Legend* (Crystal Dynamics, 2006), video game; *Tomb Raider* (Crystal Dynamics, 2013), video game. The quote from *Legend* is from the Xbox 360 version of the game, while the *Tomb Raider* (2013) quote is from the PlayStation 3 edition of the game. Crystal Dynamics developed both games, but Eidos published the 2006 version and Square Enix published the 2013 version. I do not know if the shift in marketing came from the developers or the publishers or some combination of the two.

26. *Tomb Raider* synopsis, Best Buy website, http://www.bestbuy.com/ site/tomb-raider-xbox-360/2823826.p?id=1218354577654&skuId=2823826 &st=Tomb%20Raider&lp=2&cp=1.

27. Hamilton, "Reinventing Lara Croft."

28. Pinchefsky, "Feminist Reviews *Tomb Raider.*"

29. Ibid.

30. Larsson, *Dragon Tattoo*; Larsson, *Fire*; Larsson, *Hornet's Nest.*

31. Mikula, "Gender and Videogames," 85.

32. Boudreau, "Between Play and Design."

33. Cohen, "Defining Identification."

34. Oately, "Taxonomy of the Emotions"; Zillmann, "Empathy."

35. Green, Brock, and Kaufman, "Understanding Media Enjoyment"; Cohen, "Defining Identification."

36. McCrosky, Richmond, and Daly, "Perceived Homophily"; Moyer-Guse and Nabi, "Overcoming Resistance to Persuasion."

37. Giles, "Parasocial Interaction"; Hoffner and Buchanan, "Young Adults' Wishful Identification"; Hoffner, "Children's Wishful Identification"; Horton and Wohl, "Para-Social Interaction."

38. Zillmann, "Empathy."

39. Green and Brock, "The Role of Transportation"; Green, Brock, and Kaufman, "Understanding Media Enjoyment."

40. Klimmt, "Media Psychology."

41. Eyal and Rubin, "Viewer Aggression and Homophily"; McMahan, "Immersion, Engagement and Presence."

42. Hall, "Who Needs Identity?," 6.

43. Hoffner and Buchanan, "Young Adults' Wishful Identification"; Hoffner, "Children's Wishful Identification."

44. Evans and Gamman, "Reviewing Queer Viewing," 215.

45. Media studies like Jhally and Lewis's and Lind's are limited in part because they are organized with the assumption that race and class are salient differences in audiences' interpretations of the media content. This may be reasonable, as race and class are indeed particularly salient in the texts studied, but it is also rather limiting. Jhally and Lewis, "Enlightened Racism"; Rebecca Ann Lind, "Diverse Interpretations."

46. Althusser, "Ideology," 185.

47. Turner, British Cultural, 20.

48. Foucault, "The Subject and Power," 781.

49. Ibid., 790.

50. Gilroy, "The Pitfalls of Identity," 385.

51. Butler, Gender Trouble, 190.

52. Benhabib, "Feminism and Postmodernism"; Goffman, Self in Everyday Life.

53. "Speech act" is meant in the sense used by Austin, How to Do Things with Words.

54. Butler, "Performativity, Precarity"; Butler, Precarious Life.

55. Butler, "Performativity, Precarity," xi.

56. Ibid., xii.

57. Sender, The Makeover; Ang, Watching Dallas; Bird, For Enquiring Minds; Radway, Reading the Romance.

58. Bird, Audience and Everyday Life.

59. Hall, "Who Needs Identity?"

60. Parasocial interaction is a one-sided relationship in which one person knows a lot about the other but the corollary is not true—for example, fans knowing a lot about celebrities but celebrities not knowing much about their fans. Homophily is the tendency of people to feel connected with people who share features with them. Empathy requires one to recognize the emotions of another.

61. Gilroy, Between Camps, 100.

62. Sedgwick, "Axiomatic."

63. Muñoz, Disidentifications.

64. Ibid., 6.

65. Ibid., 11.

66. Hall, "Encoding, Decoding."

67. Muñoz, 25.

68. Staiger, *Media Reception Studies,* 154.

69. Gilroy, *Between Camps,* 109.

70. *The Legend of Zelda* (Nintendo, 1986), video game; *Mario Bros.* (Nintendo, 1983), video game.

71. Hoorn and Konijn, "Perceiving and Experiencing."

72. Trepte and Reinecke, "Avatar Creation," 175.

73. Hefner, Klimmt, and Vorderer, "Identification with the Player Character"; Klimmt, Hefner, and Vorderer, "'True' Identification."

74. Klimmt et al., "Identification with Video Game Character."

75. Williams et al., "The Virtual Census."

76. Mulvey, "Visual Pleasure." I would argue, however, that psychoanalysis cannot *always* be used in digital games, due to the fact that in video games players' interactivity means they cannot always play on voyeuristic fantasy in either the scopophilic or narcissistic sense. Certainly, passive portions of games may allow this.

77. Butler, *Precarious Life,* 145.

78. Richard and Zaremba, "Gaming with Grrls"; Rehak, "Playing at Being"; McMahan, "Immersion, Engagement and Presence"; de Mul, "The Game of Life"; King and Krzywinska, *Screenplay*; Garrelts, *Meaning and Culture*; Carr et al., *Computer Games*; Slocombe, "A 'Majestic' Reflexivity"; Boudreau, "Between Play and Design."

79. Cohen, "Defining Identification"; Li, Liau, and Khoo, "Player-Avatar Identification; Van Looy et al., "Player Identification"; Hefner, Klimmt, and Vorderer, "Identification with the Player Character"; Klimmt, Hefner, and Vorderer, "'True' Identification."

80. Trepte and Reinecke, "Avatar Creation."

81. Shaw, "Rethinking Game Studies."

82. *Marvel vs. Capcom 2: New Age of Heroes* (Capcom, 2000), video game.

83. Newman, "The Myth of the Ergodic Videogame."

84. *Diablo II* (Blizzard Entertainment, 2000), video game.

85. *Wii Sports* (Nintendo, 2006), video game.

86. *Wii Fit* (Nintendo, 2008), video game.

87. In some games, probably to make animation easier, Miis' feet and hands are not attached to their bodies by arms and legs.

88. *Adventures of Lolo* (HAL Laboratory, 1989), video game.

89. *God of War* (SCE Santa Monica Studio, 2005), video game.

90. *Assassin's Creed* (Ubisoft, 2007), video game.

91. *Left 4 Dead* (Turtle Rock Studios, 2008), video game.

92. *Call of Duty2: Big Red One* (Activision, 2005), video game.

93. Cohen, "Defining Identification."

94. Hall, "Reading Realism," 635.

95. *Kingdom Hearts* (Square Enix, 2002), video game.

96. Giddens, *Modernity and Self-Identity.*
97. Hall, "Question of Cultural Identity," 598.
98. Canclini, *Consumers and Citizens,* 89.
99. Staiger, *Media Reception Studies,* 162.
100. Mouffe, "Citizenship and Political Identity."
101. Ibid., 30.
102. Ibid.
103. Ibid., 32.
104. Reagon, "Coalition Politics"; Butler, *Gender Trouble.*
105. Chin, *Purchasing Power,* 171.
106. Ibid.
107. Johansen, "Nowhere but up Girl"; Shaw, *Nowhere Girl.*
108. Green, "Transportation into Narrative Worlds."
109. Hall, "Reading Realism," 631.
110. Gee, "Cultural Models," 622.
111. Steen et al., "What Went Wrong."
112. Nardi, *Life as a Night Elf Priest,* 93.
113. Newman, *Videogames,* 139.

3. He Could Be a Bunny Rabbit for All I Care!

1. Adams, *Fundamentals of Game Design,* 128; emphasis in original.
2. Ibid., 133.
3. *God of War* (SCE Santa Monica Studio, 2005), video game.
4. Klimmt, "Media Psychology"; Grodal, "Video Games and Pleasures."
5. Jenkins, *Convergence Culture*; Bruns, *Blogs, Wikipedia and SecondLife.*
6. Bucy, "Interactivity in Society"; Myers, *Nature of Computer Games.*
7. Tronstad, "Character Identification."
8. Williams, Hendricks, and Winkler, *Gaming as Culture*; Gee, *What Video Games*; Wolf, "Introduction"; Klimmt, Hefner, and Vorderer, "'True' Identification."
9. Murphy, "'Live in Your World,'" 224.
10. King and Krzywinska, *Tomb Raiders and Space Invaders,* 169.
11. Gee, *What Video Games Have to Teach Us,* 58; emphasis in original.
12. Crawford, *Video Gamers.*
13. Calleja, *In-Game.*
14. Ibid., 169.
15. Waggoner, *My Avatar, My Self.*
16. Boudreau, *Between Play and Design.*
17. Ibid., 346.
18. Tronstad, "Character Identification," 251; *World of Warcraft* (Blizzard Entertainment, 2004), online computer game.
19. Salen and Zimmerman, *Rules of Play,* 450.

20. Ibid., 453.
21. Ibid., 455.
22. Mäyrä, *Introduction to Game Studies,* 110.
23. Tronstad, *Character Identification,* 261.
24. Juul, "Games Telling Stories?"
25. Klevjer, "What Is the Avatar?"; Tronstad, "Character Identification"; Waggoner, *My Avatar, My Self.*
26. Mathew, "The Concept of Avatar," 52.
27. These characters are from the *Tomb Raider* series (Core Design, 1996–2004; Crystal Dynamics, 2006–present), the *Mario Bros.* series (Nintendo, 1981–present), and the *Halo* series (Bungie, 2001–2009).
28. Klevjer, "Enter the Avatar."
29. Juul, *Half-Real.*
30. Tronstad, "Character Identification."
31. Juul, *Art of Failure.*
32. Bucy, "Interactivity in Society."
33. Taylor, *Play between Worlds,* 133.
34. Newman, "The Myth of the Ergodic Videogame." Though I do not analyze this type of game reception in depth here, it is worth consideration in future research.
35. Taylor, *Raising the Stakes,* 182–87; Harper, *Cultural of Digital Fighting.*
36. Newman, "The Myth of the Ergodic Videogame."
37. *Disgaea* (Nippon Ichi Software, 2003), video game.
38. *Soul Calibur 3* (Namco, 2005), video game.
39. Klimmt, "Media Psychology," 347.
40. Calleja, "Digital Games and Escapism."
41. Arsenault and Bernard Perron, "Frame of the Magic Cycle"; Schott, "Agency in and around Play."
42. Giddens, *Modernity and Self-Identity,* 64.
43. *Left 4 Dead* (Turtle Rock Studios, 2008), video game.
44. Dourish, "What We Talk About."
45. Ibid., 28.
46. Simon, "Wii Are Out of Control," 1.
47. Eladhari, "The Player's Journey"; Mortensen, "Mutual Fantasy Online"; Chee, Vieta, and Smith, "Online Gaming"; Taylor, *Play between Worlds*; Yee, "The Norranthian Scrolls"; Nardi, *My Life as a Night Elf Priest*; Pearce, *Communities of Play*; Tronstad, "Character Identification."
48. Pearce, *Communities of Play.*
49. MMORPGs are largely played on servers, belying claims that the many millions of users are actually playing online together. In reality, multiple instances of the massive online worlds exist on separate servers, tied to geographic regions and characterized by different types of game play. Play-

ers in games like *EverQuest* and *World of Warcraft* often identify themselves as members of particular servers.

50. Taylor, *Play between Worlds*, 3.

51. Nardi, *My Life as a Night Elf Priest*, 19.

52. Klevjer, "What Is the Avatar?"

53. MacCallum-Stewart, "Real Boys Carry Girly Epics," 38.

54. Steen et al., "What Went Wrong"; Consalvo, "From Dollhouse to Metaverse."

55. Steen et al., "What Went Wrong."

56. Mortensen, *Perceiving Play*, 68.

57. Storey, *Cultural Studies*, 19.

58. Juul, *A Casual Revolution*.

59. Sjöblom, "Gaming as a Situated."

60. Green, Brock, and Kaufman, "Understanding Media Enjoyment."

61. In this game players have a "sanity meter." The more they are seen by the game's enemies, the lower the bar drops. As it lowers, the avatar "goes insane" and various weird phenomena begin: the camera view tilts; shadows that look like bugs crawl across the screen; the volume on the television goes up and down; the game freezes; and even the "blue screen of death" appears, indicating a system crash. *Eternal Darkness: Sanity's Requiem* (Silicon Knights, 2002), video game.

62. Grossman and DeGaetano, *Stop Teaching Our Kids*; Sherry, "The Effects of Violent Video Games"; Gentile and Anderson, "Violent Video Games"; Dill and Dill, "Video Game Violence"; Bryce and Rutter, "Digital Game and Violence Debate"; Carnagey, Andersen, and Bushman, "Video Game Violence."

63. Interviewed in "Violence," *Game Over: Gender, Race and Violence in Video Games*, directed by Nina Huntemann (Northampton, Mass.: Media Education Foundation, 2000), DVD.

64. Smith, *Engaging Characters*.

65. Konijn and Hoorn, "Some Like It Bad."

66. Carroll, *Philosophy of Mass Art*, 313.

67. Hall, "Who Needs Identity?"

68. *Disgaea* (Nippon Ichi Software, 2003), video game.

69. *The Bard's Tale* (InXile Entertainment, 2004), video game.

70. A few interviewees used the interview setting to explore new games or modes of play. Some played in less invested ways than they normally would (e.g., not saving the game, not replaying if they lost, etc.). This was not always the case, however. Interviewees who were particularly competitive played to win regardless of the setting. Players who played on their own systems, moreover, typically played in more invested ways, as they could save the results and benefit from their successes later, than those who had to play on a borrowed system for the project.

71. Taylor, *Play between Worlds*.

72. Klevjer, "What Is the Avatar?"

73. Crick, "Game Body," 261.

74. Ibid., 266.

75. Lahti, "As We Become Machines"; Dovey and Kennedy, *Game Cultures*; Gregersen and Grodal, "Embodiment and Interface"; Behrenshausen, "(Kin)Aesthetic of Video Gaming"; Eugenie, "Corporealis Ergo Sum"; Grodal, "Stories for Eye, Ear, and Muscles"; Taylor, *Raising the Stakes*; Tucker, "Griefing"; Sjöblom, "Gaming as a Situated."

76. Foucault, *Power/Knowledge*; Bourdieu, *Distinction*; Butler, *Undoing Gender*; Grosz, *Volatile Bodies*.

77. Sjöblom, "Gaming as a Situated."

78. Juul, *A Casual Revolution*.

79. Simon, "Wii Are Out of Control," 4.

80. Behrenshausen, "(Kin)Aesthetic of Video Gaming."

81. Ibid., 353.

82. Merleau-Ponty, "Eye and Mind," 162.

83. Apperley, "Body of the Gamer," 9.

84. *Marvel vs. Capcom 2: New Age of Heroes* (Capcom, 2000), video game.

85. Due to a technical mishap, the recording of the first gaming interview was lost. Evan was kind enough to go through the process a second time.

86. Giddens, *Modernity and Self-Identity,* 64.

87. De Certeau, *Practice of Everyday Life*.

88. Ibid., 176.

89. Grossberg, "Wandering Audiences," 383.

90. Stromer-Galley, "Interactivity-as-Product."

91. Ibid., 393.

92. Malaby, "Beyond Play," 102.

93. Carol and Chuck Faygo are aliases chosen by the couple.

94. *Rock Band* (Hormonix, 2007), video game.

95. Stromer-Galley, "Interactivity-as-Product."

96. Malaby, "Beyond Play," 102.

97. Klevjer, "What Is the Avatar?"

98. Tronstad, "Character Identification."

99. *Baldur's Gate* (Bioware, 1998), video game; *The Witcher* (CD Projekt RED, 2007), video game; *Mass Effect* (Bioware, 2007), video game.

100. Klevjer, "Enter the Avatar."

101. Newman, " Myth of the Ergodic."

102. Burns, "Playing Roles."

103. Aarseth, "Genre Trouble."

104. Mäyrä, *Introduction to Game Studies*.

105. Barton, "Gay Characters."

106. McCloud, *Understanding Comics.*
107. Bogost, *Unit Operations,* 84.
108. McCloud, *Understanding Comics,* 36; emphasis in original.
109. Frome, "Identity in Comics."
110. *Space Invaders* (Taito Corporation, 1978), video game.
111. For more on intertextuality, see Kristeva, *Desire in Language*; Fiske, *Understanding Popular Culture.* For more on paratexts, see Genette, *Paratexts*; Gray, *Show Sold Separately.*
112. Jenkins, *Convergence Culture.*
113. Consalvo, "Raiding the Paratexts"; Rehak, "Mapping the Big Girl"; Pinckard, "Gender Play."
114. Newman, "Myth of the Ergodic."
115. MacCallum-Stewart, "Real Boys Carry Girly Epics," 27.
116. Kinder, *Playing with Power,* 107.
117. Newman, "Myth of the Ergodic"; Jenkins, "'X Logic.'"
118. *The Sims* (Maxis, 2000–present), video game.
119. Gee, *What Video Games Have.*
120. Boudreau, "Between Play and Design."
121. Waggoner, *My Avatar, My Self.*
122. MacCallum-Stewart, "Real Boys Carry Girly Epics," 35.
123. Klastrup and Tosca, "'Because It Just Looks Cool!,'" 4.
124. Murphy, "'Live in Your World,'" 233.
125. *Diablo II* (Blizzard Entertainment, 2000), video game.
126. He had played through this game on previous occasions and had played as all of the characters at some point.
127. *World of Warcraft* (Blizzard, 2004), video game.
128. MacCallum-Stewart, "Real Boys Carry Girly Epics," 35.
129. Ibid., 34.
130. Nakamura, "After/Images," 323.
131. Leonard, "High Tech Blackface."
132. In the interest of anonymity, I do not reproduce the entire name.
133. Turkle, *Life on the Screen.*
134. Tronstad, "Character Identification."
135. Cassell and Jenkins, *Barbie to Mortal Kombat.*
136. Williams et al., "The Virtual Census."
137. Aarseth, "Genre Trouble," 48.
138. Moultrop, "Response to Aarseth."
139. Waggoner, *My Avatar, My Self.*
140. Galloway, *Gaming,* 106.
141. Nakamura, *Cybertypes.*
142. Shaw, "On Not Becoming Gamers."
143. Nakamura, *Cybertypes,* 114.
144. Williams et al., "The Virtual Census."

4. When and Why Representation Matters to Players

1. Taylor, *Multiculturalism.*
2. Ibid., 25.
3. Ibid., 43.
4. Fraser, "Rethinking Recognition," 245.
5. *Diner Dash* (PlayFirst, 2007), video game. This is a time-management game popular on mobile devices and "casual" gaming websites.
6. Angry Black Woman, "Diner Dash."
7. Spivak, "Can the Subaltern."
8. Valdivia, "bell hooks."
9. Henderson, *Love and Money,* 72–73.
10. Jenson and de Castell, "Gender, Simulation, and Gaming," 64.
11. Canclini, *Consumers and Citizens,* 96; emphasis in original.
12. *Call of Duty 2: Big Red One* (Activision, 2005), video game; *James Bond 007: Nightfire* (EA, 2002), video game.
13. All descriptions of interviewees' identifiers are a combination of survey and interview data. Tanner identified as a heterosexual, white/Arab/Arab American female in her late thirties from the New Jersey Shore area.
14. Gregory actually filled out the survey twice and selected "gay" once and "bisexual" another time. In the interview he simply said he had been in a relationship with a man for six years and only referenced being gay over the course of both interviews.
15. Jenkins, "Complete Freedom of Movement." In this chapter Jenkins argues that video games provide alternative play spaces to children who grow up in spaces where it is increasingly difficult or unsafe to play outside.
16. Elise called herself queer over the course of the interview. She did not fill out the survey, however, so I do not know how she identified with regard to her race and gender. I read her as white and female identified.
17. Dyer, *Matter of Images*; Dyer, "Stereotyping."
18. Williams, "Virtual Census."
19. King and Krzywinska, *Tomb Raiders and Space Invaders,* 185.
20. *Perfect Dark Zero* (Rare, 2005), video game.
21. *Portal* (Valve Corporation, 2007), video game; *Mirror's Edge* (EA Digital Illusions CE, 2008), video game.
22. Free-running, also known as Parkour, is the art of moving through urban spaces by jumping, scaling, or climbing obstacles.
23. Taylor, *Multiculturalism.*
24. Dyer-Witheford and de Peuter, *Games of Empire.*
25. Shaw, "Gay in Game."
26. Chan, "Playing with Race"; Higgin, "Blackless Fantasy."
27. King and Krzywinska, *Tomb Raiders and Space Invaders,* 172.
28. Chan, "Playing with Race."
29. *Madden NFL* (Electronic Arts Tiburon, 1988–present), video game.

30. Leonard, "High Tech Blackface."

31. *NBA Live 09* (Electronic Arts Canada, 1995–2010), video game; *Madden NFL* (Electronic Arts Tiburon, 1988–present), video game.

32. Chan, "Playing with Race."

33. Galloway, *Gaming,* 72.

34. Juul, *Half Real.*

35. Chidester, "Circle Stay Unbroken."

36. Huizinga, *Homo Ludens*; Caillois, *Man, Play, and Games.*

37. Salen and Zimmerman, *Rules of Play*; Consalvo, "There Is No Magic Circle"; Malaby, "Beyond Play"; Crawford, *Video Gamers*; Nardi, *My Life as a Night Elf Priest.*

38. Shaw, "Gay in Game."

39. *Grand Theft Auto* (Rockstar North, 1997–present), video game.

40. Koster, *Theory of Fun.*

41. Ibid., 162.

42. For *Fable* and *The Sims,* he referenced the fact that it made no difference to the narrative or game outcomes if you played as a heterosexual, a homosexual, or a bisexual character.

43. Interviewed in "Mighty Real," *Further off the Straight and Narrow: New Gay Visibility on Television, 1998–2006,* directed by Katherine Sender (Northampton, Mass.: Media Education Foundation, 2006), DVD.

44. Gray, *Out in the Country.*

45. Bird, *The Audience and Everyday Life,* 115.

46. Hall, "Reading Realism."

47. Machin and Suleiman, "Arab and American Computer," 18.

48. Taylor, *Play between Worlds,* 102.

49. For this research, see Katz, Blumer, and Gurevitch, "Uses and Gratifications Research"; Ruggiero, "Uses and Gratifications Theory." For its criticism, see Severn and Tankard, *Communication Theories.*

50. In his survey response, Bryan identified as a white and Hispanic/Latino heterosexual male in his thirties.

51. *Slumdog Millionaire,* directed by Danny Boyle (2008; Beverly Hills, Calif.: 20th Century Fox Home Entertainment, 2009), DVD.

52. *The Hills* was an MTV reality television series that followed the lives of young adults in Los Angeles.

53. Shaw, "Rethinking Game Studies"; Shaw, "Putting the Gay."

54. For more information, see Hernandez, "She Tried."

55. Cassell and Jenkins, *Barbie to Mortal Kombat*; Kafai et al., *Beyond Barbie and Mortal Kombat*; Hayes, "Gendered Identities at Play."

56. Bergman, "Girls Don't Do That!," 330.

57. I have also discussed this in Shaw, "Gay in Game."

58. Morley and Robins, *Spaces of Identity,* 115.

59. Ibid., 57.

60. Shaw, "Do You Identify as a Gamer?"

61. Davies, *Cultural Studies and Beyond*, 94.
62. Plato, *The Republic*, 313–45.
63. *Super Princess Peach* (Nintendo, 2006), video game.
64. Nakamura, *Cybertypes*.
65. Leonard, "Not a Hater."
66. One of the games included in *Wii Sports* (Nintendo, 2006), video game.
67. Staiger, *Media Reception Studies*, 154.
68. Yee, *The Norranthian Scrolls*; Kennedy, "Lara Croft"; Schleiner, "Does Lara Croft Wear."
69. Leonard, "Not a Hater "; Leonard, "High Tech Blackface"; Chan, "Playing with Race"; Hall, "Representation.'"
70. Hall, "Reading Realism," 638.
71. The earliest critiques going around on game-related listservs thought the game was set in Haiti, but that was not the case. *Resident Evil 5* (Capcom, 2009), video game; Godinez, "Zombies in 'Resident Evil 5'"; McWhertor, "*Resident Evil 5* Not Redesigned."
72. Totilo, "That Notorious *Resident Evil 5*."
73. Brock, "Keeping It Real Goes Wrong," 442.
74. This history is discussed in Moreman, *Race, Oppression, and the Zombie*; McAlister, "Slaves, Cannibals"; Christie and Lauro, *Better Off Dead*; Hannabach, "Queer Intimacies."
75. Russell, "Race and Reflexivity," 4.
76. Brock, "Keeping It Real Goes Wrong," 447.
77. Geyser and Tshabalala, "Return to Darkness," 12.
78. Dyer, "Stereotyping."
79. Mäyrä, *Introduction to Game Studies*; King and Krzywinska, *Tomb Raiders and Space Invaders*.
80. Newman, "Myth of the Ergodic."
81. Carr, "Contexts, Gaming Pleasures," 478.
82. Shaw, "Talking to Gaymers"; Shaw, "Beyond Comparison."
83. *EverQuest* (Sony Online Entertainment, 1999), video game; *World of Warcraft* (Blizzard, 2004–present), video game.
84. *Tony Hawk's Underground* (Activision, 2003), video game.
85. *Marvel vs. Capcom* (Capcom, 1995–present), video game.
86. *Mercenaries* (Pandemic Studios, 2005–2008), video game.
87. Hutchinson, "Performing the Self."
88. Taylor, "Multiple Pleasures."
89. Hayes, "Gendered Identities at Play."
90. Taylor, *Play between Worlds*, 117.
91. Ibid.
92. Dietrich, "Avatars of Whiteness."
93. Taylor, *Play between Worlds*, 95.
94. Turkle, *Life on the Screen*, 180.

95. Filiciak, "Hyperidentities," 100.

96. Rose, *Powers of Freedom,* 96.

97. Charles, "Playing with One's Self," 289.

98. Malaby, "Beyond Play."

99. Dietrich, "Avatars of Whiteness"; Tucker, "Griefing"; Nardi, *My Life as a Night Elf Priest.*

100. Butler, *Gender Trouble.*

101. A discussion of this is available on the blog *WoW Musings,* written by games scholar and Internet researcher Rosa Mikeal Martey, at http://wowmusings.wordpress.com/2010/03/19/144.

102. Nakamura, "After/Images of Identity"; Nakamura, *Cybertypes*; Higgin, "Blackless Fantasy."

103. Steiner, "Nobody Knows You're a Dog."

104. Campbell, *Getting It On Online*; Miller and Slater. *The Internet*; Gray, *Out in the Country.*

105. Shaw, "Talking to Gaymers."

106. *Tetris* (Alexey Pajitnov, 1984), video game; Bogost, *Unit Operations.*

107. Murray, *Hamlet on the Holodeck.*

108. Eskelinen, "The Gaming Situation."

109. Bogost, *Unit Operations,* 100.

110. Davison, "The Third-Person Effect"; Paul, Salwen, and Dupagne, "The Third-Person Effect."

111. Bird, *Audience and Everyday Life.*

112. Clark and Clark, "Segregation as a Factor"; Clark and Clark, "Skin Color as a Factor"; *A Girl Like Me,* directed by Kiri Davis (Reel Works Teen Filmmaking, 2005).

113. Greenfield, *Mind and Media*; Kinder, *Playing with Power*; Johnston and Ettema, *Positive Images*; Steinberg and Kincheloe, *Kinderculture*; MacDonald, "Theory of Mass Culture"; Barber, *Consumed.*

114. Seiter, "Lay Theories of Media Effects"; Hoover, Schofield Clark, and Alters, *Media, Home, and Family.*

115. Nakamura, "After Images."

116. Couldry, *Media Rituals,* 45.

117. Fiske, "Understanding Popular Culture"; Hall, "Encoding, Decoding"; Hebdige, *Subculture*; Katz and Lazarsfeld, *Personal Influence.*

118. Gerbner et al., "Growing Up with Television."

119. Williams et al., "The Virtual Census."

120. Martins et al., "Female Body Imagery."

121. King and Krzywinska, *Tomb Raiders and Space Invaders.*

Conclusion

1. Pearson, "EA, Bioware Fire-Fighting."

2. EA Staff, "Full Spectrum Event."

3. Alexander, "EA's LGBT Event."

4. Shaw, "Talking to Gaymers."

5. Shaw, "Putting the Gay in Game."

6. The Human Rights Campaign has often been critiqued for trans* rights, for example, and focusing on rights like civil marriage that benefit only a subset of those who identify as LGBTQ.

7. Hanks, "Comics Becoming More Diverse?"

8. Hinkle, "How *The Sims*."

9. Alexander, "Gambit's 'A Closed World.'"

10. Allen, "Closing the Gap."

11. Corries, "Diversity Means Better Games"; Hamilton, "Video Game Industry Woke-Up."

12. Gaston, "'Women Are the New Core.'"

13. Corries, "Diversity Means Better Games."

14. Walker, "Misogyny, Sexism."

15. Hamilton, "Video Game Industry Woke Up"; Suellentrop, "Indies Grab the Controls."

16. McElroy, "IGDA Draws Backlash."

17. Pinchefsky, "Really? IGDA."

18. Corries, "Diversity Means Better Games."

19. This controversy is detailed and continually updated at the *Geek Feminism* wiki, http://geekfeminism.wikia.com/wiki/Dickwolves.

20. Hall, "*Mass Effect* Developer."

21. Gilbert, "Raven's Manveer Heir."

22. A 1985 strip of her comic *Dykes to Watch Out For* features two women discussing going to see a movie. One says she only goes to see a film if it fulfills three rules: "one, it has to have at least two women in it who, two, talk to each other about, three, something besides a man" (Bechdel, *Dykes*, 22–23).

23. Bechdel, "Testy."

24. Ibid.

25. Emphasis added to all quotes.

26. In *The Practice of Everyday Life,* de Certeau (1984) argues that people regularly remake and reimagine mass-produced products in order to individualize them. This pushes back against research that addresses only industries and products.

27. Abrams and Giles, "Ethnic Identity"; Davis and Gandy Jr., "Racial Identity and Media Orientation."

28. Taylor, "Multiple Pleasures," 36.

29. Foucault, *History of Sexuality,* 45.

30. Ibid., 83.

31. Nichols, *Beyond Uhura,* 164.

32. Gilroy, "Pitfalls of Identity," 393.

33. Riggs, "Signifyin' Snap! Queen," 64.

34. Jackson, *Racial Paranoia,* 11.

35. Gramsci, *Letters from Prison.*
36. D'Acci, "Television, Representation, and Gender."
37. Ibid., 380.
38. Ibid.
39. Mouffe, "Citizenship and Political Identity," 30.
40. This point is also made in Sender, *Business, Not Politics.*
41. Taylor, *Multiculturalism,* 72.
42. Ibid., 104.
43. Becker, *Gay TV and Straight America.*
44. McLelland, "Local Meanings"; McLelland, "Japanese Girls' Comics."
45. Henderson, "Lesbian Pornography."
46. Tate, *Everything but the Burden*; Leonard, "Virtual Gangstas"; Leonard, "High Tech Blackface"; Leonard, "To the White Extreme."
47. Lorde, *Sister Outsider,* 112; emphasis in original.
48. Ibid.
49. Shaw, "Gay in Games."
50. Taylor, *Play between Worlds,* 124.
51. Hamm, "Unique Video Game Characters."
52. Images from Hamm's designs are available at Shaylyn Hamm, "The Aesthetics of Unique Video Game Characters," May 20, 2010, *GameCareerGuide,* http://gamecareerguide.com/features/854/features/854/the_aesthetics_of_unique_video_.php.
53. Hamm, "Unique Video Game Characters," 39.
54. Gilroy, *After Empire,* 3.
55. Dyer, *Only Entertainment,* 168.
56. Dovey and Kennedy, *Game Cultures,* 93.
57. Williams et al., "The Virtual Census."
58. Juul, *Casual Revolution.*
59. Ibid., 152; emphasis in original.
60. Shaw, "Identify as a Gamer"; Shaw, "On Not Becoming Gamers."
61. Ibid.
62. Laramée, *Secrets of the Game Business,* xvii.
63. Ibid., xxi.
64. Ibid.
65. Games.net, "Racism in Games."
66. Ray, *Gender Inclusive Game Design*; Cassell and Jenkins, *Barbie to Mortal Kombat.*
67. Shaw, "Ethic of Representation," 172.
68. Salen and Zimmerman, *Rules of Play,* 526.
69. Ibid.
70. Flanagan, *Critical Play.*
71. Braithwaite and Schreiber, *Challenges for Game Designers,* 177–78.
72. Anthropy, *Rise of the Videogame Zinesters.*
73. Juul, *Art of Failure.*

Gameography

Adventures of Lolo. Nintendo Entertainment Systems. Developed by HAL Laboratory. HAL American, 1989.

Assassin's Creed. PlayStation 3. Developed by Ubisoft Montreal. Ubisoft, 2007.

Baldur's Gate. Windows. Developed by Bioware. Interplay Entertainment, 1998.

California Games. Nintendo Entertainment System. Developed by Epyx. Epyx Games, 1987.

Call of Duty 3. PlayStation 2. Developed by Treyarch. Activision, 2006.

Castlevania. Nintendo Entertainment System. Developed by Konami. Konami, 1987.

Custer's Revenge. Atari 2600. Developed by Mystique. Mystique, 1982.

Diablo II. Windows. Developed by Blizzard North. Blizzard Entertainment, 2000.

Diner Dash. Windows. Developed by GameLab. PlayFirst, 2007.

Disgaea: Hour of Darkness. PlayStation 2. Developed by Nippon Ichi Software. Altus, 2003.

Doom. Sega 32X. Developed by id Software. Sega, 1994.

Duke Nukem. Sega Saturn. Developed by Lobotomy Software. Sega, 1997.

Eternal Darkness: Sanity's Requiem. Nintendo Game Cube. Developed by Silicon Knights. Nintendo, 2002.

EverQuest. Windows. Developed by Sony Online Entertainment. Sony Online Entertainment, 1999.

Fable: The Lost Chapters. Xbox 360. Developed by Lionhead Studios. Microsoft Game Studios, 2005.

Fable II. Xbox 360. Developed by Lionhead Studios. Microsoft Game Studios, 2008.

Fable III. Xbox 360. Developed by Lionhead Studios. Microsoft Game Studios, 2010.

Fallout 3. Xbox 360. Developed by Bethesda Game Studios. Bethesda Softworks, 2008.

God of War. PlayStation 2. Developed by SCE Santa Monica Studio. Sony Computer Entertainment, 2005.

Grand Theft Auto III. PlayStation 2. Developed by DMA Design. Rockstar Games, 2001.

Indigo Prophecy (Fahrenheit). PlayStation 2. Developed by Quantic Dream. Atari, 2005.

James Bond 007: Nightfire. PlayStation 2. Developed by Eurocom. Electronic Arts, 2002.

Kingdom Hearts. PlayStation 2. Developed by Square Enix. Square Enix, 2002.

LA Noire. PlayStation 3. Developed by Team Bondi. Rockstar Games, 2011.

Left 4 Dead. Xbox 360. Developed by Turtle Rock Studios. Valve Corporation, 2008.

Madden NFL 09. PlayStation 3. Developed by Electronic Arts Tiburon. Electronic Arts Sports, 2008.

Marvel vs. Capcom 2: New Age of Heroes. PlayStation 2. Developed by Capcom. Capcom Production Studio, 2000.

Mass Effect. Windows. Developed by Bioware. Microsoft Game Studios, 2007.

Mercenaries: Playground of Destruction. PlayStation 2. Developed by Pandemic Studios. LucasArts, 2005.

Metroid. Nintendo Entertainment System. Developed by Nintendo's Research and Development 1 and Intelligent Systems. Nintendo, 1986.

Mirror's Edge. Xbox 360. Developed by EA Digital Illusions CE. Electronic Arts, 2008.

Ms. Pac-Man. Arcade game. Developed by Bally Midway. Namco, 1982.

NBA Street. PlayStation 2. Developed by Electronic Arts Canada. Electronic Arts Sports BIG, 2001.

NBA Live 09. PlayStation 3. Developed by Electronic Arts Canada. Electronic Arts, 2009.

ESPN NHL 2K5. PlayStation 2. Developed by Kush Games. Sega, 2004.

Othello. Nintendo Entertainment System. Developed by HAL Laboratory. Kawada, 1986.

Perfect Dark Zero. Xbox 360. Developed by Rare. Microsoft Game Studios, 2005.

Portal. Xbox 360. Developed by Valve Corporation. Valve Corporation, 2007.

Resident Evil 5. PlayStation 3. Developed by Capcom. Capcom, 2009.

Rock Band. Xbox 360. Developed by Harmonix. MTV Games/Electronic Arts, 2007.

Soul Calibur 3. PlayStation 2. Developed by Project Soul. Namco, 2005.

Space Invaders. Arcade. Developed by Taito Corporation. Midway, 1978.

Super Mario Bros. Nintendo Entertainment System. Developed by Nintendo EAD. Nintendo, 1985.

Super Princess Peach. Nintendo DS. Developed by TOSE. Nintendo, 2006.

Team Fortress 2. Windows. Developed by Valve Corporation. Valve Corporation, 2007.

Tetris. Nintendo Game Boy. Developed by Alexey Pajitnov. Nintendo, 1989.

The Bard's Tale. PlayStation 2. Developed by InXile Entertainment. Vivendi Universal Games, 2004.

The Legend of Zelda. Nintendo Entertainment System. Developed by Nintendo R&D 4. Nintendo, 1986.

The Sims. Windows. Developed by The Sims Studio. Electronic Arts, 2009.

The Sims Online. Windows. Developed by Maxis. Electronic Arts, 2002.

The Witcher. Windows. Developed by CD Projekt RED. Atari, 2007.

Tiny Toon Adventures. Nintendo Entertainment System. Developed by Konami. Konami, 1991.

Tomb Raider. Windows. Developed by Core Design. Eidos Interactive, 1996.

Tomb Raider: Legend. Xbox 360. Developed by Crystal Dynamics. Eidos Interactive, 2006

Tomb Raider. PlayStation 3. Developed by Crystal Dynamics. Square Enix, 2013.

Tony Hawk's Underground. Xbox 360. Developed by Neversoft. Activision, 2003.

Wii Sports. Nintendo Wii. Developed by Nintendo EAD Group Number 2. Nintendo, 2006.

Wii Fit. Nintendo Wii. Developed by Nintendo EAD Group Number 5. Nintendo, 2008.

World of Warcraft. Windows. Developed by Blizzard Entertainment. Blizzard Entertainment, 2004.

Bibliography

Aarseth, Espen. *Cybertext: Perspectives on Ergodic Literature.* Baltimore, Md.: Johns Hopkins University Press, 1997.

———. "Genre Trouble: Narrativism and the Art of Simulation." In *First Person: New Media as Story, Performance, and Game,* edited by Pat Harrigan and Noah Wiardrip-Fruin, 45–55. Cambridge, Mass.: MIT Press, 2004.

Abbate, Janet. *Recoding Gender: Women's Changing Participation in Computing.* Cambridge, Mass.: MIT Press, 2012.

Abrams, Jessica R., and Howard Giles. "Ethnic Identity Gratifications Selection and Avoidance by African Americans: A Group Vitality and Social Identity Gratifications Perspective." *Media Psychology* 9 (2007): 115–34.

Abu-Lughod, Lila. *Dramas of Nationhood: The Politics of Television in Egypt.* Cairo, Egypt: American University in Cairo Press, 2005.

Adams, Ernest. *Fundamentals of Game Design.* 2nd ed. Berkeley, Calif.: New Riders, 2010.

Alexander, Leigh. "Interview: How Gambit's 'A Closed World' Tackles Sexuality, Identity." *Gamasutra,* September 26, 2011. http://www.gamasutra.com/view/news/36951.

———. "Opinion: In the Sexism Discussion, Let's Look at Game Culture." *Gamasutra,* July 16, 2012. http://www.gamasutra.com/view/news/174145.

———. "EA's LGBT Event Aims to Be a First Step towards Cultural Change." *Gamasutra,* March 7, 2013. http://www.gamasutra.com/view/news/187769.

Allen, Samantha. "Closing the Gap between Queer and Mainstream Games." *Polygon,* April 2, 2014. http://www.polygon.com/2014/4/2/5549878/closing-the-gap-between-queer-and-mainstream-games.

Allor, Martin. "Relocating the Site of the Audience." *Critical Studies in Mass Communication* 5 (1988): 217–33.

Althusser, Louis. "Ideology and the Ideological State Apparatuses." In *Cultural Theory and Popular Culture: A Reader.* 4th ed., edited by John Storey, 302–12. New York: Pearson, 2009.

Anderson, Benedict. *Imagined Communities: Reflections on the Origin and Spread of Nationalism*. London: Verso, 1983.

Ang, Ien. *Watching "Dallas": Soap Opera and the Melodramatic Imagination*. London: Routledge, 1989.

———. *Desperately Seeking the Audience*. New York: Routledge, 1991.

Angry Black Woman. "Diner Dash and the Angry Black Women." *The Angry Black Woman Blog*, November 7, 2007. http://theangryblackwoman .com/2007/11/07/diner-dash-and-the-angry-black-women.

Anthropy, Anna. *Rise of the Videogame Zinesters: How Freaks, Normals, Amateurs, Artists, Dreamers, Drop-outs, Queers, Housewives, and People Like You Are Taking Back an Art Form*. New York: Seven Stories Press, 2012.

Apperley, Thomas H. "Genre and Game Studies: Toward a Critical Approach to Video Game Genres." *Simulation and Gaming* 37, no. 1 (2006): 6–23.

———. "The Body of the Gamer: Game Art and Gestural Excess." *Digital Creativity* (September 2013). DOI: 10.1080/14626268.2013.808967.

Appiah, Anthony. *The Ethics of Identity*. Princeton, N.J.: Princeton University Press, 2005.

Armstrong, G. Blake, and Kimberly A. Neunendorf. "TV Entertainment, News, and Racial Perceptions of College Students." *Journal of Communication* 42, no. 3 (1992): 153–76.

Arsenault, Dominic, and Bernard Perron. "In the Frame of the Magic Cycle: The Circle(s) of Gameplay." In *The Video Game Theory Reader 2*, edited by Bernard Perron and Mark J. P. Wolf, 109–31. London: Routledge, 2009.

Austin, J. L. *How to Do Things with Words*. 2nd ed. Oxford: Oxford University Press, 1975.

Barber, Benjamin R. *Consumed: How Markets Corrupt Children, Infantilize Adults, and Swallow Citizens Whole*. New York: W. W. Norton, 2007.

Barker, Martin. "Taking the Extreme Case: Understanding a Fascist Fan of Judge Dredd." In *Trash Aesthetics: Popular Culture and Its Audience*, edited by Deborah Cartmell, Heidi Kaye, Ian Hunter, and Imelda Whelehan, 14–30. London: Pluto Press, 1997.

Barton, Matthew D. "Gay Characters in Video Games." *Armchair Arcade*, April 1, 2004. http://www.armchairarcade.com/aamain/content.php ?article.27.

Basil, Michael D. "Identification as a Mediator of Celebrity Effects." *Journal of Broadcasting and Electronic Media* 40 (1996): 478–95.

Beam, Joseph. "Making Ourselves from Scratch." In *The Columbia Reader on Lesbians and Gay Men in Media, Society, and Politics*, edited by Larry Gross and James D. Woods, 79–80. New York: Columbia University Press, 1999.

Bechdel, Alison. *Dykes to Watch Out For*. New York: Firebrand Books, 1986.

———. "Testy." *Alison Bechdel Blog*, November 8, 2013. http://dykestowatch outfor.com/testy.

Becker, Ron. *Gay TV and Straight America.* New Brunswick, N.J.: Rutgers University Press, 2006.

Behrenshausen, Bryan G. "Toward a (Kin)Aesthetic of Video Gaming." *Games and Culture* 2, no. 4 (2007): 335–54.

Benhabib, Seyla. "Feminism and Postmodernism." In *Feminist Contentions,* edited by Seyla Benhabib, Judith Butler, Drucilla Cornell, and Nancy Fraser, 17–34. New York: Routledge, 1995.

Benshoff, Harry M., and Sean Griffin. *Queer Images: A History of Gay and Lesbian Film in America.* Lanham, Md.: Rowman and Littlefield, 2006.

Bergman, Stephanie. "But . . . Girls Don't Do That!" In *From Barbie to Mortal Kombat: Gender and Computer Games,* edited by Justine Cassell and Henry Jenkins, 329–31. Cambridge, Mass.: MIT Press, 2000.

Bernstein, Mary. "Celebration and Suppression: The Strategic Uses of Identity by the Lesbian and Gay Movement." *American Journal of Sociology* 103, no. 3 (1997): 531–65.

Bird, S. Elizabeth. "Travels in Nowhere Land: Ethnography and the 'Impossible' Audience." *Critical Studies in Mass Communication* 9 (1992): 250–60.

———. *For Enquiring Minds: A Cultural Study of Supermarket Tabloids.* Knoxville: University of Tennessee Press, 1992.

———. *The Audience and Everyday Life: Living in a Media World.* New York: Routledge, 2003.

Bobo, Jacqueline. "*The Color Purple*: Black Women as Cultural Readers." In *Say It Loud! African-American Audiences, Media, and Identity,* edited by Robin R. Means Coleman, 205–27. New York: Routledge, 2002.

Boellstorff, Tom. "A Ludicrous Discipline? Ethnography and Game Studies." *Games and Culture* 1, no. 1 (2006): 29–35.

Bogost, Ian. *Unit Operations: An Approach to Videogame Criticism.* Cambridge, Mass.: MIT Press, 2006.

———. "Atari Porn Games." *Kotaku,* November 17, 2007. http://www.kotaku.com.au/2007/11/atari_porn_games.

———. *Persuasive Games: The Expressive Power of Videogames.* Cambridge, Mass.: MIT Press, 2010.

Boudreau, Kelly. "Between Play and Design: The Emergence of Hybrid-Identity in Single-Player Videogames." Montreal: Université de Montréal, 2012.

Bourdieu, Pierre. *Distinction: A Social Critique of the Judgement of Taste.* Translated by Richard Nice. Cambridge, Mass.: Harvard University Press, 1984.

Braithwaite, Andrea. "'Seriously, Get Out': Feminists on the Forums and the War(craft) on Women." *New Media and Society,* June 12, 2013. doi:10.1177/1461444813489503.

Braithwaite, Brenda, and Ian Schreiber. *Challenges for Game Designers.* Boston: Course Technology, 2009.

Breslaw, Anna. "Another Racist Shitstorm Brews over Casting *Hunger Games'* Finnick." *Jezebel,* May 5, 2012. http://jezebel.com/5907900/casting-of-the-hunger-games-finnick-is-stirring-up-another-race-shitstorm.

Brock, André. "When Keeping It Real Goes Wrong: *Resident Evil 5,* Race, and Gamers." *Games and Culture* 6, no. 5 (2011): 429–52.

Bruns, Axel. *Blogs, Wikipedia, SecondLife, and Beyond: From Production to Produsage.* New York: Peter Lang, 2008.

Bryce, Jo, and Jason Rutter. *Understanding Digital Games.* London: Sage, 2006.

Bucy, Erik P. "Interactivity in Society: Locating an Elusive Concept." *Information Society* 20 (2004): 373–83.

Bull, Sarah. "*The Hunger Games* Hit by Racism Now as Movie Fans Tweet Vile Slurs over Casting of Black Teen Actress as Heroine Rue." *MailOnline,* March 30, 2012. http://www.dailymail.co.uk/news/article-2122714/The-Hunger-Games-hit-racism-row-movie-fans-tweet-vile-slurs-casting-black-teen-actress-heroine-Rue.html.

Burns, Andrew. "Playing Roles." In *Computer Games: Text, Narrative, and Play,* edited by Diane Carr, David Buckingham, Andrew Burn, and Gareth Schott, 72–87. Malden, Mass.: Polity Press, 2006.

Burrill, Derek A. *Die Tryin': Videogames, Masculinity, Culture.* New York: Peter Lang, 2008.

Butler, Judith. "Collected and Fractured." In *Identities,* edited by Kwame Anthony Appiah and Henry Louis Gates Jr., 439–47. Chicago: University of Chicago Press, 1995.

———. *Undoing Gender.* New York: Routledge, 2004.

———. *Precarious Life: The Powers of Mourning and Violence.* New York: Verso, 2004.

———. *Gender Trouble.* 3rd ed. New York: Routledge, 2006.

———. "Performativity, Precarity, and Sexual Politics." *Revista de Antropoligia Iberoamericana* 4, no. 3 (2009): i-xii.

Butsch, Richard. *The Making of American Audiences: From Stage to Television, 1750–1990.* Cambridge: Cambridge University Press, 2000.

Caillois, Roger. *Man, Play, and Games.* Translated by Meyer Barash. New York: Free Press of Glencoe, 1961.

Calleja, Gordon. "Digital Games and Escapism." *Games and Culture* 5, no. 4 (2010): 335–53.

———. *In-Game: From Immersion to Incorporation.* Cambridge, Mass.: MIT Press, 2011.

Campbell, John Edward. *Getting It On Online: Cyberspace, Gay Male Sexuality, and Embodied Identity.* New York: Harrington Park Press, 2004.

Canclini, Néstor García. *Consumers and Citizens: Globalization and Multicultural Conflicts.* Minneapolis: University of Minnesota Press, 2001.

Caperton. "*HungerGames*: WhatDoYouMean,theBlackGirlWasBlack?" *Femin-

iste, March 27, 2012. http://www.feministe.us/blog/archives/2012/03/27/hunger-games-what-do-you-mean-the-black-girl-was-black.

Carnagey, Nicholas L., C. A. Andersen, and B. J. Bushman. "The Effect of Video Game Violence on Physiological Desensitization to Real-Life Violence." *Journal of Experimental Psychology* 43, no. 3 (2007): 489–96.

Carr, Diane. "Contexts, Gaming Pleasures, and Gendered Preferences." *Simulation Gaming* 36, no. 4 (2005): 478.

Carr, Diane, David Buckingham, Andrew Burn, and Gareth R. Schott. *Computer Games: Text, Narrative, and Play.* Malden, Mass.: Polity Press, 2006.

Carroll, Noël. *A Philosophy of Mass Art.* Oxford: Oxford University Press, 1998.

Cassell, Justine, and Henry Jenkins. *From Barbie to Mortal Kombat: Gender and Computer Games.* Cambridge, Mass.: MIT Press, 2000.

Castronova, Edward. *Synthetic Worlds: The Business and Culture of Online Games.* Chicago: University of Chicago Press, 2005.

Caughey, John L. "Gina as Steven: The Social and Cultural Dimensions of a Media Relationship." *Visual Anthropology Review* 10, no. 1 (1994): 126–35.

Chalk, Andy. "A Short History of Race in Games." *Escapist,* August 16, 2007. http://www.escapistmagazine.com/articles/view/columns/the-needles/1353-A-Short-History-of-Race-in-Games.

———. "*Dragon Age* Writer: Same-Sex Romance Is Here to Stay." *Escapist,* December 23, 2010. http://www.escapistmagazine.com/news/view/106414-Dragon-Age-Writer-Same-Sex-Romance-is-Here-to-Stay.

Chambers, Becky. "The All-Too-Familiar Harassment against Feminist Frequency and What the Gaming Community Can Do about It." *Mary Sue,* June 12, 2012. http://www.themarysue.com/the-all-too-familiar-harassment-against-feminist-frequency-and-what-the-gaming-community-can-do-about-it.

Chan, Dean. 2005. "Playing with Race: The Ethics of Racialized Representations in E-games." *IRIE* 4 (2005): 24–30.

Charles, Alec. "Playing with One's Self: Notions of Subjectivity and Agency in Digital Games." *Eludamos* 3, no. 2 (2009): 281–94.

Chee, Florence, Marcelo Vieta, and Richard Smith. "Online Gaming and the Interactional Self." In *Gaming as Culture: Essays on Reality, Identity, and Experience in Fantasy Games,* edited by J. Patrick Williams, Sean Q. Hendricks, and W. Keith Winkler, 154–74. Jefferson, N.C.: McFarland and Company, 2006.

Chidester, Phil. "May the Circle Stay Unbroken: *Friends,* the Presence of Absence, and the Rhetorical Reinforcement of Whiteness." *Critical Studies in Media Communication* 25, no. 2 (2008): 157–74.

Chin, Elizabeth. *Purchasing Power: Black Kids and American Consumer Culture.* Minneapolis: University of Minnesota Press, 2001.

Christie, Deborah, and Sarah Juliet Lauro, eds. *Better Off Dead: The*

Evolution of the Zombie as Post-human. New York: Fordham University Press, 2011.

Clark, Kenneth B., and Mamie K. Clark. "Segregation as a Factor in the Racial Identification of Negro Preschool Children: A Preliminary Report." *Journal of Experimental Education* 8, no. 2 (1939): 161–63.

———. "Skin Color as a Factor in Racial Identification of Negro Preschool Children." *Journal of Social Psychology* 11 (1940): 159–69.

Cohen, Jonathan. "Defining Identification: A Theoretical Look at the Identification of Audiences with Media Characters." *Mass Communication and Society* 4, no. 3 (2001): 245–64.

Collins, Suzanne. *The Hunger Games.* New York: Scholastic, 2008.

Consalvo, Mia. 2003. "Hot Dates and Fairy-tale Romances: Studying Sexuality in Video Games." In *The Video Game Theory Reader,* edited by Mark J. P. Wolf and Bernard Perron, 171–94. New York: Routledge.

———. *It's a Queer World after All: Studying "The Sims" and Sexuality.* New York: GLAAD Center for the Study of Media and Society, 2003. https://www.academia.edu/654441/Its_a_queer_world_after_all_Studying_The_Sims_and_sexuality.

———. *Cheating: Gaining Advantage in Videogames.* Cambridge, Mass.: MIT Press, 2007.

———. "From Dollhouse to Metaverse: What Happened When *The Sims* Went Online." In *The Players' Realm: Studies on the Culture of Video Games and Gaming,* edited by J. Patrick Williams and Jonas Heide Smith, 203–22. Jefferson, N.C.: McFarland and Company, 2007.

———. "Hardcore Casual: Game Culture *Return(s) to Ravenhearst*." Proceedings of the Fourth International Conference of Foundations of Digital Games, 2009.

———. "There Is No Magic Circle." *Games and Culture* 4, no. 4 (2009): 408–17.

———. "Confronting Toxic Gamer Culture: A Challenge for Feminist Game Studies Scholars." *Ada: A Journal of Gender, New Media, and Technology,* no. 1 (2012). doi: 10.7264/N33X84KH.

———. "Raiding the Paratexts of Lara Croft." *InMediaRes,* March 12, 2013. http://mediacommons.futureofthebook.org/imr/2013/03/12/raiding-paratexts-lara-croft.

Corries, Alexa Ray. "Character Diversity Means Better Games, Says Microsoft Studios Writer." *Polygon,* March 26, 2013. http://www.polygon.com/2013/3/26/4150538/character-diversity-means-better-games-says-microsoft-studios-writer.

Couldry, Nick. *Inside Culture: Re-imagining the Method of Cultural Studies.* London: Sage, 2000.

———. *Media Rituals: A Critical Approach.* New York: Routledge, 2003.

———. "Theorising Media as Practice." *Social Semiotics* 14, no. 2 (2004): 115–32.

————. *Media, Society, World: Social Theory and Digital Media Practice.* London: Polity Press, 2012.

Crawford, Garry. *Video Gamers.* London: Routledge, 2012.

Crawford, Garry, and Jason Rutter. "Playing the Game: Performance in Digital Game Audiences." In *Fandom: Identities and Communities in a Mediated World,* edited by Jonathan Gray, Cornel Sandvoss, and C. Lee Harrington, 271–81. New York: New York University Press, 1997.

Crenshaw, Kimberlé. "Mapping the Margins: Intersectionality, Identity Politics, and Violence against Women of Color." *Stanford Law Review* 43 (1991): 1241–99.

Crick, Timothy. "The Game Body: Toward a Phenomenology of Contemporary Video Gaming." *Games and Culture* 6, no. 3 (2011): 259–69.

D'Acci, Julie. *Defining Women: Television and the Case of Cagney and Lacey.* Chapel Hill, N.C.: University of North Carolina Press, 1994.

————. "Television, Representation, and Gender." In *The Television Studies Reader,* edited by Robert C. Allen and Annette Hill, 373–88. New York: Routledge, 2004.

Dasgutpa, Nilanjana, and Shaki Asgari. "Seeing Is Believing: Exposure to Counterstereotypic Women Leaders and Its Effect on the Malleability of Automatic Gender Stereotyping." *Journal of Experimental Psychology* 40 (2004): 642–58.

Davies, Ioan. *Cultural Studies and Beyond: Fragments of Empire.* New York: Routledge, 1995.

Davis, Jessica L., and Oscar II. Gandy Jr. "Racial Identity and Media Orientation: Exploring the Nature of Constraint." *Journal of Black Studies* 29, no. 3 (1999): 367–97.

Davison, W. Phillips. "The Third-Person Effect in Communication." *Public Opinion Quarterly* 47, no. 1 (1983): 1–15.

Dayan, Daniel. "Paticularistic Media and Diasporic Communications." In *Media, Ritual, and Identity,* edited by Tamar Liebes and James Curran, 103–13. London: Routledge, 1998.

de Certeau, Michel. *The Practice of Everyday Life.* Translated by Stephen F. Rendall. Berkeley: University of California Press, 2011.

de Mul, Jos. "The Game of Life: Narrative and Ludic Identity Formation in Computer Games." In *Handbook of Computer Game Studies,* edited by Joost Raessens and Jeffery Goldstein, 251–66. Cambridge, Mass.: MIT Press, 2006.

DeVane, Ben, and Kurt D. Squire. "The Meaning of Race and Violence in Grand Theft Auto: San Andreas." *Games and Culture* 3, nos. 3–4 (2008): 264–85.

Dietrich, David. "Avatars of Whiteness: Racial Expression in Video Game Characters." *Sociological Inquiry* 83, no. 1 (2013): 82–105.

Dill, Karen E., and Jody C. Dill. "Video Game Violence: A Review of the

Empirical Literature." *Aggression and Violent Behavior* 3, no. 4 (1998): 407–28.

Dornfeld, Barry. *Producing Public Television, Producing Public Culture.* Princeton, N.J.: Princeton University Press, 1998.

Doty, Alexander. *Making Things Perfectly Queer: Interpreting Mass Culture.* Minneapolis: University of Minnesota Press, 1993.

Douglas, Susan J. *Where the Girls Are: Growing Up Female with the Mass Media.* New York: Times Books, 1994.

Dourish, Paul. "What We Talk about When We Talk about Context." *Personal and Ubiquitous Computing* 8, no. 1 (2004): 19–30.

Dovey, Jonathan, and Helen W. Kennedy. *Game Cultures: Computer Games as New Media.* New York: Open University Press, 2006.

Dyer, Richard. *Only Entertainment.* London: Routledge, 1992.

———. *The Matter of Images: Essays on Representation.* 2nd ed. London: Routledge, 1993.

———. "Stereotyping." In *The Columbia Reader on Lesbians and Gay Men in Media, Society, and Politics,* edited by Larry Gross and James D. Woods, 297–301. New York: Columbia University Press, 1999.

Dyer-Witheford, Nick, and Greig de Peuter. 2009. *Games of Empire: Global Capitalism and Video Games.* Minneapolis: University of Minnesota Press.

EA Staff. "EA Hosts LGBT Full Spectrum Event." *EA News,* March 4, 2013. http://www.ea.com/news/ea-hosts-lgbt-full-spectrum-event.

Eladhari, Mirjam. "The Player's Journey." In *The Players' Realm: Studies on the Culture of Video Games and Gaming,* edited by J. Patrick Williams and Jonas Heide Smith, 171–87. Jefferson, N.C.: McFarland and Company, 2007.

Enevold, Jennifer, and C. Hagstrom. "Mothers, Play, and Everyday Life: Ethnology Meets Games Studies." *Ethnologia Scandinavica* 39 (2009): 29–41. http://gamingmoms.files.wordpress.com/2009/09/ethnologia -2009.pdf.

Eskelinen, Markku. "The Gaming Situation." *Game Studies* 1, no. 1 (2001). http://www.gamestudies.org/0101/eskelinen.

Eugenie, Shinkle. "Corporealis Ergo Sum: Affective Response in Digital Games." In *Digital Gameplay: Essays on the Nexus of Game and Gamer,* edited by Nate Garrelts, 21–35. Jefferson, N.C.: McFarland and Company, 2005.

Evans, Caroline, and Lorraine Gamman. "Reviewing Queer Viewing." In *Queer Cinema: The Film Reader,* edited by Harry Benshoff and Sean Griffin, 209–24. New York: Routledge, 2004.

Ewen, Stuart. *Captains of Consciousness: Advertising and the Social Roots of the Consumer Culture.* New York: McGraw-Hill, 1976.

Eyal, Keren, and Alan M. Rubin. "Viewer Aggression and Homophily, Identification, and Parasocial Relationship with Television Characters." *Journal of Broadcasting and Electronic Media* 47, no. 1 (2003): 77–98.

Filiciak, Mirosław. "Hyperidentities: Postmodern Identity Patterns in Massively Multiplayer Online Role-playing Games." In *Video Game Theory Reader,* edited by Mark J. P. Wolf and Bernard Perron, 87–102. New York: Routledge, 2003.

Fine, Gary Alan. "Frames and Games." In *The Game Design Reader: A Rules of Play Anthology,* edited by Katie Salen and Eric Zimmerman, 578–601. Cambridge, Mass.: MIT Press. 2006.

Fisherkiller, JoEllen. "Everday Learning about Identities among Young Adolescents in Television Culture." *Anthropology and Education Quarterly* 28, no. 4 (1997): 467–92.

Fiske, John. *Understanding Popular Culture.* Boston: Routledge, 1989.

Fitzgerald, Joe. "At San Francisco Convention, Gay Gamers Are Diversifying the Industry." *San Francisco Examiner,* August 5, 2013. http://www.sfexaminer.com/sanfrancisco/at-san-francisco-convention-gay-gamers-are-diversifying-the-industry/Content?oid=2535082.

Flanagan, Mary. *Critical Play: Radical Game Design.* Cambridge, Mass.: MIT Press, 2009.

Foucault, Michel. *Power/Knowledge: Selected Interviews and Other Writings, 1972–1977.* Edited by Colin Gordon, Translated by Colin Gordon, Leo Marshall, John Mepham, and Kate Soper. New York: Pantheon Books, 1980.

———. "The Subject and Power." *Critical Inquiry* 8, no. 4 (1982): 777–95.

———. *An Introduction.* Vol. 1, *The History of Sexuality.* Translated by Robert Hurley. New York: Vintage Books, 1990.

Frasca, Gonzalo. "Simulation versus Narrative: Introduction to Ludology." In *Video Game Theory Reader,* edited by Mark J. P. Wolf and Bernard Perron, 221–35. New York: Routledge, 2003.

Fraser, Nancy. "Rethinking Recognition." In *Cultural Studies: From Theory to Action,* edited by Pepi Leistyna, 243–51. Malden, Mass.: Blackwell, 2005.

Freedman, Eric. "8-Bit Porn: Atari after Dark." *Flow,* June 9, 2007. http://flowtv.org/2007/06/atari-video-games-adult-freud.

Frome, Johnathan. "Identity in Comics." *Comics Journal,* no. 211 (1999): 82–86.

Frum, Larry. "Nearly Half of All Video-Gamers Are Women." *CNN Tech,* August 11, 2013. http://www.cnn.com/2013/08/08/tech/gaming-gadgets/female-gamers.

Fung, Richard. "Looking for My Penis: The Eroticized Asian in Gay Video Porn." In *The Columbia Reader on Lesbians and Gay Men in Media, Society, and Politics,* edited by Larry Gross and James D. Woods, 517–25. New York: Columbia University Press, 1999.

Galloway, Alexander R. *Gaming: Essays on Algorithmic Culture.* Minneapolis: University of Minnesota Press, 2006.

Games.net. "Racism in Games." *Games.net,* October 26, 2008. http://www.youtube.com/watch?v=imqDprGVzfM.

Gaming in Color. "Gaming in Color: The Queers & Gaymers of the Pixelated World." Kickstarter, March 6, 2013. http://www.kickstarter.com/projects/gamingincolor/gaming-in-color-queers-and-gaymers-of-the-pixelate.

Garrelts, Nate. *The Meaning and Culture of Grand Theft Auto: Critical Essays.* Jefferson, N.C.: McFarland and Company, 2006.

Gaston, Martin. "'Women Are the New Core,' Says Microsoft Narrative Designer." *Gamespot,* March 27, 2013. http://www.gamespot.com/news/women-are-the-new-core-says-microsoft-narrative-designer-6406037.

Gauntlett, David. *Creative Explorations: New Approaches to Identities and Audiences.* New York: Routledge, 2007.

Gee, James Paul. *What Video Games Have to Teach Us about Learning and Literacy.* 1st ed. New York: Palgrave Macmillan, 2003.

——. "Cultural Models: Do You Want to Be the Blue Sonic or the Dark Sonic?" In *The Game Design Reader: A Rules of Play Anthology,* edited by Katie Salen and Eric Zimmerman, 610–39. Cambridge, Mass.: MIT Press, 2006.

Geertz, Clifford. *Interpretation of Cultures.* New York: Basic Books, 1973.

Genette, Gérard. *Paratexts: Thresholds of Interpretation.* Cambridge: Cambridge University Press, 1997.

Gentile, Douglas A., and Craig A. Anderson. "Violent Video Games: Effects on Youth and Public Policy Implications." In *Handbook of Children, Culture, and Violence,* edited by N. E. Dowd, D. G. Singer, and R. F. Wilson, 225–46. Thousand Oaks, Calif.: Sage, 2006.

Gerbner, George, Michael Morgan, Larry Gross, Nancy Signorielli, and James Shanahan. "Growing Up with Television: Cultivation Processes." In *Media Effects: Advances in Theory and Research,* edited by Jennings Bryant and Dolf Zillmann, 43–67. Mahwah, N.J.: Lawrence Erlbaum Associates, 2002.

Gerbner, George, and Larry Gross. "Living with Television: The Violence Profile." *Journal of Communication* 26 (1976): 172–99.

Geyser, Hanli, and Pippa Tshabalala. "Return to Darkness: Representations of African in *Resident Evil 5.*" Paper presented at DiGRA 2011: Think, Design, Play, Utrecht, the Netherlands, 2011.

Giddens, Anthony. *Modernity and Self-Identity: Self and Society in the Late Modern Age.* Stanford: Stanford University Press, 1991.

Giddings, Seth. "Events and Collusions: A Glossary for the Microethnography of Video Game Play." *Games and Culture* 4, no. 2 (2009): 144–57.

Gilbert, Ben. "Raven's Manveer Heir Urges Industry to Address Ethnic Misrepresentation." *Joystiq,* March 6, 2010. http://www.joystiq.com/2010/03/06/ravens-manveer-heir-urges-industry-to-address-ethnic-misreprese.

Giles, David C. "Parasocial Interaction: A Review of the Liteartuare and a Model for Future Research." *Media Psychology* 4, no. 3, (2002): 279–305.

Gilroy, Paul. "British Cultural Studies and the Pitfalls of Identity." In *Black*

British Cultural Studies: A Reader, edited by Houston A. Baker, Manthia Diawara, and Ruth H. Lindeborg, 223–39. Chicago: University of Chicago Press, 1996.

———. *Between Camps: Nations, Cultures, and the Allure of Race.* Cambridge, Mass.: Harvard, 2001.

———. *After Empire: Melancholia or Convivial Culture?* London: Routledge, 2004.

Ginsburg, Faye. "Culture/Media: A (Mild) Polemic." *Anthropology Today* 10, no. 2 (1994): 13.

Gitlin, Todd. *Inside Prime Time.* New York: Pantheon Books, 1983.

Glaser, Barney, and Anselm Strauss. *The Discovery of Grounded Theory: Strategies for Qualitative Research.* New Brunswick, N.J.: Aldune Transaction, 2006.

Godinez, Victor. "Zombies in 'Resident Evil 5' Become Issue of Race." *Dallas News,* April 12, 2008. http://www.dallasnews.com/sharedcontent/dws/ent/stories/DN-gamer_0412gl.ART.State.Edition1.466a558.html.

Goffman, Erving. *The Presentation of Self in Everyday Life.* Garden City, N.Y.: Doubleday, 1959.

Goldberg, Stephanie. "*Hunger Games* and Hollywood's Racial Casting Issue." *CNN Entertainment,* March 28, 2012. http://www.cnn.com/2012/03/28/showbiz/movies/hunger-games-black-actors.

Gorriz, Cecilia M., and Claudia Medina. "Engaging Girls with Computers through Software Games." *Communications of the ACM* 43, no. 1 (2000): 42–49.

Gramsci, Antonio. *Letters from Prison.* 2 vols. Translated by Frank Rosengarten. New York: Columbia University Press, 1994.

Graner Ray, Sheri. *Gender Inclusive Game Design: Expanding the Market.* Hingham, Mass.: Charles River Media, 2004.

Gray, Jonathan. *Show Sold Separately: Promos, Spoilers, and Other Media Paratexts.* New York: New York University Press, 2010.

Gray, Mary L. *Out in the Country: Youth, Media, and Queer Visibility in Rural America.* New York: New York University Press, 2009.

Green, Melanie C. "Transportation into Narrative Worlds: The Role of Prior Knowledge and Perceived Realism." *Discourse Processes* 38, no. 2 (2004): 247–66.

Green, Melanie C., and Timothy K. Brock. "The Role of Transportation in the Persuasiveness of Public Narratives." *Journal of Personality and Social Psychology* 79, no. 5 (2000): 701–21.

Green, Melanie C., Timothy K. Brock, and Geoff F. Kaufman. "Understanding Media Enjoyment: The Role of Transportation into Narrative Worlds." *Communication Theory* 14, no. 4 (2004): 311–27.

Greenfield, Patricia Marks. *Mind and Media: The Effects of Television, Video Games, and Computers on the Developing Child.* Cambridge, Mass.: Harvard University Press, 1984.

Greenhouse, Emily. "Twitter's Free-Speech Problem." *New Yorker,* August 1, 2013. http://www.newyorker.com/online/blogs/elements/2013/08/how-free-should-speech-be-on-twitter.html.

Gregersen, Andreas, and Torben Grodal. "Embodiment and Interface." In *Video Game Theory Reader 2,* edited by Bernard Perron and Mark J. P. Wolf, 65–83. New York: Routledge, 2009.

Grodal, Troben. "Video Games and the Pleasures of Control." In *Media Entertainment: The Psychology of Its Appeal,* edited by Dolf Zillmann and Peter Vorderer, 197–212. Mahwah, N.J.: Lawrence Erlbaum Associates, 2000.

———. "Stories for Eye, Ear, and Muscles: Video Games, Media, and Embodied Experiences." In *Video Game Theory Reader,* edited by Mark J. P. Wolf and Bernard Perron, 129–55. New York: Routledge, 2003.

Gross, Larry. "Minorities, Majorities, and the Media." In *Media, Ritual, and Identity,* edited by Tamar Liebes and James Curran, 87–102. New York: Routledge, 1998.

———. *Up from Invisibility: Lesbians, Gay Men, and the Media in America.* New York: Columbia University Press. 2001.

Gross, Larry P., and James D. Woods. *The Columbia Reader on Lesbians and Gay Men in Media, Society, and Politics.* New York: Columbia University Press, 1999.

Grossberg, Larry. "Wandering Audiences, Nomadic Critics." *Cultural Studies* 2, no. 3 (1988): 377–91.

Grossman, Dave, and Gloria DeGaetano. *Stop Teaching Our Kids to Kill: A Call to Action against TV, Movie, and Video Game Violence.* New York: Crown, 1999.

Grosz, Elizabeth A. *Volatile Bodies: Toward a Corporeal Feminism.* Bloomington: Indiana University Press, 1994.

Hall, Alice. "Reading Realism: Audiences' Evaluations of the Reality of Media Texts." *Journal of Communication* 53, no. 4 (2003): 624–41.

Hall, Charlie. "*Mass Effect* Developer Makes Emotional Plea to Eliminate Social Injustice in Games." *Polygon,* March 19, 2014. http://www.polygon.com/2014/3/19/5528066/mass-effect-manveer-heir-gdc-social-injustice.

Hall, Stuart. "What Is This 'Black' in Black Popular Culture?" *Social Justice* 20, nos. 1–2 (1993): 104–11.

———. "The Question of Cultural Identity." In *Modernity: An Introduction to Modern Societies,* edited by Stuart Hall, David Held, Don Hubert, and Kenneth Thompson, 596–632. Boston: Blackwell, 1996.

———. "Who Needs Identity?" In *Questions of Cultural Identity,* edited by Stuart Hall and Paul du Gay, 1–18. London: Sage, 1996.

———. *Representation: Cultural Representations and Signifying Practices.* Thousand Oaks, Calif.: Sage, 1997.

———. "Encoding, Decoding." In *The Cultural Studies Reader,* edited by Simon During, 90–103. London: Routledge, 1997.

Hamilton, Kirk. "The Perilous Process of Reinventing Lara Croft." *Kotaku,*

December 4, 2012. http://kotaku.com/5965680/the-perilous-process-of-reinventing-lara-croft.

———. "And Then the Video Game Industry Woke Up." *Kotaku,* April 1, 2013. http://kotaku.com/and-then-the-video-game-industry-woke-up-464888949.

Hamm, Shaylyn. "The Aesthetics of Unique Video Game Characters." Master's thesis, Southern Methodist University, 2009.

Hanks, Henry. "Are Comics Becoming More Diverse?" *CNN.com,* September 7, 2011. http://geekout.blogs.cnn.com/2011/09/07/are-comics-becoming-more-diverse.

Hannabach, Cathy. "Queer Intimacies at the End of the World: Disability, Sex, and Zombies in *The Walking Dead.*" In *Zombies, Sex, and Sexuality,* edited by Shaka McGlotten and Steve Jones. Jefferson, N.C.: MacFarland, forthcoming.

Harper, Todd. *The Culture of Digital Fighting Games: Performance and Practice.* New York: Routledge, 2014.

Hayes, Elisabeth. "Gendered Identities at Play: Case Studies of Two Women Playing *Morrowind.*" *Games and Culture* 2, no. 1 (2007): 23–48.

Hebdige, Dick. *Subculture: The Meaning of Style.* London: Methuen, 1979.

Hefner, Dorothee, Christoph Klimmt, and Peter Vorderer. "Identification with the Player Character as Determinant of Video Game Enjoyment." Paper presented at the International Conference on Entertainment Computing, 2007.

Henderson, Lisa. "Storyline and the Multicultural Middlebrow: Reading Women's Culture on National Public Radio." *Critical Studies in Mass Communication* 16, no. 3 (1999): 329–46.

———. "Lesbian Pornography: Cultural Transgression and Sexual Demystification." In *The Columbia Reader on Lesbians and Gay Men in Media, Society, and Politics,* edited by Larry Gross and James D. Woods, 173–91. New York: Columbia University Press, 1999.

———. *Love and Money: Queers, Class, and Cultural Production.* New York: New York University Press, 2013.

Hermes, Joke. *Reading Women's Magazines: An Analysis of Everyday Media Use.* Cambridge, Mass.: Polity Press, 1995.

Hernandez, Patricia. "She Tried to Make Good Video Games for Girls, Whatever That Meant." *Kotaku,* March 28, 2012. http://kotaku.com/5913019/she-tried-to-make-good-video-games-for-girls-whatever-that-meant.

Herz, J. C. *Joystick Nation: How Computer Games Ate Our Quarters, Won Our Hearts, and Rewired Our Minds.* Boston: Little, Brown, 1997.

Higgin, Tanner. "Blackless Fantasy: The Disappearance of Race in Massively Multiplayer Online Role-playing Games." *Games and Culture* 4, no. 3 (2009): 3–26.

———. "*Fallout 3*'s Curious System of Race." *Gaming the System,* 2012. http://www.tannerhiggin.com/fallout-3s-curious-system-of-race.

Hinkle, David. "How *The Sims* Got Its Same-Sex Relationship Update." *Joystiq,* August 5, 2013. http://www.joystiq.com/2013/08/05/how-the-sims-got-its-same-sex-relationships.

Hoffner, Cynthia. "Children's Wishful Identification and Parasocial Interaction with Favorite Television Characters." *Journal of Broadcasting and Electronic Media* 40, no. 3 (1996): 389–402.

Hoffner, Cynthia, and Martha Buchanan. "Young Adults' Wishful Identification with Television Chracters: The Role of Perceived Similarity and Character Attributes." *Media Psychology* 7, no. 4 (2005): 325–51.

hooks, bell. "Postmodern Blackness." In *Cultural Theory and Popular Culture,* edited by John Storey, 417–41. Athens: University of Georgia Press, 1998.

Hoorn, Johan F., and Elly A. Konijn. "Perceiving and Experiencing Fictional Characters: An Integrative Account." *Japanese Psychological Research* 45, no. 4 (2003): 250–68.

Hoover, Stewart, Lynn Schofield Clark, and Diane F. Alters. *Media, Home, and Family.* New York: Routledge, 2003.

Horton, Donald, and R. Richard Wohl. "Mass Communication and Parasocial Interaction: Observations on Intimacy at a Distance." *Psychiatry* 19, no. 1 (1956): 215–29.

Hutchinson, Rachel. "Performing the Self: Subverting the Binary in Combat Games." *Games and Culture* 2, no. 4 (2007): 283–99.

Huizinga, Johan. *Homo Ludens: A Study of the Play-Element in Culture.* Boston: Beacon Press, 1955.

Irresistible-Revolution. "And WOC Are Invisible Yet Again: Anita Sarkeesian." Irresistible-Revolution's Tumblr page, March 11, 2013. http://irresistible-revolution.tumblr.com/post/45143183984/and-woc-are-invisible-yet-again-anita-sarkeesian.

Jackson Jr., John L. "Toward an Ethnography of a Quotation-Marked-Off-Place." *Souls* 1, no. 1 (1999): 23–35.

———. "A Little Black Magic." *South Atlantic Quarterly* 104, no. 3 (2005): 393–402.

———. "Toward an Ethnographic Lingua Franca: Communication and Anthropology." *Journal of Communication* 58 (2008): 664–78.

———. *Racial Paranoia: The Unintended Consequences of Political Correctness.* New York: Basic Civitas, 2008.

Jenkins, Henry. "'Complete Freedom of Movement': Games as Gendered Play Spaces." In *From Barbie to Mortal Kombat: Gender and Computer Games,* edited by Justine Cassell and Henry Jenkins, 262–97. Cambridge, Mass.: MIT Press, 2000.

———. "'X Logic': Repositioning Nintendo in Children's Lives." *Quarterly Review of Film and Video* 14, no. 4 (2003): 55–70.

———. *Convergence Culture: Where Old and New Media Collide.* New York: New York University Press, 2006.

———. *Fans, Bloggers, and Gamers: Exploring Participatory Culture*. New York: New York University Press, 2006.

Jenson, Jennifer, and Suzanne de Castell. "Gender, Simulation, and Gaming: Research Review and Redirections." *Simulation and Gaming* 41, no. 1 (2010): 51–71.

Jhally, Sut, and Justin Lewis. "Enlightened Racism: *The Cosby Show*, Audiences, and the Myth of the American Dream." In *The Audience Studies Reader*, edited by Will Brooker and Deborah Jermyn, 279–86. New York: Routledge, 2003.

Johansen, Erin. "Nowhere but up Girl: An Interview with Justine Shaw, Creator of *Nowhere Girl*." *Technodyke.com*, March 12, 2002. http://www.technodyke.com/features/031202_nowheregirl.asp?page=1.

Johnston, Jerome, and James Ettema. *Positive Images: Breaking Stereotypes with Children's Television*. Beverly Hills, Calif.: Sage, 1987.

Juul, Jesper. "Games Telling Stories?" *Game Studies* 1, no. 1 (2001). http://www.gamestudies.org/0101/juul-gts.

———. *Half-Real: Video Games between Real Rules and Fictional Worlds*. Cambridge, Mass.: MIT Press, 2005.

———. *A Casual Revolution: Reinventing Video Games and Their Players*. Cambridge, Mass.: MIT Press, 2010.

———. *The Art of Failure: An Essay on the Pain of Playing Video Games*. Cambridge, Mass.: MIT Press, 2013.

Kafai, Yasmin B., C. Heeter, J. Denner, and J. Y. Sun, eds. *Beyond Barbie and Mortal Kombat: New Perspectives on Gender and Gaming*. Cambridge, Mass.: MIT Press, 2008.

Kalata, Kurt. "*Final Fight*: The Story of Poison," *Hardcore Gaming 101*, May 7, 2009. http://www.hardcoregaming101.net/finalfight/finalfight2.htm.

Katz, Elihu, Jay G. Blumer, and Michael Gurevitch. "Uses and Gratifications Research." *Public Opinion Quarterly* 37, no. 4 (Winter 1973–74): 509–23.

Katz, Elihu, and Paul F. Lazarsfeld. *Personal Influence: The Part Played by People in the Flow of Mass Communications*. 2nd ed. New Brunswick, N.J.: Transaction, 2006.

Kennedy, Helen W. "Lara Croft: Feminist Icon or Cyberbimbo? On the Limits of Textual Analysis." *Game Studies* 2, no. 2, (2002). http://gamestudies.org/0202/kennedy.

Kent, Steven L. *The Ultimate History of Video Games*. New York: Prima Publishing, 2001.

Kerr, Aphra. *The Business and Culture of Digital Games: Gamework/Gameplay*. London: Sage, 2006.

Kerr, Aphra, Pat Brereton, Julian Kucklich, and Roddy Flynn. "New Media: New Pleasures?" STeM working paper, Dublin City University, July 2004. http://www.academia.edu/2694086/New_Media_New_Pleasures_STeM_Working_Paper_Dublin_City_University.

Kinder, Marsha. *Playing with Power in Movies, Television, and Video Games:*

From Muppet Babies to Teenage Mutant Ninja Turtles. Berkeley: University of California Press, 1993.

King, Geoff, and Tanya Krzywinska. *Screenplay: Cinema/Videogames/Interfaces.* London: Wallflower, 2002.

———. *Tomb Raiders and Space Invaders: Videogame Forms and Contexts.* New York: I. B. Tauris, 2006.

Klastrup, Lisbeth, and Susana Tosca. "'Because It Just Looks Cool!' Fashion as Character Performance: The Case of *WoW*." *Journal of Virtual Worlds Research* 1, no. 3 (2009): 4–17.

Klevjer, Rune. "What Is the Avatar? Fiction and Embodiment in Avatar-Based Computer Games." PhD diss., University of Bergen, 2006.

———. "Enter the Avatar: The Phenomenology of Prosthetic Telepresence in Computer Games." In *The Philosophy of Computer Games* 7 (2012): 17–38.

Klimmt, Christoph. "Media Psychology 'Is Not yet There': Introducing Theories on Media Entertainment to the Presence Debate." *Presence* 12, no. 4 (2003): 346–59.

Klimmt, Christoph, Dorothee Hefner, and Peter Vorderer. "The Video Game Experience as 'True' Identification: A Theory of Enjoyable Alteration of Players' Self-Perception." *Communication Theory* 19 (2009): 351–73.

Klimmt, Christoph, Dorothee Hefner, Peter Vorderer, Christian Roth, and Christopher Blake. "Identification with Video Game Character as Automatic Shift of Self-Perception." *Media Psychology* 13, no. 4 (2010): 323–38.

Kline, Stephen, Nick Dyer-Witheford, and Greig de Peuter. *Digital Play: The Interaction of Technology, Culture, and Marketing.* Montreal: McGill-Queen's University Press, 2003.

Konijn, Elly A., and Johan F. Hoorn. "Some Like It Bad: Testing a Model for Perceiving and Experiencing Fictional Characters." *Media Psychology* 7 (2005): 107–44.

Koster, Raph. *A Theory of Fun for Game Design.* Scottsdale, Ariz.: Paraglyph Press, 2005.

Kraidy, Marwan. *Hybridity, or the Cultural Logic of Globalization.* Philadelphia: Temple University Press, 2005.

Kristeva, Julia. *Desire in Language: A Semiotic Approach to Literature and Art.* New York: Columbia University Press, 1980.

Lahti, Martti. "As We Become Machines." In *Video Game Theory Reader,* edited by Mark J. P. Wolf and Bernard Perron, 157–70. New York: Routledge, 2003.

Langness, L. L., and Gelya Frank, *Lives: An Anthropological Approach to Biography.* Novato, Calif.: Chandler and Sharp Publishers, 1965.

Laramée, Francois Dominic, ed. *Secrets of the Game Business.* Hingham, Mass.: Charles River Media, 2003.

Larsson, Stieg. *The Girl with the Dragon Tattoo*. New York: Vintage Books, 2009.

———. *The Girl Who Played with Fire*. New York: Vintage Books, 2009.

———. *The Girl Who Kicked the Hornet's Nest*. New York: Vintage Books, 2009.

Latour, Bruno. *Reassembling the Social*. Oxford: Oxford University Press, 2005.

Leonard, David J. "High Tech Blackface: Race, Sports, Video Games and Becoming the Other." *Intelligent Agent* (2004). http://www.intelligentagent.com/archive/IA4_4gamingleonard.pdf.

———. "To the White Extreme: Conquering Athletic Space, White Manhood, and Racing Virtual Reality." In *Digital Gameplay: Essays on the Nexus of Game and Gamer,* edited by Nate Garrelts, 110–29. Jefferson, N.C.: MacFarland and Company, 2005.

———. "Not a Hater, Just Keepin' It Real: The Importance of Race- and Gender-Based Game Studies." *Games and Culture* 1, no. 1 (2006): 83–88.

———. "Virtual Gangstas, Coming to a Suburban House Near You: Demonization, Commodification, and Policing Blackness." In *The Meaning and Culture of "Grand Theft Auto,"* edited by Nate Garrelts, 49–69. Jefferson, N.C.: McFarland and Company, 2006.

Lewis, Helen. "Game Theory: Making Room for the Women." *New York Times*, December 25, 2012. http://artsbeat.blogs.nytimes.com/2012/12/25/game-theory-making-room-for-the-women.

———. "This Is What Online Harassment Looks Like." *NewStatesman*, July 6, 2012. http://www.newstatesman.com/blogs/internet/2012/07/what-online-harassment-looks.

Li, Dong Dong, Albert Kien Liau, and Angeline Khoo. "Player–Avatar Identification in Video Gaming: Concept and Measurement." *Computers in Human Behavior* 29 (2013): 257–63.

Lind, Rebecca Ann. "Diverse Interpretations: The 'Relevance' of Race in the Construction of Meaning in, and the Evaluation of, a Television News Story." *Howard Journal of Communication* 7 (1996): 53–74.

Lorde, Audre. *Sister Outsider: Essays and Speeches*. Trumansburg, N.Y.: Crossing Press, 1984.

MacCallum-Stewart, Esther. "Real Boys Carry Girly Epics: Normalising Gender Bending in Online Games." *Eludamos* 2, no. 1 (2008): 27–40.

MacDonald, Dwight. "A Theory of Mass Culture." In *Mass Culture: The Popular Arts in America,* edited by Bernard Rosenberg and David Manning White, 59–73. New York: Free Press, 1957.

MacDonald, Keza. "A Gay History of Gaming." *IGN,* January 25, 2012. http://www.ign.com/articles/2012/01/25/a-gay-history-of-gaming.

Machin, David, and Usama Suleiman. "Arab and American Computer War Games: The Influence of Global Technology on Discourse." *Critical Discourse Studies* 3, no. 1 (2006): 1–22.

Malaby, Thomas. "Beyond Play." *Games and Culture* 2, no. 2 (2007): 95–113.

Manekekar, Purnima. "National Texts and Gendered Lives: An Ethnography of Television Viewers in a North Indian City." *American Ethnologist* 20, no. 3 (1993): 543–63.

Martins, Nicole, Dmitri Williams, Kristen Harrison, and Rabindra A. Ratan. "A Content Analysis of Female Body Imagery in Video Games." *Sex Roles* 61 (2009): 824–36.

Mathew, Oruvattithara Mathew. "The Concept of Avatar or Avatara (Incarnation) in Hinduism." *Annales de philosophie and des sciences humaines* 21, no. 1 (2005): 51–67.

Mäyrä, Frans. *An Introduction to Game Studies: Games in Culture.* London: Sage, 2008.

McAlister, Elizabeth. "Slaves, Cannibals, and Infected Hyper-whites: The Race and Religion of Zombies." *Anthropological Quarterly* 85, no. 2 (2012): 457–86.

McCarthy, Anna. *Ambient Television: Visual Culture and Public Space.* Durham, N.C.: Duke University Press, 2001.

McCloud, Scott *Understanding Comics: The Invisible Art.* Northampton, Mass.: Kitchen Sink Press, 1993.

McCrosky, James C., Virginia P. Richmond, and John A. Daly. "The Development of a Measure of Perceived Homophily in Interpersonal Communication." *Human Communication Research* 1, no. 4, (1975): 323–32.

McElroy, Griffin. "IGDA Draws Backlash, Member Resignations over Female Dancers at GDC Party." *Polygon,* March 28, 2013. http://www.polygon.com/2013/3/28/4157266/igda-gdc-party-brenda-romero-resignation.

McLaughlin, Rus. "The History of *Tomb Raider.*" *IGN,* March 1, 2008. http://www.ign.com/articles/2008/03/01/ign-presents-the-history-of-tomb-raider.

McLelland, Mark. "Why Are Japanese Girls' Comics Full of Boys Bonking?" *Intensities: The Journal of Cult Media* 1 (2001). http://intensities.org/Essays/McLelland.pdf.

———. "Local Meanings in Global Space: A Case Study of Women's 'Boy Love' Web Sites in Japanese and English." *Mots Pluriels,* no. 19 (2001). http://motspluriels.arts.uwa.edu.au/MP1901mcl.html.

McMahan, Alison. "Immersion, Engagement and Presence: A Method for Analyzing 3-D Video Games." In *The Video Game Theory Reader,* edited by Mark J. P. Wolf and Bernard Perron, 67–86. New York: Routledge, 2003.

McRobbie, Angela. *The Uses of Cultural Studies.* London: SAGE, 2005.

McWhertor, Michael. "*Resident Evil 5* Not Redesigned after Racism Criticism, Says Producer." *Kotaku,* June 3, 2008. http://kotaku.com/5012678/resident-evil-5-not-redesigned-after-race-criticism-says-producer.

Means Coleman, Robin R. *Say It Loud! African American Audiences, Media, and Identity.* New York: Routledge, 2002.

Mercer, Kobena. "Dark and Lovely Too: Black Gay Men in Independent Film." In *Queer Looks: Perspectives on Lesbian and Gay Film and Video*, edited by Martha Gever, John Greyson, and Pratibha Parmar, 238–56. New York: Routledge, 1993.

Merleau-Ponty, Maurice. "Eye and Mind." Translated by D. Carelton. In *The Primacy of Perception*, edited by J. M. Edie, 159–90. Evanston, Ill.: Northwestern University Press, 1961.

Mikula, Maja. "Gender and Videogames: The Political Valency of Lara Croft." *Continuum: Journal of Media and Cultural Studies* 17, no. 1 (2010): 79–87.

Miller, Daniel, and Don Slater. *The Internet: An Ethnographic Approach*. New York: Berg, 2000.

Moreman, Christopher M., and Cory James Rushton, eds. *Race, Oppression, and the Zombie: Essays on the Cross-cultural Appropriations of the Caribbean Tradition*. Jefferson, N.C.: McFarland and Company, 2011.

Morley, David. *Television, Audiences, and Cultural Studies*. London: Routledge, 1992.

Morley, David, and Kevin Robins, *Spaces of Identity: Global Media, Electronic Landscapes, and Cultural Boundaries*. London: Routledge, 1995.

Mortensen, Torill Elvira. "Mutual Fantasy Online: Playing with People." In *The Players' Realm: Studies on the Culture of Video Games and Gaming*, edited by J. Patrick Williams and Jonas Heide Smith, 188–202. Jefferson, N.C.: McFarland and Company, 2007.

———. *Perceiving Play: The Art and Study of Computer Games*. New York: Peter Lang, 2009.

Mouffe, Chantal. "Citizenship and Political Identity." *October* 61 (1992): 28–32.

Moultrop, Stuart. "Response to Aarseth." In *First Person: New Media as Story, Performance, and Game*, edited by Pat Harrigan and Noah Wiardrip-Fruin, 47–48. Cambridge, Mass.: MIT Press, 2004.

Moyer-Guse, Emily, and Robin L. Nabi. "Explaining the Effects of Narrative in an Entertainment Television Program: Overcoming Resistance to Persuasion." *Human Communication Research* 36, no. 1 (2009): 26–52.

Mulvey, Laura. "Visual Pleasure and Narrative Cinema." *Screen* 16, no. 3 (1975): 6–18.

Muñoz, José Esteban. 1999. *Disidentifications: Queers of Color and the Performance of Politics*. Minneapolis: University of Minnesota Press.

Murphy, Patrick D., and Marwan M. Kraidy. "International Communication, Ethnography, and the Challenge of Globalization." *Communication Theory* 13, no. 3 (2003): 304–23.

Murphy, Sheila C. "'Live in Your World, Play in Ours': The Spaces of Video Game Identity." *Journal of Visual Culture* 3 (2004): 223–38.

Murray, Janet H. *Hamlet on the Holodeck: The Future of Narrative in Cyberspace*. Cambridge, Mass.: MIT Press, 1997.

Myers, David. *The Nature of Computer Games: Play as Semiosis*. New York: Peter Lang, 2003.

Nakamura, Lisa. "After/Images of Identity: Gender, Technology, and Identity Politics." In *Reload: Rethinking Women and Cyberculture*, edited by Mary Flanagan and Austin Booth, 321–31. Cambridge, Mass.: MIT Press, 2002.

———. *Cybertypes: Race, Ethnicity, and Identity on the Internet*. New York: Routledge, 2002.

Nardi, Bonnie. *My Life as a Night Elf Priest: An Anthropological Account of "World of Warcraft."* Ann Arbor: University of Michigan Press, 2009.

Nasaw, David. *Going Out: The Rise and Fall of Public Amusements*. New York: Basic Books, 1993.

Newman, James. "The Myth of the Ergodic Videogame: Some Thoughts on Player–Character Relationships in Videogames." *Game Studies* 2, no. 1 (2002). http://www.gamestudies.org/0102/newman.

———. *Videogames*. New York: Routledge, 2013.

Nichols, Nichelle. *Beyond Uhura: Star Trek and Other Memories*. London: Boxtree, 1995.

"Nintendo's Shining Star: The History of Mario." *Gamecubicle*, August 23, 2008. http://www.gamecubicle.com/features-mario-nintendo_shining_star.htm.

NowGamerTube. "Metroid Samus Reveal." December 5, 2011. http://www.youtube.com/watch?feature=player_embedded&v=08gy74Yx4tY.

Oakes, Penelope J., S. Alexander Haslam, and John C. Turner. *Stereotyping and Social Reality*. Cambridge, Mass.: Blackwell, 1994.

Oately, Keith. "A Taxonomy of the Emotions of Literary Response and a Theory of Identification in Fictional Narrative." *Poetics* 23 (1994): 53–74.

Ochalla, Bryan. "Boy on Boy Action: Is Gay Content on the Rise?" *Gamasutra*, December 8, 2006. http://www.gamasutra.com/features/20061208/ochalla_01.shtml.

———. "Are Video Games Getting Gayer?" *Advocate*, August 26, 2009. http://www.advocate.com/arts-entertainment/features/2009/08/26/are-video-games-getting-gayer-0.

O'Donovan, Betsy. "Reading for Race." *Durham (N.C.) Herald-Sun*, April 1, 2012.

O'Leary, Amy. "Fighting Harassment in Video Game World." *International Herald Tribune*, August 2, 2012.

Paul, Bryant, Michael B. Salwen, and Michel Dupagne. "The Third-Person Effect: A Meta-analysis of the Perceptual Hypothesis." *Mass Communication and Society* 3, no. 1 (2000): 57–85.

Pearce, Celia. "Productive Play: Game Culture from the Bottom Up." *Games and Culture* 1, no. 1 (2006): 17–24.

———. *Communities of Play: Emergent Cultures in Multiplayer Games and Virtual Worlds*. Cambridge, Mass.: MIT Press, 2009.

Pearson, Dan. "EA, Bioware Fire-fighting Reactions to SWTOR's 'Gay Ghetto' Planet." *Games Industry International,* January 15, 2013. http://www.gamesindustry.biz/articles/2013-01-15-ea-bioware-fire-fighting-reactions-to-swtors-gay-ghetto-planet.

Peterman, Erika. "Opinion: Hysteria over *Hunger Games* Characters' Race Is Misguided." *InAmerican,* April 9, 2012. http://inamerica.blogs.cnn .com/2012/04/09/opinion-hysteria-over-hunger-games-characters-race-is-misguided.

Plato. *The Republic.* Translated by Tom Griffith. Edited by G. R. F. Ferrari. Cambridge: Cambridge University Press, 2000.

Phelan, Shane. *Identity Politics: Lesbian Feminism and the Limits of Community.* Philadelphia: Temple University Press, 1989.

Pinchefsky, Carol. "A Feminist Reviews *Tomb Raider*'s Lara Croft." *Forbes,* March 12, 2013. http://www.forbes.com/sites/carolpinchefsky/2013/03/12/a-feminist-reviews-tomb-raiders-lara-croft/2.

———. "Really? IGDA Party at GDC Brings on the Female Dancers." *Forbes,* March 27, 2013. http://www.forbes.com/sites/carolpinchefsky /2013/03/27/really-igda-party-at-gdc-brings-on-the-female-dancers.

Pinckard, Jane. "Gender Play: Successes and Failures in Character Designs for Videogames." *Game Girl Advance,* April 16, 2003. http://www .gamegirladvance.com/archives/2003/04/16/genderplay_successes_and_ failures_in_character_designs_for_videogames.html.

Plunkett, Luke. "Rape, Racism and Repetition: This Is Probably the Worst Game Ever Made." *Kotaku,* October 7, 2011. http://kotaku.com/ 5847507/rape-racism—repetition-this-is-%20probably-the-worst-game-ever-made.

———. "Awful Things Happen When You Try to Make a Video about Video Game Stereotypes." *Kotaku,* June 12, 2012. http://kotaku.com/5917623/ awful-things-happen-when-you-try-to-make-a-video-about-video-game-stereotypes.

Pollack, Andrew. "What's New in Video Games: The Brouhaha over X-rated Games." *New York Times,* October 24, 1982. http://www.nytimes. com/1982/10/24/business/what-s-new-in-video-games-the-brouhaha-over-x-rated-games.html.

Radway, Janice. *Reading the Romance: Women, Patriarchy, and Popular Literature.* Chapel Hill: University of North Carolina Press, 1984.

———. "Reception Study: Ethnography and the Problems of Dispersed Audiences and Nomadic Subjects." *Cultural Studies* 2, no. 3 (1988): 359–76.

Rao, Anjali. "Shigeru Myamoto Talk Asia Interview." *CNN.com,* February 15, 2007. http://www.cnn.com/2007/WORLD/asiapcf/02/14/miyamoto .script/index.html.

Reagon, Bernice Johnson. "Coalition Politics: Turning the Century." In *Home Girls: A Black Feminist Anthology,* edited by Barbara Smith, 356–68. New York: Kitchen Table Press, 1983.

Rehak, Bob. "Mapping the Big Girl Lara Croft and New Media Fandom." *Information, Communication, and Society* 6, no. 4 (2003): 477–96.

———. "Playing at Being: Psychoanalysis and the Avatar." In *The Video Game Theory Reader,* edited by Mark J. P. Wolf and Bernard Perron, 103–27. New York: Routledge, 2003.

Richard, Birgit, and Jutta Zaremba. "Gaming with Grrls: Looking for Sheroes in Computer Games." In *Handbook of Computer Game Studies,* edited by Joost Raessens and Jeffery Goldstein, 283–300. Cambridge, Mass.: MIT Press, 2006.

Riggs, Marlon. "Notes of Signifyin' Snap! Queen." *Art Journal* 50, no. 3 (1991): 64.

Robins, Kevin, and Asu Aksoy. "Whoever Looks Always Finds: Transnational Viewing and Knowledge-Experience." In *Transnational Television Worldwide: Towards a New Media Order,* edited by Jean K. Chalaby, 14–42. New York: I. B. Tauris, 2005.

Rose, Nikolas S. *Governing the Soul: The Shaping of the Private Self.* New York: Routledge, 1990.

———. *Powers of Freedom: Reframing Political Thought.* New York: Cambridge University Press, 1999.

Ruggiero, Thomas E. "Uses and Gratifications Theory in the 21st Century." *Mass Communication and Society* 3, no. 1 (2000): 3–37.

Russell, John. "Race and Reflexivity: The Black Other in Contemporary Japanese Mass Culture." *Cultural Anthropology* 6 (1991): 3–25.

Rutherford, Jonathan. *Identity: Community, Culture, Difference.* London: Lawrence and Wishart, 1990.

Salen, Katie, and Eric Zimmerman. *Rules of Play: Game Design Fundamentals.* Cambridge, Mass.: MIT Press, 2004.

Saltsman, Adam. "Opinion: We Have an Empathy Problem." *Polygon,* April 12, 2013. http://www.polygon.com/2013/4/12/4216834/opinion-we-have-an-empathy-problem.

Sarkeesian, Anita. "Harassment, Misogyny and Silencing on YouTube." *Feminist Frequency,* June 7, 2012. http://www.feministfrequency.com/2012/06/harassment-misogyny-and-silencing-on-youtube.

———. "Tropes vs. Women in Video Games." Kickstarter, May 17, 2012. http://www.kickstarter.com/projects/566429325/tropes-vs-women-in-video-games.

Sayles, Rick. "Classic Game: *Rick Dangerous.*" *Retro Spirit,* December 3, 2013. http://www.retrospiritgames.co.uk/2012/12/classic-game-rick-dangerous.html.

Schleiner, Anne-Marie. "Does Lara Croft Wear Fake Polygons? Gender and Gender Role-Subversion in Computer Adventure Games." *Leonardo* 34, no. 3 (2001): 221–26.

Schott, Gareth. "Agency in and around Play." In *Computer Games: Text,*

Narrative, and Play, edited by Diane Carr, David Buckingham, Andrew Burn, and Gareth Schott, 133–48. Malden, Mass.: Polity Press, 2006.

Schott, Gareth R., and Kirsty R. Horrell. "Girl Gamers and Their Relationship with the Gaming Culture." *International Journal of Research into New Media Technologies* 6, no. 4 (2000): 36–53.

Sedgwick, Eve Kosofsky. "Axiomatic." In *The Cultural Studies Reader,* edited by Simon During, 321–39. New York: Routledge. 1993.

Seiter, Ellen. "Lay Theories of Media Effects: Power Rangers at Preschool." In *Gender, Race, and Class in Media: A Text Reader,* edited by Gail Dines and Jean McMahon Humez, 367–84. Thousand Oaks, Calif.: Sage, 2003.

Sender, Katherine. *Business, Not Politics: The Making of the Gay Market.* New York: Columbia University Press, 2004.

———. *The Makeover: Reality Television and the Reflexive Audience.* New York: New York University Press, 2012.

Severn, Werner J., and James W. Tankard. *Communication Theories: Origins, Methods, and Uses in the Mass Media.* 4th ed. New York: Longman, 1997.

Shaheen, Jack G. *Reel Bad Arabs: How Hollywood Vilifies a People.* New York: Olive Branch Press, 2001.

Sharam, Charles. "Native Americans in Video Games: Racism, Stereotypes, and the Digitized Indian." *Project COE,* April 4, 2011. http://www.projectcoe.com/2011/04/04/native-americans-in-video-games-racism-stereotypes-and-progress.

Shaw, Adrienne. "In-Gayme Representation?" Paper presented at the Seventh International Digital Arts and Culture Conference: The Future of Digital Media Culture, Perth, Australia, September 2007.

———. "Peliharrastaja, or What Gaming in Finland Can Tell Us about Gaming in General." Paper presented at Under the Mask: Perspectives on the Gamer, University of Bedfordshire, Luton, United Kingdom, June 2009.

———. "Putting the Gay in Game: Cultural Production and GLBT Content in Video Games." *Games and Culture* 4 no. 3 (2009): 228–53.

———. "Beyond Comparison: Reframing Analysis of Video Games Produced in the Middle East." *Global Media Journal* 9, no. 16 (2010). http://lass.purduecal.edu/cca/gmj/sp10/graduate/gmj-sp10-grad-article-shaw.htm.

———. "What Is Video Game Culture? Cultural Studies and Game Studies." *Games and Culture* 5, no. 4 (2010): 403–24.

———. "Toward an Ethic of Representation: Ethics and the Representation of Marginalized Groups in Video Games." In *Designing Games for Ethics: Models, Techniques and Frameworks,* edited by Karen Schrier and David Gibson, 159–77. Hershey, Penn.: IGI Global, 2011.

———. "Do You Identify as a Gamer? Gender, Race, Sexuality, and Gamer Identity." *New Media and Society* 14, no. 1 (2012): 25–41.

———. "Talking to Gaymers: Questioning Identity, Community, and Media

Representation." *Westminster Papers in Culture and Communication* 9, no. 1 (2012): 69–89.

———. "Rethinking Game Studies: A Case Study Approach to Video Game Play and Identification." *Critical Studies in Media Communication* 30, no. 5 (2013): 347–61.

———. "On Not Becoming Gamers: Moving beyond the Constructed Audience." *Ada: A Journal of Gender, New Media, and Technology*, no. 2 (June 2013). http://adanewmedia.org/2013/06/issue2-shaw.

Shaw, Justine. *Nowhere Girl.* Online comic. 2001. http://nowheregirl.com.

Sherry, John L. "The Effects of Violent Video Games on Aggression: A Meta-analysis." *Human Communication Research* 27, no. 3 (2001): 309–31.

Sieczkowski, Cavan. "*Hunger Games* Movie's Rue Responds to Racist Tweets as Jennifer Lawrence's 'Curvy' Figure Is Criticized." *International Business Times*, March 29, 2012. http://www.ibtimes.com/'hunger-games'-movie's-rue-responds-racist-tweets-jennifer-lawrence's-'curvy'-figure-criticized.

Silberman, Steve. "Neurodiversity Requires Conventional Thinking about Brains." *Wired,* April 16, 2013. http://www.wired.com/magazine/2013/04/neurodiversity.

Simon, Bart. "Wii Are Out of Control: Bodies, Game Screens, and the Production of Gestural Excess." *Loading . . .* 3, no. 4 (2009): 1–17.

Sisler, Vit. "Representation and Self-Representation: Arabs and Muslims in Digital Games." In *Gaming Realities: A Challenge for Digital Culture,* edited by Manthos Santoineous, 85–92. Athens, Ga.: Fournos, 2006.

Sjöblom, Bjorn. "Gaming as a Situated Collaborative Practice." *Human IT* 9, no. 3 (2008): 128–65.

Slocombe, Will. "A 'Majestic' Reflexivity: Machine-Gods and the Creation of the Playing Subject in *Deus Ex* and *Deus Ex: Invisible War.*" In *Digital Gameplay: Essays on the Nexus of Game and Gamer,* edited by Nate Garrelts, 36–51. Jefferson, N.C.: McFarland and Company, 2005.

Smith, Andrea. *Conquest: Sexual Violence and American Indian Genocide.* Cambridge, Mass.: South End Press, 2005.

Smith, Murray. *Engaging Characters: Fiction, Motion, and the Cinema.* Oxford: Clarendon, 1995.

Snider, Mark. "'Mario' Creator Shigeru Miyamoto." *USA Today,* November 10, 2010. http://content.usatoday.com/communities/gamehunters/post/2010/11/qa-mario-creator-shigeru-miyamoto/1#.UUDd81s4X6U.

Spelman, Elizabeth V. *Inessential Woman: Problems of Exclusion in Feminist Thought.* Boston: Beacon Press, 1988.

Spivak, Gayatri Chakravorty. *In Other Worlds: Essays in Cultural Politics.* New York: Routledge, 1987.

———. "Can the Subaltern Speak?" In *Marxism and the Interpretation of Culture,* edited by Cary Nelson and Lawrence Grossberg, 271–313. Urbana: University of Illinois Press, 1988.

Staiger, Janet. *Media Reception Studies*. New York: New York University Press, 2005.

Steele, Jeanne R., and Jane D. Brown. "Adolescent Room Culture: Studying Media in the Context of Everyday Life." *Journal of Youth and Adolescence* 24, no. 5 (1995): 551–76.

Steen, Francis F., Patricia Marks Greenfield, Mari Sian Davies, and Brendesha Tynes. "What Went Wrong with *The Sims Online*: Cultural Learning and Barriers to Identification in a Massively Multiplayer Online Role-playing Game." In *Playing Video Games: Motives, Responses, and Consequences*, edited by Peter Vorderer and Bryant Jennings, 307–23. Mahwah, N.J.: Lawrence Erlbaum Associates, 2006.

Steinberg, Shirley R., and Joe L. Kincheloe. *Kinderculture: The Corporate Construction of Childhood*. 2nd ed. Boulder, Colo.: Westview Press, 2004.

Steiner, Peter. "On the Internet, Nobody Knows You're a Dog." *New Yorker*, July 5, 1993.

Storey, John. *Cultural Studies and the Study of Popular Culture*. 2nd ed. Athens: University of Georgia Press, 2003.

Stromer-Galley, Jennifer. "Interactivity-as-Product and Interactivity-as-Process." *Information Society* 20 (2004): 391–94.

Suellentrop, Chris. "Indies Grab the Controls at a Game Conference." *New York Times*, March 31, 2013. http://www.nytimes.com/2013/04/01/arts/video-games/game-developers-conference-celebrates-indie-creators.html?pagewanted=all&_r=1&

Tate, Greg. *Everything but the Burden: What White People Are Taking from Black Culture*. New York: Broadway Books, 2003.

Taylor, Charles. *Multiculturalism: Examining the Politics of Recognition*. Princeton, N.J.: Princeton University Press, 1994.

Taylor, T. L. "Multiple Pleasures: Women and Online Gaming." *Convergence* 9, no. 1 (2003): 21–46.

———. *Play between Worlds: Exploring Online Game Culture*. Cambridge, Mass.: MIT Press, 2006.

———. *Raising the Stakes: E-sports and the Professionalization of Computer Gaming*. Cambridge: MIT Press, 2012.

Thompson, Clive. "The Game of Wife." *Slate*, April 7, 2004. http://www.slate.com/id/2098406.

Totilo, Stephen. "That Notorious *Resident Evil 5* and the People I Met in Africa." *Multiplayer Blog*, August 3, 2007. http://multiplayerblog.mtv.com/2007/08/03/that-notorious-resident-evil-5-trailer-and-the-people-i-met-in-africa.

Trepte, Sabine, and Leonard Reinecke. "Avatar Creation and Video Game Enjoyment: Effects of Life-Satisfaction, Game Competitiveness, and Identification with the Avatar." *Journal of Media Psychology* 22, no. 4 (2010): 171–84.

Tronstad, Ragnhild. "Character Identification in *World of Warcraft*: The

Relationship between Capacity and Apperance." In *Digital Culture, Play, and Identity: A "World of Warcraft" Reader,* edited by Hilde G. Corneliussen and Jill Walker Rettberg, 249–64. Cambridge, Mass.: MIT Press, 2008.

Tuchman, Gaye. "The Symbolic Annihilation of Women by the Mass Media." In *Hearth and Home: Images of Women in the Mass Media,* edited by Gaye Tuchman, Arelene Kaplan Daniels, and James Benet, 3–38. Oxford: Oxford University Press, 1978.

Tucker, Staci. "Griefing: Policing Masculinity in Online Games." PhD, diss., University of Oregon, 2011.

Turkle, Sherry. *Life on the Screen: Identity in the Age of the Internet.* New York: Simon and Schuster, 1995.

Turner, Graeme. *British Cultural Studies: An Introduction.* 2nd ed. New York: Routledge, 1996.

Turow, Joseph. *Breaking Up America: Advertisers and the New Media World.* Chicago: University of Chicago Press, 1997.

Valdivia, Angharad N. "bell hooks: Ethics from the Margins." *Qualitative Inquiry* 8, no. 4 (2002): 429–47.

Valentine, David. *Imagining Transgender: An Ethnography of a Category.* Durham, N.C.: Duke University Press, 2007.

Van Looy, Jan, Cedric Courtois, Melanie De Vocht, and Lieven De Marez. "Player Identification in Online Games: Validation of a Scale for Measuring Identification in MMORPGs." *Media Psychology* 2, no. 2 (2012): 197–221.

Voorhees, Gerald. "The Character of Difference: Procedurality, Rhetoric, and Roleplaying Games." *Game Studies* 9, no. 2 (2009): http://gamestudies.org/0902/articles/voorhees.

Waggoner, Zach. *My Avatar, My Self: Identity in Video Role-playing Games.* Jefferson, N.C.: McFarland and Company, 2009.

Walker, John. "Misogyny, Sexism, and Why RPS Isn't Shutting Up." *Rock, Paper, Shotgun,* April 6, 2013. http://www.rockpapershotgun.com/2013/04/06/misogyny-sexism-and-why-rps-isnt-shutting-up.

Walker, Lisa. *Looking Like What You Are: Sexual Style, Race, and Lesbian Identity.* New York: New York University Press, 2001.

Weeks, Patrick. "Same-sex Relationships in *Mass Effect 3.*" Bioware blog, May 2, 2012. http://blog.bioware.com/2012/05/07/same-sex-relationships-in-mass-effect-3.

Williams, Dmitri, Nicole Martins, Mia Consalvo, and James D. Ivory. "The Virtual Census: Representations of Gender, Race, and Age in Video Games." *New Media and Society* 11, no. 5 (2009): 815–34.

Williams, J. Patrick, Sean Q. Hendricks, and W. Keith Winkler. *Gaming as Culture: Essays on Reality, Identity, and Experience in Fantasy Games.* Jefferson, N.C.: McFarland and Company, 2006.

Wolf, Mark J. P. Introduction to *The Medium of the Video Game,* edited by Mark J. P. Wolf, 1–10. Austin: University of Texas Press, 2001.

Worley, Joyce. "Women Join the Arcade Revolution." *Electronic Games* 1, no. 3 (1982): 30–33.

Yang, Robert. "Not That There's Anything Wrong with That." *Escapist Magazine,* October 6, 2009. http://www.escapistmagazine.com/articles/view/issues/issue_222/6614-Not-That-Theres-Anything-Wrong-With-That.

Yee, Nick. 2005. *The Norranthian Scrolls: A Study of EverQuest.* http://www.nickyee.com/eqt/report.html.

Zillmann, Dolf. 1991. "Empathy: Affect from Bearing Witness to the Emotions of Others." In *Responding to the Screen: Reception and Reaction Processes,* edited by Jennings Bryant and Dolf Zillmann, 135–68. Hillsdale, N.J.: Lawrence Erlbaum Associates.

Zimmerman, Bonnie. "The Politics of Transliteration: Lesbian Personal Naratives." *Signs: Journal of Women in Culture and Society* 9, no. 4 (1984): 663–82.

Index

Italicized page numbers refer to figures.

Adrienne Shaw is assistant professor of media and communication at Temple University.